KUNSTMUSEUM BASEL

1 Hans Holbein the Younger (1497/98-1543)
Portrait of Bonifacius Amerbach (1495-1562), Basel Jurist
(Bildnis des Basler Rechtsgelehrten Bonifacius Amerbach). 1519
Tempera on pine, varnished, 28.5 x 27.5 cm
Inv. no. 314. Amerbach Kabinett, 1662

Christian Geelhaar

KUNSTMUSEUM BASEL

The History of the Paintings Collection
and
a Selection of 250 Masterworks

A Palladion Book
Distributed by Harry N. Abrams, Inc., Publishers

*A publication of The Friends of the Kunstmuseum Basel
in association with Palladion Publishers (Zürich)
and supported by The Baloise Insurance Group*

Publications of The Friends of the Kunstmuseum Basel, Volume 7

Publisher: Karl-Ulrich Majer, Michael P. Maegraith
Translation: John Mitchell, Isabel Feder
Editors: Meret Meyer, Pamela Pinto
Photography: Martin Bühler (Öffentliche Kunstsammlung Basel)
with the exception of pages 8, 14, 15, 180, 181, 201 (Ewald Graber)
and 58, 116, 139, 271 (Hans Hinz)
Color separations: Schwitter AG, Allschwil
Production: Benziger AG, Einsiedeln

Distributed in 1993 by Harry N. Abrams, Incorporated, New York
A Times Mirror Company
Library of Congress Catalog Card Number: 93–70646
ISBN 0–8109–3133–8 (Abrams)

Printed and bound in Switzerland

Contents

Acknowledgments

The author wishes to express his sincere thanks to Professor Wilhelm Hill, Chairman of The Friends of the Kunstmuseum Basel, and to Mr. Luzius Gloor, President of the Executive Committee of The Baloise Insurance Group, for having given their support to the present publication.

He also wishes to thank the following for the information and assistance they have given him: Professor Henry-Louis de La Grange, Bibliothèque Musicale Gustav Mahler, Paris, Dr. Christian Klemm, Kunsthaus, Zürich, Carolyn Lanchner, The Museum of Modern Art, New York, Dr. Franz Meyer, Mrs. Annalee Newman, Mrs. E. Raillard-Oeri, Astrid Schirmer, Andreas Speiser, Agathe Straumann, Margrit Suter and Dr. Hans Theler, as well as Peter Berkes, Martin Bühler, Klaus Hess and Nikolaus Meier of the Kunstmuseum in Basel.

The City of Basel to Its Works of Art

The Museum (1844-49) in the Augustinergasse designed by Melchior Berri (now the Natural History Museum and the Museum of Ethnology, *top left*)

The "Haus zur Mücke" (1545) on the Schlüsselberg (*top right*)

The "Bachofen House" (1841-45) on the Münsterplatz (now occupied by the Education Department)

O f all the towns of the Swiss Confederation none deserves more praise than the City of Basel and its worthy elders for their great expenditure and diligence in collecting and highly honouring studies and the arts, especially excellent paintings, drawings and the like", wrote Joachim von Sandrart in 1679 in his *Teutsche Academie*. And he went on to report how those worthy city elders had prevented the inheritors of the "Amerbach Kabinett" from removing that important collection from the city by "buying it, apparently in 1661, for 9,000 crowns in cash and handing it over to the University, where, together with a world-famous library that boasts an abundance of manuscripts, it can now be enjoyed by all. The jewel of this art treasure consists of 20 original paintings by Holbein, in which his genius and skill are beyond praise."[1]

With the purchase of the Amerbach Kabinett - whose origins date back to before the Reformation and which stems from the passionate interest in collecting not of a prince but of a middle-class citizen educated in the humanities-Basel came into the possession of an art collection in 1661, the first urban community to do so. The University, which bore part of the cost of the purchase, was then given the collection to administer. The books and manuscripts of the Amerbach library were incorporated into Basel University Library. The bronzes, goldsmiths' models and coins were separated from the rest of the collection in 1856 and were incorporated into the newly founded "Mediaeval Collection", which in 1894 was housed in the Historical Museum in the Barfüsserkirche. The natural history and ethnological objects later went to the Natural History Museum and the Museum of Ethnology. Finally, the paintings, drawings and prints, the most numerous and the most significant part of the Amerbach Kabinett, form the nucleus of the Öffentliche Kunstsammlung (Public Art Collection), the development of which is the subject of this publication, and which became an independent entity when the Kunstmuseum (Museum of Fine Arts) was opened in 1936.

The "Haus zur Mücke"

The "University Collections" were housed in the "Haus zur Mücke", an old meeting place of the Basel nobility on the Schlüsselberg near the Münsterplatz (Cathedral Square), which had been specially fitted out to take the art collection and the University Library. They were opened to the public as early as 1671. At that time no other city in Europe possessed a public institution of this kind. Princely art collections were only opened to the public as from the middle of the 18th century, and new museums were not founded until the 19th century.[2]

From then on, the art treasures exhibited in the "Haus zur Mücke", and especially Holbein's works, were one of the sights of Basel, which visitors interested in art seldom failed to see. From 1681 onwards, the art collection was open to the public free of charge on Thursday afternoons, and on payment of a modest fee scholars and visitors passing through Basel could be admitted at any time on application. The remarks of Joachim von Sandrart quoted above are among the earliest accounts of the Basel art collection, which was subsequently mentioned in much other travel literature. The Library's visitors' book, in which visitors were asked to sign their names from 1662 to 1822, when it was filled up, shows that pride of place among non-local visitors went to the Germans, for whom Basel is the gateway to Switzerland. Next came the Swiss, followed by the English, French, Dutch, Scandinavians, Poles, Russians and Balts. It is not apparent how keen the citizens of Basel were on visiting the art collection because they seldom signed the visitors' book. There are illustrious names among the signatures: on 26 November 1764 the Scottish lawyer and writer James Boswell, whose travel journals on his Grand Tour also describe his stay in Basel; Johann Caspar Lavater, who signed his name no fewer than eight times between 1774 and 1794; on 25 July 1776 Sir William Hamilton, the British Minister to the Court of Naples and a celebrated collector of Greek vases; on 31 October 1776, and again on 12 August 1785, the British travel writer William Coxe, whose accounts comment in detail on the sights of Basel; on 19 July 1777 Emperor Joseph II of Austria, who passed through Basel on his way back from Paris; in October 1779 the 22 year-old Duke Carl Augustus of Saxony-Weimar, who travelled to Switzerland in the company of his Minister of State Johann Wolfgang von Goethe - who had already entered his name on 8 July 1775; on 11 July 1784 Prince Henry of Prussia, the younger brother of Frederick the Great, on his way to Paris; on 21 December 1801 Heinrich von Kleist, and finally, on 14 January 1814, Emperor Francis I of Austria and King Frederick William III of Prussia, who came to Basel for a meeting with Czar Alexander of Russia.[3]

In 1823 another magnificent private collection, the "Faesch Museum" - like the Amerbach Kabinett, this will be described in the next chapter - was acquired by the University, and the paintings it included were immediately transferred to the "Haus zur Mücke". In 1833 the first catalogue of the collection, compiled by the Basel painter Hieronymus Hess (1799-1850), was printed. The growing interest of the citizens of Basel in their art collection was now more frequently expressed in donations of paintings and drawings, which were presented by individual patrons or purchased by groups of art-lovers as the opportunity arose. The shortage of space in both the Library and the art collection consequently became ever more pressing. Plans were made to transfer the art treasures to the Reinacher Hof, but these were frustrated by the City's defeat in its fight against the rural areas of the Canton of Basel, and the Canton's division into two half-cantons: the City and the rural areas.

The existence of the University and its art collection were jeopardised by this division of the Canton. Like the Cathedral Treasure, the art collection was initially supposed to be added to the public assets of the former Canton of Basel and then to be divided between the two half-cantons in proportion to their respective populations, with the more populous rural areas receiving two-thirds and the City one-third. However, it was then decided that the City should retain all the University's assets and pay 64% of their value - or 331,451 Swiss francs - in compensation to the rural areas. A special committee of experts, comprising two specialists nominated by each of the two half-cantons, was appointed to value the art collection. The City's experts estimated it at 16,000 Swiss francs and those from the rural areas at 113,000 Swiss francs. A court of arbitration subsequently set its value at 22,000 Swiss francs. The art collection was thus spared the fate of the Basel Cathedral Treasure, which was scattered to the four winds after the rural areas disposed of their share by auction.[4]

The Old Museum

As a result of the losses it suffered when the Canton of Basel was divided into two and the payments that were necessary to retain what it salvaged, the City of Basel became more aware of the value of the University's assets and the academic collections. In 1835 the Freiwillige Akademische Gesellschaft (Voluntary Academic Association) was formed and, as part of the reorganisation of the University that it initiated, a law on the administration and utilisation of the University's assets was passed in 1836. Thought was also immediately given to the provision of suitable accommodation for the collections.[5] As early as 1837 the site of the Augustinian Monastery was considered for an extensive museum building to house all the collections. On 30 March 1841 a printed leaflet called upon the citizens of Basel to pledge voluntary contributions for the planned construction. A year later the 455 subscribers, who in a very short time had guaranteed the impressive sum of 70,308 Swiss francs, were invited to found a Freiwilliger Museumsverein (Voluntary Museum Association). It was now also possible to announce a competition for the project. In June 1842 the plans submitted by Melchior Berri were selected as the most appropriate and were recommended for execution. On 21 March 1843 the Basel Parliament approved a credit of 180,000 Swiss francs to finance the building costs, which were estimated at 255,000 Swiss francs, and awarded Berri the contract. The construction work was begun in the spring of 1844. The ceremonial inauguration took place only five and a half years later, on 26 November 1849. One of the speakers on that occasion said "there has always been a lively interest in scientific and intellectual life in Basel. This interest was maintained even in the darkest days, when Basel's power seemed broken." The speaker then went on to state with pride that this interest "is still strong among our citizens, as is witnessed by the superb building whose inauguration is being celebrated today".[6]

The reliefs by the Schaffhausen sculptor Johann Jakob Oechslin (1802-1873) that adorn the frieze on the Museum's main façade - the city goddess Basilea, flanked by Rhenus, Mercury and Helvetia, reigns as the patroness of the fine arts and the promoter of scientific disciplines, industry and trade - make it clear that the newly erected building was intended to serve several purposes, rather than to be just a museum of fine arts. It housed not only the galleries for the collections of paintings and plaster casts and the Kupferstichkabinett (Department of Prints and Drawings), as well as the antiquarian and ethnographical rooms that were on the second floor, but also exhibition rooms for the scientific collections, a physics and chemistry laboratory with a lecture theatre, the library and a prestigious auditorium.

In his task of combining within a multi-purpose building different rooms that had quite disparate functions and housed art and scientific collections as well as university institutes, Melchior Berri (1801-1854), a pupil of Friedrich Weinbrenner in Karlsruhe, could not base himself on traditional museum design. As the most important architect of late Classicism in Switzerland, he created the "Temple of Science" required of him in the competition specifications by using neo-Classical forms, for instance "Greek" beams and "Pompeian" decorative painting. Berri's museum in the Augustinergasse is not the first dedicated museum building in Switzerland. 1826 saw the opening in Geneva of Samuel Vaucher's Musée Rath on the Place Neuve - the same year as the foundation stone was laid in Munich for Leo von Klenze's Alte Pinakothek.

Before the new Museum was inaugurated, fears were expressed that the modest collection might be lost in the monumental rooms but these fears were silenced - and shown to be quite unfounded - by the abundant donations prompted by the Museum's inauguration and by those in succeeding years. In 1856 the rapid growth of the collections led to the removal of the mediaeval objects from the Museum and to the foundation of the independent "Basel Mediaeval Collection" in the Bischofshof. And yet the Museum's Annual Report for 1862 complains about "the shortage of space that increases each year and last year almost became intolerable". The authorities expected soon "to reach the point where we do not know whether continued growth should be welcomed or dreaded".[7] In 1866 the transfer of the physics and chemistry institutes made it possible for the corner rooms on the second floor, which had previously been occupied by the antiquarian and ethnographical collections, to be allocated to the art collection. In the five rooms of the Painting Gallery, which were lit by skylights, the Amerbach Kabinett with the Holbein collection, the Faesch Museum with its early German painting, the donations of Emilie Linder and the Birmann Collection were all initially shown more or less separately, but in the late 1880s thought was given to the idea of a chronological hanging by school, to take more account of art historical development. However, these endeavours to achieve a clearer presentation were also hampered by the pressing shortage of space.

In October 1880 a reader's letter appeared in the *Schweizerischer Volksfreund* raising the question of "how our city could be elevated to an arts centre, bearing in mind the example of other places where art has found a home, received nurture and support, and brought forth rich fruit. What for instance was Munich before King Ludwig attracted art to it? It was a small town with a court and about 60,000 inhabitants, and now through the attraction and cultivation of the arts it has become a fine metropolis with over 200,000 inhabitants." And the writer went on to ask: "What would become of Paris if it were abandoned by the arts? They have raised not only Paris but the whole of French industry to their high standing. Mother art is like the sun - through its warmth and light even the remotest branches of industry are made to blossom." The correspondent felt that as far as Basel was concerned: "It would, at the very least, be easy for Basel to become the arts centre of German-speaking Switzerland, as Geneva is for French-speaking Switzerland, for Basel has just as much wealth. Its Government spends 15,000 Swiss francs a year on supporting the theatre; if it voted as much for acquisitions by the Museum this would certainly be a rewarding investment. Basel could thus acquire a rich and important gallery and would attract a host of artists and foreigners."[8]

It was not until 1903 that the Basel Government finally started making a regular annual grant of 3,000 Swiss francs to the Öffentliche Kunstsammlung. This was later increased several times and by 1991 amounted to 400,000 Swiss francs for acquisitions by the Painting Gallery. However, it has never come anywhere close to the subsidies that the City gives to its theatre. All the same, in the second half of the 19th century, the generosity of certain citizens interested in art - such as the bequest of Samuel Birmann, who died in 1847, the foundation in the name of Mr. and Mrs. Rudolf and Margaretha Bleiler-Mieg (1858) and the fund of Mayor Felix Sarasin (1862) - as well as the annual contributions made by the Freiwilliger Museumsverein and the Gesellschaft zur Förderung des Guten und Gemeinnützigen (Society for the Promotion of Public Welfare and Utility) - made it possible also to extend the collection by purchases. In 1889 thought was for the first time given to certain guidelines for acquisitions, and it was laid down that: "just as Holbein and the Upper Rhine painters are particularly well represented among the Old Masters, so among contemporary painters special attention should be paid to Böcklin".[9] The art of Arnold Böcklin, a native of Basel, was singled out as a new speciality of the Basel collection, alongside Holbein.

In the autumn of 1897 Basel celebrated the 400th anniversary of the birth of Hans Holbein the Younger with an exhibition in the Museum, and at the same time marked Arnold Böcklin's seventieth birthday with a large jubilee exhibition held in the Kunsthalle from 20 September to 24 October. The Museum managed to acquire ten of Böcklin's paintings during his lifetime. Moreover, in 1901, following Böcklin's death in January of that year, it was given four more pictures in the artist's memory, as well as three paintings on long-term loan from the Federal Gottfried Keller Foundation. After the turn of the century Böcklin's work became an additional attraction to that of Holbein.[10] "Here I *immersed* myself in Holbein and Böcklin", wrote the composer and pianist Ferruccio Busoni (1866-1924) on 25 February 1900 after visiting the Basel Museum. On that Sunday evening he performed Beethoven's Fifth Piano Concerto, Brahms' Variations on a Theme by Paganini and, as an encore, Chopin's Polonaise in A flat major in the eighth subscription concert of Basel's Music Society. "By Holbein: his wife and children and the dead (recumbent) Christ. Unbelievable drawings. As for Böcklin: I will simply mention Vita somnium breve (Life is a brief dream) in which childhood, youth, old age and death are brought together in one picture... What colours! And then 'The Sacred Grove'. - 'Self-Portrait' (the last he did). A whole troup of mermaids and mermen playing in the water around a rock. And more too."[11] Gustav Mahler (1860-1911) also went to the Museum in the course of a visit he paid to Basel to stage a performance of his Second Symphony in C minor with the Basel Orchestra and the Choral Society in the Cathedral on 15 June 1903 on the occasion of the 39th Musicians' Festival. He was accompanied by his wife, Alma, as well as by the two friends Carl Moll and Kolo Moser, who then went on to see Ferdinand Hodler and Cuno Amiet in order to invite them to take part in the exhibition of the Vienna "Secession" in January and February 1904. Mahler noted on 13 or 14 June 1903: "Today we shall look around the city a little - Böcklin, Holbein, etc. So far we have just been taking it easy."[12] Paul Klee (1879-1940) wrote to his fiancée on 11 June 1904: "Basel is unfortunately not a beautiful city, but the collection of paintings is well worth seeing: Holbein, early German masters, as well as Böcklin. And there is a nice zoo."[13]

The shortage of space in the Museum in the Augustinergasse grew increasingly critical.[14] The construction of the University Library made some additional room available for the natural history collections in 1896 and meant that the art collection could occupy the entire second floor. However, even then the available rooms were inadequate and did not satisfy reasonable safety standards. Warning had already been given on an earlier occasion of the danger of fire and of the impossibility, should one break out, of evacuating the irreplaceable art treasures from the Painting Gallery, which was situated at the top of several flights of stairs. An extension of the Museum, whether for the art collection or for the natural sciences sections, had become inevitable. In 1898 the Basel Government therefore bought the Rollerhof, which was adjacent to the Museum. The Akademische Gesellschaft was able to acquire three additional properties between the Museum and the Münsterplatz, so that a suitable site was now available for an extension.

A New Kunstmuseum

On 15 August 1903 a reader's letter in the *Basler Nachrichten* drew attention to the "Great danger for our paintings and other collections in the Museum". This warning was precipitated by a news item that had appeared in that newspaper on 12 August commenting on a rail accident in Paris the previous day and recalling the disastrous fire at a large charity bazaar, which on 4 May 1897 had cost the lives of over one hundred people. It was not only in Paris that the precautions against accidents were woefully inadequate, the correspondent complained, but also in the Basel Museum: the collection of amphibians displayed on the ground floor, which were preserved in hundreds of glass bottles filled with spirit, the ethnographical collection consisting mainly of well-dried objects, and the stuffed mammals kept on the first floor all represented a great fire hazard for the "collection of paintings worth many millions" situated above them on the top floor. The correspondent urged the parties responsible to move that collection to separate premises, for the Museum contained treasures "of which all the citizens of Basel are proud and which are sacred to them; treasures bearing witness to how, from time immemorial, art and science have been highly honoured in Basel".[15]

This letter clearly had an effect, for in October 1903 a number of citizens set up a committee to examine the museum issue. In March 1904, with the agreement of the Basel Council (Regierungsrat), it invited seven Basel architects to an exchange of ideas about an extension to the Museum on the site of the Rollerhof. However, doubts were expressed about this site because of the fire hazard associated with the proximity of apartment buildings and shops in the Freie Strasse. It was therefore suggested that a building should be constructed for the art collection - the Elisabethenschanze being proposed as the site - while the old Museum should be given over entirely to the natural history and ethnology collections. At first the Basel Council did not wish to surrender the Elisabethenschanze, but subsequently, on 2 October 1907, it gave its support to this site. The citizens' committee then organised a collection of voluntary contributions for the proposed new building and the extension of the old Museum, through which over one million Swiss francs was raised within three months. Of this, 745,551 Swiss francs was to be made available for a new museum of fine arts.

This encouraging result enabled planning to begin. A Museum Building Commission set up in June 1908 again examined the site question at length. Two experts were brought in, the Munich architect Theodor Fischer (1862-1938), who built the Stuttgart Kunsthalle and the museums in Kassel and Wiesbaden, and Professor Alfred Lichtwark (1852-1914), the famous director of the Kunsthalle in Hamburg. They preferred the Elisabethenschanze. On 11 February 1909 Lichtwark wrote from Basel: "We had to deliver an opinion as to the selection of the site, and in this Fischer and I, as impartial outsiders, had the major say. The site next to the Cathedral on the terrace overlooking the Rhine, indescribably beautiful in itself, we rejected at once and without second thoughts. The Cathedral is delicate and not big. A large palace of a museum right alongside it would dwarf it by its massiveness. We enjoyed the quiet beauty of the site very much... As for the Schützenmatte site, we found it acceptable only if there was nothing better. But we were unanimous in finding the site on an old 'Schanze' (fortification wall), which is now in the centre of the city, to be suitable."[16]

Although a competition among Swiss architects for the construction of a museum on the Elisabethenschanze was announced on 7 July 1909, the site problem had still by no means been conclusively settled: the site of the Lese-gesellschaft (Readers' Circle) on the Münsterplatz and the Rollerhof were both still being considered as possibilities. In order to put an end to the debate, the architects Rudolf Linder and Emil Bercher worked out a project for the large, open site of the Schützenmatte, which had earlier already been considered as a possible location, and in August 1912 they exhibited their plans in the Kunsthalle. As a result, the Basel Parliament decided on 15 May 1913 that a new museum of fine arts should be constructed in the Schützenmatt Park and that a competition should be announced.[17] The competition jury awarded equal first prize to the architects Emil Faesch and Hans Bernoulli. The two competitors were invited to revise and improve their proposals. The Basel Council

The Kunstmuseum (1932-36) in the St. Alban-Graben, designed by Rudolf Christ and Paul Bonatz; view from the North-East.

decided in favour of Bernoulli's project and on 27 January 1916 authorised a credit of 2,422,500 Swiss francs for its construction. Hans Bernoulli (1876-1959) subsequently made several changes to his project and tried to translate the wishes and suggestions of the various commissions into the plans. On 18 June 1918 a building contract was finally concluded with him. But the project was still not sufficiently advanced for the work to begin. New suggestions for alterations brought new difficulties. Then in April 1920 the Basel Council decided to postpone the new building indefinitely - which in practice meant abandoning the plans that had already been drawn up.

To alleviate the Öffentliche Kunstsammlung's shortage of space, even if only temporarily, the Basel Parliament passed a resolution on 23 June 1921 under which the Bachofen House on the Münsterplatz, which had been acquired earlier from Mrs. Louise Bachofen-Burckhardt and which, following her death in February 1920, had now become free, was made available as a branch gallery. This step was taken, in particular, so that the works in the Professor Jakob Bachofen-Burckhardt Foundation, the bequest of Hans Vonder Mühll and the Emilie Linder collection could be accommodated there. At the same time, the Augustinerhof (Augustinergasse 19) was fitted out to house the Kupferstichkabinett. On 4 November 1922 both premises were officially inaugurated and started to be used for their new purpose.[18]

The main courtyard of the Kunstmuseum with sculptures by Alexander Calder (*The Big Spider*), Bernhard Luginbühl (*Wyss Ma*), Eduardo Chillida (*Around The Void IV*) and Auguste Rodin (*The Burghers of Calais*).

From then on, the Basel painting collection was hence to be seen in two separate locations. The French painter Maurice Denis (1870-1943), a member of the Nabis, recorded in his diary in the summer of 1926: "I visited the museum, the main one and the one on the Münsterplatz where there is a very beautiful Madonna by Cranach, large and noble, and a fine Bocaccino, a Virgin in a curious landscape." Both *The Virgin and Child Holding a Piece of Bread* (*Maria mit dem ein Brotstück haltenden Kind*. Ill.22, p.46) by Lucas Cranach the Elder and the *Madonna and Child with St. Veronica* (*Madonna mit dem Kinde und der hl. Veronika*), previously attributed to Boccaccio Boccaccino but now thought to be by Lorenzo Lotto, were part of the Bachofen bequest. But Maurice Denis was particularly enthusiastic about a work by El Greco that he saw in Basel, about which he observed: "The techniques of Cézanne rather than those of Tintoretto, with romanticism as well. Dramatic hallucination. Intensity in a narrow, very limited series of relationships. Intensity of expression. A frenzied, sick man. Plastic balance by someone who is unbalanced." And he went on to say: "This is striking in this museum of the reasonable Holbein, the robust Witz, where Schongauer and Baldung Grien themselves have the same concern as their audience, a certain humanism."[19] This painting by El Greco - the famous *Laocoon* (now in the National Gallery of Art in Washington) - was not, however, a permanent component of the Basel Museum's collection, but hung there in the years 1923 to 1930 on long-term loan from the Fischer-von Mendelssohn family.

With the appointment of the architect Karl August Burckhardt-Koechlin (1879-1960) as the chairman of the Kunstkommission (Board of Trustees) in 1923, the project of a new museum of fine arts was revived. The new chairman recommended that one should be built on the St. Alban-Graben, on the site of the Württembergerhof, which had in any case been impaired by the Swiss National Bank's new premises, and of the neighbouring Railway Bank (Eisenbahnbank). On 27 May 1926, at the request of the Basel Council, the Basel Parliament approved the credit of 775,000 Swiss francs needed to purchase the Württembergerhof. The problem of a site for the Kunstmuseum was thus finally resolved.

The removal of the major part of the art collection from the second storey of the Museum in the Augustinergasse, where the fire risk was considerable, seemed increasingly urgent. Following a proposal from the Kunstverein (Art Association), which was in financial straits, the majority of the exhibition rooms in the Kunsthalle (the Kunstverein's exhibition hall) on the Steinenberg were rented in 1927 to accommodate the Öffentliche Kunst-sammlung temporarily. The move took place in May and June 1928. In return for a subsidy from the Basel Government for the extension and renovation of the Kunsthalle, fourteen paintings from the Kunstverein's collec-tion were, in addition, transferred to the Museum's possession in July 1927, including Böcklin's *Idealised Portrait of Angela Böcklin as a Muse* (*Idealbildnis der Angela Böcklin als Muse*. Ill.105, p.127), Rudolf Koller's *Coming Home from the Fields* (*Heimkehr vom Felde*) and also three pictures by Ferdinand Hodler: *Craftsman Reading* (*Lesender Handwerker*. c.1881), *Disappointed Soul* (*Enttäuschte Seele*. Ill.116, p.137) and *View into Infinity* (*Blick in die Unendlichkeit*. Ill.123, pp. 144-145). With the latter, the first version of Hodler's monumental picture, the Öffentliche Kunstsammlung now acquired a work whose purchase for the new Kunstmuseum had been contemplated as long ago as 1917 - at which time the Schützenmatte site was still being proposed - when in February and March of that year it had been displayed in a Hodler exhibition at the Kunsthalle. The discussions about the desirability of buying *View into Infinity* had provoked a veritable art battle, which had been conducted not only within the Kunstkommission but also within the Kunstverein, and which had divided Basel artistic circles and large sections of the public into hostile camps. The purchase of the painting by the Kunstverein had finally put an end to the controversy but Hodler's *View into Infinity* did not find its final home until 1936, when it was hung in the entrance hall on the second floor of the newly constructed Kunstmuseum on the St. Alban-Graben.[20]

In 1927 a Commission for the Building of the Kunstmuseum was set up. It was chaired by Karl August Burckhardt-Koechlin and counted among its members Paul Bonatz (1877-1951), a professor at Stuttgart's Technical University and one of Germany's most experienced architects in the field of monumental buildings. In the summer of 1928 a competition was announced among Swiss architects, the closing date for which was 15 February 1929. Of the 107 projects submitted, none was totally satisfactory or in a fit state for execution. Prizes were awarded to six projects and the winners were invited to take part in a restricted competition. Once again none of the projects was totally satisfactory. Nevertheless, the architects Rudolf Christ (1895-1975) and Paul Büchi were given a prize and were asked to revise their project once more. In the spring of 1930 the two architects were then commissioned to prepare the final building design and to work out a detailed cost estimate. The Building Commission decided to give its member Paul Bonatz an executive role in the further planning and carrying-out of the work. On 19 September 1931 the final plans were available, as was a detailed breakdown estimating the cost at 7.35 million Swiss francs. On 10 December a proposal was submitted to the Basel Parliament and the project was announced in the press.

Before the debate in the Basel Parliament, a controversy blew up in the press, of which Georg Schmidt - the art critic of the *National-Zeitung* and later the director of the Kunstmuseum - made himself the spokesman. For reasons of cost, Schmidt favoured the functionalism of a skeletal building in the modern style, such as that designed by his brother Hans, and rejected the monumentalism of the massive building that was planned, which he saw as expressing an outdated glorification of money and power. In the debate held in the Basel Parliament on 14 January 1932, only the Communists fiercely opposed the building project; when the Parliament approved the building of the Kunstmuseum on the St. Alban-Graben by an overwhelming majority, the Communists resorted to a referendum. Another battle broke out. However, when the referendum was voted upon on 7 and 8 May 1932, there was a turnout of only 30 per cent: 6,836 votes were cast in favour of the new museum building and 6,190 against. On 21 June the direction of the building work was entrusted to the architects Rudolf Christ of Basel and Paul Bonatz of Stuttgart. The shell of the building was completed by May 1934. After thirty years of planning, the consideration of five different sites, and four competitions, the Kunstmuseum of Basel, on whose façade is incised the dedication "The City of Basel to Its Works of Art", was ceremonially inaugurated on 29 August 1936.

The ceremony in the front courtyard of the Kunstmuseum - at which a performance of Antonio Vivaldi's Concerto Grosso in D minor was given by the Basel Chamber Orchestra conducted by Paul Sacher - was attended by representatives of the Basel authorities, delegates from the University and official committees, patrons and benefactors and also by numerous museum officials and art historians, who had congregated for the XIVth International Congress for Art History, which was meeting in Basel the following day. The guest list was marred by only one imperfection: no one had remembered to invite the artists living in Basel. The Museum received several gifts to mark its inauguration: the Winterthur collector Oskar Reinhart donated *Portrait of a Lady in Furs* (*Bildnis einer Dame im Pelz*) by Wilhelm Trübner, Maja Sacher-Stehlin donated *Rest in the Jura* (*Rast im Jura*. 1908) by Jean-Jacques Lüscher, Marguerite Müller-Müller donated the *Self-Portrait* painted by her brother Albert Müller in 1918, and the Kunstverein presented *Girl Reading* (*Lesendes Mädchen*) by Sebastian Gutzwiller, which it had lent to the old Museum to mark its opening in 1849.[21] Museums in Geneva, Berlin, Naples, Dijon and Strasbourg sent the paintings by Konrad Witz in their possession and these, together with those in the Basel collection, made it possible to hold an exhibition of practically the entire preserved oeuvre of this painter.

The two main local daily newspapers, the *Basler Nachrichten* and the *National-Zeitung*, brought out special issues for the Kunstmuseum's inauguration.[22] Writing in the *National-Zeitung*, Georg Schmidt described his impressions on his first visit: he in particular "who had never made a secret of his disagreement with the mentality expressed in this building" felt he should "simply not keep silent" on this day. Schmidt admitted that his worst fears had not been realised: "the galleries have been refined from the monumental style that is so inappropriate for the urban, democratic art of the 15th and 16th centuries, the main strength of our collection, to something more intimate. One is totally, and very pleasantly, surprised to find that, in striking contrast to the building, with its external façades, courtyard façades and above all its least successful feature, the completely excessive and disproportionate staircase ... the rooms themselves are on a truly human scale and the materials, although expensive, are used with a restraint that completely suits the nature of our most valuable pictures."[23]

Although the building might initially have seemed far too large for the collection, its size soon proved to be "fundamentally correct", as Georg Schmidt stated in 1952, "because the modern section, being particularly designed for expansion, made the growth of this part of the collection to its current size not only possible but necessary".[24] 20th century painting now became another highly regarded and famous speciality of the collection, in addition to Holbein and Böcklin. The American painter Mark Tobey (1890-1976), who in 1960 was to settle in Basel for the rest of his life, wrote to his friend and fellow painter Lyonel Feininger in August 1954: "Pardon le crayon mais ma plume est sèche and je suis dans Basle et aujourd'hui I have seen beaucoup des Tableaux in the Museum here. Quite a peu Marées - many Holbein but I prefer in toto his drawings (portraits). Böcklin who still has a charm for me because in him I recapture the idealism of my youth. He was a bad muralist! They have excellent moderns, many good Léger, Braque and Picasso and their excellent cubist period. The Otto Dix of two old people which I saw in Cologne in '36. The handsome Franz Marc - Munch - 2 but not the best - many fine Klees - very late Kirchner - Mountains (sic) scenes in rose and blue almost cerise. Miles of nondescript native painters of the 19th Century..."[25]

The rapid growth of the modern collection and also the large formats popular among postwar painters, particularly Americans, ultimately resulted in a renewed shortage of space in the Kunstmuseum. On 7 February 1980, thirty-four years after the Kunstmuseum had been inaugurated, the Museum für Gegenwartskunst (Museum for Contemporary Art) - at that time the first museum in Europe exclusively dedicated to contemporary art - was opened in the St. Alban-Tal. The Museum für Gegenwartskunst, a branch of the Kunstmuseum, owes its existence to the generosity of the Basel art patron and the founder of the Emanuel Hoffmann Foundation, Maja Sacher-Stehlin (1896-1989), and her family.[26]

The Kunstkommission

The Amerbach Kabinett had been part of the University Library since it was housed in the "Haus zur Mücke" and was administered by the university authorities. It was not until a law concerning the administration and utilisation of the University's assets was passed on 6 April 1836 that the art collection became a separate entity independent of the Library. The administration of the "Öffentliche Kunstsammlung" (Public Art Collection) - as it was now officially called - was the responsibility of the Kunstkommission, a committee of experts whith functions similar to those of the Board of Trustees in Anglo-Saxon museums: "The art collection is under the control of a committee of at least three members, which will be responsible for the administration and use of this collection."

On 2 June 1836 the University authorities appointed a Kunstkommission consisting of five members. Professor W.M.L. de Wette (1780-1849), a theologian, was chosen as chairman, and the philologist and director of the University Library, Professor Franz Gerlach (1793-1876) was appointed as a further representative of the University. Those selected to represent the City were the art collector and founder of the Basel Künstlergesellschaft (Artists' Society) Peter Vischer-Passavant (1779-1851), the Councillor and Mayor Felix Sarasin-Brunner (1797-1862), who was a great art-lover, and the painter and art dealer Samuel Birmann (1793-1847). From 1854 to 1866 the Kunstkommission was chaired by Professor Wilhelm Wackernagel (1806-1869), a specialist in German philology, who founded the "Basel Mediaeval Collection" in the Bischofshof in 1856. He was followed as chairman of the Kunstkommission by Dr. Edward His-Heusler (1820-1905). Although a ribbon manufacturer by trade, Dr. His-Heusler won great recognition through his documentary research - he was the leading Holbein expert of his time - and rendered valuable services by arranging the prints and engravings of the Öffentliche Kunstsammlung and making them accessible.

In March 1848 the university authorities suggested that a curator should be appointed to look after the collection and that this post should be offered to the Basel historian and art scholar Jacob Burckhardt (1818-1897). He apparently welcomed the offer at first, but never took up the post. Jacob Burckhardt became a member of the Kunstkommission in 1859, a capacity in which, as will be shown later, he was able to exert far greater influence over the fortunes of the Öffentliche Kunstsammlung and its administration than he would ever have been able to do in the subordinate position of curator. In January 1859 the engraver Johann Jakob Falkeisen was finally apppointed the first curator of the collection. He carried out his duties conscientiously until his death in 1883, without exerting any influence over the development of the collection. The responsibility for managing the collection and acquiring pictures remained entirely in the hands of the Kunstkommission.

The independence - many critics called it "high-handedness"[27] - with which the Kunstkommission performed its task and made its decisions may be illustrated by two episodes concerning the loan of works from the collection to exhibitions held outside Basel. On 22 February 1868 - because of unfortunate experiences the previous year over the loan to the Paris World's Fair of Benjamin Vautier's picture *Courtier and Peasants*[28] - the Kunstkommission decided to forbid all future loans of paintings. Accordingly, in June 1874 it refused a request from the Société Vaudoise des Beaux-Arts (Fine Arts Society of the Canton of Vaud) that the two paintings *Pentheus pursued by* the Maenads (*Pentheus von den Maenaden verfolgt*. Ill.93, p.118) and *The Charmer* (*La Charmeuse*. Ill.94, p.119) by Charles Gleyre should be made available to the Musée Arlaud for an exhibition in memory of the artist, who had died on 5 May. The Council of the Canton of Vaud thereupon tried to make the Basel Government put pressure on the Kunstkommission and "to force it to yield up the Gleyre pictures for the projected Gleyre exhibition",[29] but without success, for the Kunstkommission stuck to its position. Then on 14 July Federal Councillor Paul Cérésole supported the request of his Vaudois compatriots and addressed a personal letter to Jacob Burckhardt. In his reply to Cérésole, Burckhardt immediately reiterated the reasons that prevented the Kunstkommission from complying with the request "...we as a committee are bound by *seven precedents* among them a refusal to Gleyre himself while he was alive, other refusals made to our best artists here, etc.! The rule in question was not adopted light-heartedly at the time; it was a matter of protecting ourselves against the periodic depletion of our museum and of protecting our pictures against the *very serious* dangers they run every time they are transported." He explained that the exceptional waiving of this rule would require a "precise order from the Basel Government which relieves us of all responsibility". The Kunstkommission would of course not oppose such an order, Burckhardt stated.[30] In the end it yielded to political pressure and sent the two pictures to Lausanne in August.[31]

Half a century later the two pictures by Gleyre were again sent on loan, this time to Paris for the "Exhibition of Swiss Art from the XVth to the XIXth Centuries (from Holbein to Hodler)", which was held in June and July 1924 in the Musée du Jeu de Paume. "So many difficulties...to solve, so much resistance to overcome, so many scruples to assuage, acceptances to collect, good will to inspire!"[32] complained Léonce Bénédite, the curator of the Musée du Luxembourg in his introduction to the catalogue of the exhibition he had organised - although he was not referring to the loan of the Basel Gleyre pictures. At first this exhibition was due to have included paintings by Holbein and Konrad Witz, which were requested from the Basel Museum. As far as loan requests for works by Böcklin and other 19th and 20th century artists were concerned, the Kunstkommission declared itself "in favour of far-reaching agreement in all areas", but it made it clear from the outset that it could "not lend pictures by Witz and Holbein".[33] And yet the question of what loans could be made to support this exhibition, which was acknowledged to be in the national interest, was discussed in numerous sessions in the weeks that followed. The selection proposed by the organisers included the panel by Konrad Witz *Joachim and Anna by the Golden Gate* (*Joachim und Anna an der Goldenen Pforte*. Ill.8, p.35) as well as *The Body of the Dead Christ in the Tomb* (*Der Leichnam Christi im Grabe*. Ill.38, pp.59-60) and *Double Portrait of Jakob Meyer zum Hasen, Mayor of Basel, and his Wife Dorothea Kannengiesser* (*Doppelbildnis des Basler Bürgermeisters Jakob Meyer zum Hasen und seiner Gattin Dorothea Kannengiesser*. Ill.36, p.57) by Hans Holbein.[34] On 28 May, two weeks before the exhibition opened, the Kunstkommission was still categorically refusing to lend these wooden panels and offering some portrait drawings by Holbein instead. The scenario of the summer of 1874 was now repeated: Federal Councillor Jean-Marie Musy sent a protest to the Basel Councillor Fritz Hauser and, as a result, the Basel Government issued an order to the Kunstkommission on 3 June requiring it to send the two Holbein pictures to Paris. This was the first and last time they left the place where they were painted and their traditional home in the Basel Museum.[35]

Curators and Directors

Chairmen of the Kunstkommission like Wilhelm Wackernagel and Eduard His-Heusler still functioned more or less as superintendents of the Öffentliche Kunstsammlung and managers of the Museum. Not until Dr. Daniel Burckhardt-Werthemann, a pupil of Jacob Burckhardt, was appointed curator in November 1887 did a certain change occur, insofar as he was the first art historian to occupy the position. Dr. Burckhardt-Werthemann made a name for himself as an expert in painting by artists from the Upper Rhine, his principal achievement being the discovery of Konrad Witz. After assuming office in May 1888 his first concern was to rearrange the collection; he also tried to expand its contents in an appropriate way. In January 1901 he took over the chairmanship of the Kunstkommission from Heinrich Wölfflin (1864-1945), who in 1893 had succeeded Jacob Burckhardt in the chair of art history at Basel University, had been a member of the Kunstkommission since 1896, and who now accepted a position in Berlin. The Zürich art historian Paul Ganz (1872-1954) was appointed curator to succeed Burckhardt. He was primarily interested in the Kupferstichkabinett, and he turned the Basel collection of drawings and prints into a public institution. To promote the latter, the Verein der Freunde des Kupferstichkabinetts (Association of Friends of the Print Room) was founded in 1912, from which the Verein der Freunde des Kunstmuseums Basel (Association of Friends of the Museum of Fine Arts Basel) evolved in 1937.[36]

Paul Ganz retired from his position in the spring of 1919 to devote himself completely to teaching at the University. His place was taken by the Basel art historian Heinrich Alfred Schmid (1863-1951), the biographer of Grünewald and Böcklin and an expert on early German painting and Holbein. He had succeeded Heinrich Wölfflin in 1901 as Professor for Art History and he was also a member of the Kunstkommission until his departure for Prague in 1904. In July 1925 Schmid exchanged the post of curator for the chair of art history at Basel University, while the previous holder of the chair, Professor Friedrich Rintelen (1881-1926), gave up his professorship in order to head the Öffentliche Kunstsammlung. He was its curator for only a few months because he died in May 1926, at the age of only 45, in Catania.[37] Otto Fischer (1886-1948), who since 1921 had been Director of the Staatliche Gemäldegalerie in Stuttgart, was appointed to succeed him.[38] As a member of the "Neue Künstler-Vereinigung München"(New Artists' Association of Munich), from which "Der Blaue Reiter" evolved, Fischer had, from early on, taken a lively interest in the contemporary art scene in Munich. The second main focus of his research was East Asian, particularly Chinese, art. Fischer played a leading role in deciding the internal organisation of the Kunstmuseum's premises on the St. Alban-Graben, which were planned and constructed during his period of office. He also laid the foundations for the modern section of the Öffentliche Kunstsammlung, which was later systematically expanded by his successors Georg Schmidt[39] - who headed the Kunstmuseum from 1939 until the end of 1961 and who in 1955 was the first curator allowed to use the title of director - and Franz Meyer[40], director from 1962 until the end of 1980. Their contributions in this area will be dealt with in the chapters of this book that are devoted to 20th century art.

Paul Ganz was the author of the volume *Meisterwerke der Öffentlichen Kunstsammlung in Basel* (*Masterpieces of the Public Art Collection in Basel*), which appeared in 1924 as one of the series *Meisterwerke der bedeutendsten Galerien Europas* (*Masterpieces of the Most Important Galleries in Europe*) published in Munich by Franz Hanfstaengl. Otto Fischer rendered extraordinary services to the Öffentliche Kunstsammlung by his account of its history, which he published in 1936 in the *Festschrift zur Eröffnung des Kunstmuseums* (*Volume to Commemorate the Inauguration of the Kunstmuseum*). Finally, Georg Schmidt, in his last book, *Museum of Fine Arts, Basle, 150 paintings 12th - 20th century*, sought to sketch a history of the development of art according to the criteria of social history; this appeared in 1964 as a volume to commemorate the centenary of The Baloise Insurance Company Limited. The Baloise Insurance Group is also to be thanked for the generous support it has given to the present publication.

2 Master from Constance, 1445
The Saintly Hermits Paul and Anthony are Fed by a Raven.
(*Die Speisung der hl. Einsiedler Paulus und Antonius*). 1445
Tempera on canvas laid down on pine, varnished, 133.5 x 77.5 cm
Inv. no. 1598. Acquired with a special grant from the City of Basel, 1933

For those who can see and appreciate the charm of things past, there is never a moment to waste in Basel. Despite the passing of the centuries and its busy modern commerce, this curious town has preserved something of its ancient spirit. The enterprising mentality of its current inhabitants is, although in a totally different realm of activity, the authentic successor to that which, in the 16th century, stimulated and transmitted to thinkers throughout Europe the irony of a philosopher such as Erasmus and the immortal genius of a painter such as Holbein.

There is something touching in the apparently impossible combination of these two forces - the sheer intellectual merit of some, and the doggedly tenacious and practical willpower of others. It may seem exaggerated to talk of the genius of Basel, but how else can one express the effort to do well, the continual striving to excel which is, in the golden periods of its history, the hallmark of Basel's valiant population, small in numbers though it may be. This genius has, above all, been able to turn to account unexpected gifts of fortune, the windfalls brought to it by chance.

To Erasmus of Rotterdam, to Vesalius, to Johann Buxtorf, and to a host of other scholars it gave Oporin and Froben, the famous typographers and printers. The books created by these men were so perfect that many which are now out of date and worthless and which would, without their workmanship, have been consigned like so many others to the dust of oblivion are still sought after today.

To Hans Holbein it gave the only thing appropriate to a painter of his calibre: the support of a rich and cultivated bourgeoisie, the encouragement of sound advice and, what is even more important, the generous purse of Bonifacius Amerbach, the Maecenas of his time, the jurist and man of taste to whom, after three centuries, Basel owes its most precious asset, its inestimable collection of the great painter's works, that score of paintings and those six dozen drawings which the whole world has come to call 'The Holbeins of Basel'."[41]

These comments introduce two newspaper articles which, in the autumn of 1892, the painter Félix Vallotton (1865-1925) devoted to the works of Hans Holbein the Younger in the Basel Museum. Of these twenty-one paintings not all were "of equal value, and several hardly offer any interest beyond the purely documentary and comparative", Vallotton said. However, he added: "The Munich Pinakothek, so rich in masterpieces of the schools of Upper Germany, has only two; on the other hand, it has nineteen by Holbein the Elder. Dresden has four, but among those four is the portrait of *Morette*, a first-class work and in my humble opinion the painter's masterpiece. In Vienna there are seven at the Belvedere, of which the portraits of Jane Seymour and John Chambers are without equal. And finally at the Louvre there are eight, of which several are also famous.

Basel is therefore ahead of these four great galleries in terms of quantity, and this is a blessing in which the whole of Switzerland, which has never been considered an art centre, can rejoice. As for quality, if it had only the *Dead Christ* and the portrait of the painter's wife and children, that would be enough to maintain its status. Other museums - those already mentioned and the great collections of England - have canvases that may be more perfect and more definitive, but Basel alone possesses the entire master, that is to say, culminating masterpieces in all the genres he attempted and in which he excelled, examples of all his styles, records of the various directions in which he went and the way in which his genius fluctuated."[42]

The writer and philosopher Friedrich Schlegel (1772-1829) also praised the variety of Basel's collection of Holbeins. In his travel report from Switzerland in September 1804 he noted that Basel possessed "many very remarkable paintings by Holbein in its public collection, which show him from a different side than do his portraits, in which he is so excellent but almost always in the same manner. There are historical paintings here, too, and indeed of very different kinds", while among the portraits there are "several excellently finished in Holbein's well-known, superb and absolutely objective style".[43]

A century later, Joris-Karl Huysmans (1848-1907), the author of the novels *A Rebours* (1884) and *Là-bas* (1891) - in the first he described works by the visionaries Gustave Moreau and Odilon Redon, and in the second he expressed, as one of the first to do so, his admiration for the art of Mathias Grünewald[44] - was rather disappointed by the Basel Museum. "Holbeins, yes - but I've seen equally good ones everywhere. They have nothing to teach us." However, he made one exception: "There is one, the portrait of a woman, his wife apparently, with red eyes and a distressed air, together with two children, that holds you because of the life it expresses. It is a superb portrait." And: "A beautiful recumbent Christ, too."

In any case, Huysmans did not find everything to his liking in Protestant Basel: he considered the Three Kings Hotel to be "noisy, without intimacy and very expensive", the City Hall to be "a stage set - it looks rather like old Paris at the World's Fair"; finally, and worst of all for a Catholic convert: "You have to pray in your hotel room here ... One does not feel at home when there are no churches, when one can no longer go to God's house." Huysmans also found Grünewald's small Basel *Crucifixion* (Ill.20, p.44) mediocre, and considered it the work of a pupil. As the entries in his travel notebooks of the autumn of 1903 indicate, his attention was also caught by some pictures by other masters, such as Hans Baldung's *The Crucified Christ with Saints* (*Christus am Kreuz mit Heiligen*. Ill.25, p.49), about which he noted: "A shrew of a virgin, the good thief with his hair pomaded and parted, and little waxed moustaches. It looks like a joke, an addition by a hack." He said the following about Baldung's two small panels *Death and the Maiden* and *Death and the Matron* (*Der Tod und das Mädchen. Der Tod und die Frau*. Ills.26-27, p.50): "A naked woman turning round is embraced by Death, who is biting her chin. Another woman, also naked, whom Death has seized by the hair - she is holding her hands together, is weeping and pleading with the yellowish Death who is showing her the earth with his other arm. Primitive women, cheap, as if made of lard. As for their sex, that is barely concealed by a thin veil." The portraits of the Zürich Banneret Jacob Schwytzer and his wife (Ills.46-47, p.67) caused him to exclaim: "This Stimmer is a fine painter." And on Konrad Witz's representation of *Joachim and Anna by the Golden Gate* (*Joachim und Anna an der Goldenen Pforte*. Ill.8, p.35) he had this to say: "Near a cloister, on a golden ground, Joachim with a halo, in a blue robe with heavy shoes and a red cloak up over his head, embraces a woman with a halo, a white headdress and clad in green. A shrew with something of Redon about her. - He has an almost roguish look. There is something base, indecent in the face of that man with his air of a bad monk." Huysmans concluded: "Some good painting - but this Witz must have been a lecher."[45]

Hans Holbein was born in 1497 or 1498 in Augsburg, but in a signed self-portrait drawn in 1543, after he had worked in England for ten years, he still called himself "Ioannes Holpenius Basileensis", a citizen of Basel. Like his elder brother Ambrosius (1494?-1519?), he was trained as a painter by his father Hans (1460/70-1524). In 1516, shortly after having moved to Basel as a journeyman, the 18 year-old had the honour of being commissioned to paint a double portrait of Jakob Meyer zum Hasen, who in that year was chosen as Basel's first mayor not belonging to the nobility, and his second wife Dorothea Kannengiesser (Ill.36, p.57). In 1521, when the rear part of the new City Hall was finished, the construction of which had been decided on by the City in 1504, Holbein was commissioned to decorate the Parliament Chamber. The City Hall was also the place where the eight scenes from Holbein's Passion of Christ (Ill.37, p.58) were kept, until in 1770 these were incorporated into the public collection by a decision of the Basel Government - although this had been expressly rejected in 1713 - so that they could be shown together with the Holbein works from the Amerbach Kabinett in the "Haus zur Mücke".

In the 17th and 18th centuries the Passion pictures were considered Hans Holbein's masterpiece, and they constituted one of the major sights of the city, which no visitor from outside Basel failed to see. Joachim von Sandrart (1606-1688) admired the paintings here in 1635 when he passed through Basel. In his *Teutsche Academie der Edlen Bau-, Bild- und Mahlerey-Künste* (1675/79), one of the first works on art history written in German, he wrote enthusiastically: "The most excellent piece and the crown of all his art is the Passion of Christ in eight sections painted on a panel, which is well preserved in the Basel City Hall. This is a work in which every achievement of our art is to be found: piety, the spiritual and worldly beauty of the pictures, the noble and low-born figures, buildings, landscapes, day and night. This panel proclaims its master's honour and fame; it is surpassed by none either in Germany or Italy and easily wins the laurels among the works of Old Masters."[46] He went on to recount the attempt made by Elector Maximilian of Bavaria, a passionate art collector, to acquire the Passion panels in 1641 by offering Basel 30,000 guilders worth of salt deliveries. Basel refused, but the Elector's offer made it "all the more convinced of the high value of these paintings", and of course their fame must have been spread further by Sandrart's account of the incident. Later on, the esteem in which the Passion panels were held declined, and Félix Vallotton for instance said: "I do not much like the *Passion*, an altar painting in eight parts, and I have the courage to confess it." But he nonetheless admitted: "this is a question of taste and cannot be discussed. I simply know that if I were given the choice, I would take not this one but the painting next to it, the *Dead Christ*."[47]

For Sandrart it was just the other way round. He considered that Holbein's "naked recumbent body of our Lord taken down from the cross" was "not as well done as other works of his", and he was astonished that "1,000 ducats should nonetheless have been offered for it".[48] There is hardly an 18th century travel account that, if it deals with Basel's Holbein collection, does not endorse Sandrart's comments on *The Body of the Dead Christ in the Tomb (Der Leichnam Christi im Grabe.* Ill. 38,pp.59-60)! However, it is understandable that such a sentimental age should take exception to a manner of representation that disregarded every ideal of beauty. Thus, Karl Spazier asked in his *Wanderungen durch die Schweiz (Travels through Switzerland)*, "why do people want to have their stomachs turned by bleeding corpses?" And he made the controversial suggestion: "If only they had taken the thousand ducats that are supposed to have been offered for this work and put them into a fund for country schoolmasters! That would have been more religious from every point of view."[49] Johann Gerhard Reinhard Andreä noted in his letters written from Switzerland to Hanover in 1764 that this picture of death stirred the viewer to compassion - "one cannot look at it enough, but one cannot look at it without horror".[50] For his part, Johann Rudolf von Sinner confessed in his Swiss travel descriptions: "This painting inspires more horror than piety. Of all the ways of representing the Saviour of the world, this one seems the least worthy of the majesty of the subject."[51] And Christoph Meiners expressed a similar view: "The Christ taken down from the cross does not in my judgment have the dignity or majesty of the Saviour of the world...Also the bleeding wounds inspire not pity but horror and disgust."[52]

A hundred years later *The Body of the Dead Christ in the Tomb* also inspired "aversion and horror" in Anna Grigoryevna, the young wife of Fyodor M. Dostoyevsky (1821-1881), as she confided to her diary in August 1867. Her husband, on the other hand, regarded the painting "with enthusiasm and wanted to examine it close up. So he climbed on a chair, and I was afraid he would be punished because there is a punishment for everything here." The painting had a deeply disturbing effect on Dostoyevsky and he reportedly called out: "Holbein was a great painter and poet."[53] Anna Grigoryevna thought her husband was about to have an epileptic fit and took the precaution of conducting him out of the room. However, before leaving the Museum, Dostoyevsky insisted on seeing Holbein's *The Body of the Dead Christ in the Tomb* again.[54] The couple made an overnight stop in Basel on 23 August 1867 on the way from Baden-Baden to Geneva. Dostoyevsky knew about the city on the Rhine from the *Letters of a Russian Traveller* (1791-1795) by the poet and historian Nikolai Karamsin (1766-1826) and on the next day he and his wife followed in Karamsin's footsteps by visiting the Cathedral, the hill on which it stands and the Museum in the Augustinergasse.

"I saw a similar picture in Basel not long ago", Prince Myshkin recalls in the novel *The Idiot*: "It left an indelible impression on me."[55] The reference is to Holbein's *The Body of the Dead Christ in the Tomb*. Dostoyevsky incorporated his impressions of the picture into his novel, the first draft of which was written in Geneva. His reminiscences in the sixth chapter of Part Three may be considered the first sympathetic appreciation of Holbein's masterpiece. The description of the mercilessly realistic picture causes Dostoyevsky to raise the question of the existence of God: "if such a corpse (and it must have been just like that) was seen by all ... who believed in Him and worshipped him, then how could they possibly have believed, as they looked at the corpse, that the martyr would rise again? Here one cannot help being struck by the idea that if death is so horrible and if the laws of nature are so powerful, then how can they be overcome?"

The novel *The Idiot*, published in 1869, must have caused many a reader to wish to see Holbein's *The Body of the Dead Christ in the Tomb* in the original. Lenin is one example. When he came to Basel in November 1916 to deliver a lecture to a small circle of Russian academics on the position in Russia at the time, he suddenly remembered the painting and was prompted to visit the Museum.[56]

The Body of the Dead Christ in the Tomb and the *Portrait of the Artist's Wife and her Two Oldest Children (Bildnis von Holbeins Frau mit den beiden älteren Kindern.* Ill. 42, p.64) were part of the Amerbach Kabinett. The origin of the religious work is unknown, and it is possible that Bonifacius Amerbach (1495-1562) saved it from the ravages of the iconoclasts in February 1529.[57] The *Family Portrait,* on the other hand, is one of the few works in the Amerbach Kabinett whose provenance is certain. At some unknown point in time it came into the possession of the Zürich painter Hans Asper (1499-1571), from whom Basilius Amerbach (1533-1591) tried to buy it. However, Asper did not want to part with the picture and it was not until after Asper's death in 1579 that Amerbach succeeded in acquiring the painting, for 6 crowns, with the help of Jacob Clauser (1520/25-1579), a Zürich-born painter who often acted as Amerbach's intermediary in the search for and acquisition of items for his collection.[58] In the collection inventory that Basilius Amerbach drew up between 1585 and 1587, probably as an appendix to his will, the *Family Portrait* and the *Dead Christ*, in keeping with their importance, appear at the top of the list of 49 large and small paintings: "Holbein's wife and two children by H. Holbein painted on paper with oil paints and mounted on wood. A picture of a 'dead man' by H. Holbein on wood with oil paints."[59]

It was only Basilius Amerbach, the last representative of his line, who was a collector in the true sense of the word, although his father Bonifacius and his grandfather Johannes helped to create the Amerbach Kabinett.[60] Johannes Amerbach (c.1440-1513), the founder of the Basel family, was born and grew up in the Lower Franconian monastery town of Amorbach in the bishopric of Würzburg. His real name was Johann Welcker but he later took the name of his birthplace as his family name. He studied at the University of Paris, where he acquired a Master of Arts degree in 1462, before moving to Venice, a centre of early book printing, where he was active as a printer. His presence in Basel is documented from 1478 onwards. In 1479 he bought the house "Zur Ellenden Herberge" in the Rheingasse in "Kleinbasel", and three years later the imposing residence "Zum Kaiserstuhl" situated diagonally across from it. There he created an excellent printing office that made a name for itself by publishing the Latin church fathers; it was this that later induced Erasmus of Rotterdam (1469-1536) to settle in Basel. Johannes Amerbach was in close contact not only with the most important scholars of his time but also with artists. Through him and his partner and successor Johannes Froben (c. 1460-1527) - who took over the Amerbach printing office in 1507 - Basel became a thriving centre of book printing and humanistic literature in the decades around 1500.

Johannes Amerbach owned an extensive library but he was not an art collector. All the same, one of the most precious objects in the Amerbach Kabinett, an ornately decorated Late Gothic ceremonial dagger, belonged to him.[61] His son Bonifacius, too, clearly did not have a strong interest in collecting but cared more about history. This presumably prompted him to follow the custom of humanistic circles throughout Europe, and to put together a small, highly selective collection of antique coins and medals, which was then further expanded by his son Basilius. Bonifacius loved precious items worked in gold, and was prepared to spend considerable sums on them. In 1555 he paid the large sum of 124 guilders for a silver-gilt globe goblet, which is still preserved.[62] He also left behind him a number of paintings, among them two portraits by Hans Holbein the Younger, whom he knew personally: a portrait of himself painted in 1519 when he was in his youth (Ill.1, p.2) and *Portrait of Erasmus in Profile, Writing (Bildnis des schreibenden Erasmus im Profil)*, which was painted in 1523 and which he had acquired in 1542 from among the works owned by Holbein's wife.

After taking his Master of Arts degree at Basel University, Bonifacius Amerbach turned to the study of law, first at the University of Freiburg im Breisgau, and subsequently in Avignon, where he obtained a Doctor of Law degree in 1525. Following his return to Basel he taught Roman Law at the University there and earned himself an eminent reputation as the "Syndikus" (legal adviser) of the Basel Council. When Erasmus of Rotterdam stayed in the house of the Froben family in Basel from the summer of 1514 to the spring of 1516 - he also often lived there later - a deep friendship developed between the scholar and Bonifacius Amerbach, which moulded the young man intellectually. In June 1535 he fetched Erasmus back to Basel from Freiburg, where he had taken refuge when the Reformation started. Erasmus died in Basel on 13 July 1536. The "Prince of Humanists" commemorated his association with Amerbach, who was 26 years his junior, by making him his heir. Bonifacius inherited coins, medals and plaquettes, various gold and silver utensils and other objects of artistic value from Erasmus, together with some paintings and drawings, presumably including the sketch Hans Holbein made for the portrait of Sir Thomas More and his family.[63]

The legacy left by Erasmus - for the storage of which Bonifacius Amerbach had an elaborately carved chest made, which is still preserved today[64] - and Bonifacius' numismatic collection were inherited by Bonifacius' only son, Basilius, in 1562, together with the paintings, drawings and gold artefacts which were in the family's possession. Basilius followed his father's example in taking up law, and he studied extensively in Tübingen, Padua, Bologna and Bourges. In 1561 he obtained a doctorate from Bologna. In the following year he was appointed to the "Chair for the Codex" at the University of Basel. From 1564 until his death he occupied the "Chair for the Pandects". He also followed in his father's footsteps by being the legal adviser to the Basel Council as well as to a private clientèle from Basel and elsewhere.

In 1562, only a year after his marriage, Basilius Amerbach lost his young wife and newly born son on the same day, and in the same month, on 24 or 25 April, his father, Bonifacius, also died. These losses must have been a turning-point in his life. He was not yet thirty but he never married again. With growing resoluteness he withdrew to his study, and from then on completely dedicated himself to reverently maintaining his artistic inheritance and to expanding, compiling an inventory of and displaying his own collection. His critical examination of the material in his collection was assisted by his extensive correspondence with experts and scholars throughout Europe. In the late 1580s Basilius, who as a student had travelled to Rome and Naples in 1556 to see the Roman antiquities there, undertook the first systematic excavation of the Roman theatre in Augusta Rauracorum (Kaiseraugst, just a few miles outside Basel), together with the Basel merchant and Councillor Andreas Ryff (1550-1603). They were assisted by the Basel painter Hans Bock the Elder, who drew the sketches and plans. This was the first scientific excavation on any significant scale north of the Alps.

The growth of the collection can be followed in various inventories and a list of annual expenses for purchases which was drawn up by Basilius' nephew and heir Ludwig Iselin (1559-1612) using notes made by his uncle, which have since been lost. Basilius' collecting activity seems to have begun around 1562 at an initially modest rate, for expenses in that year amounted to less than one pound. However, they increased rapidly, reaching a three-figure amount for the first time around 1568. Between 1569 and 1575/76 the totals were again below the one hundred pound mark. In the years 1576 to 1578, when the plague raged in Basel and numerous artists' studios and households were liquidated, they reached highs of up to 448 pounds.[65]

At the beginning of his collecting activity, Basilius added to the numismatic holdings inherited from his father. His first major purchase, in 1576, was of the coin and medal collection of the Savoyard personal physician Ludovic Demoulin de Rochefort, who was born in Blois in 1515, settled in Basel in 1576 and died there in 1582.[66] In the last years of Basilius' life, too, numismatics occupied a central place in his collecting. His extensive purchases of the stock-in-trade of three goldsmiths' workshops, which he made particularly in the plague years 1576-78, and which brought him goldsmiths' designs, models and tools, testify to a strong interest in the goldsmith's craft.[67] However, the collection's main strength lies in the area of fine arts, in its paintings (of which there are more than 50), drawings and prints. Of the fifteen paintings by Holbein the Younger, some were already in the family's possession and others, as is demonstrated by the example of the *Portrait of the Artist's Wife and her Two Oldest Children*, were acquired by Basilius by dint of patience and persistence.

In the case of the paintings, two distinct chronological periods can be observed in the collection. Firstly, there are works from an earlier period by artists such as Niklaus Manuel (c.1484-1530), Ambrosius Holbein (1494?-1519?) and his brother Hans, who were born between 1480 and 1500, and belonged to the generation of Bonifacius Amerbach. Secondly, there are pictures by contemporaries of Basilius, artists born between 1520 and 1550, such as Hans Bock the Elder (c.1550/52-1624). Similarly, two distinct geographical regions are represented. On the one hand, Basilius Amerbach concentrated on artists working in Basel and the Upper Rhine area with whom either his father or his grandfather had been connected, or of whom he himself was an acquaintance or a friend. On the other, the collection includes representatives of the Swiss Renaissance such as Hans Leu the Younger from Zürich and Niklaus Manuel from Berne, who in his large "cloths" (paintings on canvas) such as *The Judgment of Paris* (*Das Urteil des Paris*. Ill.31, p.53) dealt on a monumental scale with themes from antiquity and the nude.[68]

The collection of some 1600 to 1800 sheets of drawings likewise principally focuses on the art of the Upper Rhine area, which at the end of the 15th and the beginning of the 16th century experienced one of the golden ages in the history of European art, with its great masters Martin Schongauer, Mathias Grünewald, Urs Graf, Hans Baldung Grien and, above all, Hans Holbein the Younger and his father Hans Holbein the Elder. Basilius Amerbach not only sought to collect individual drawings by well established artists; he also acquired the entire contents of workshops and part of the drawings left behind upon their death by artists such as Urs Graf, Niklaus Manuel and Hans Holbein the Younger. The extent to which individual artists are represented reveals the importance of the collection, which was unique in its time. For instance, Amerbach possessed about 50 drawings by Hans Holbein the Elder, 12 by Hans Baldung, about 115 by Urs Graf, about 70 by Niklaus Manuel, and about 240 by Hans Holbein the Younger, if one includes the marginal drawings in the copy of Erasmus of Rotterdam's *In Praise of Folly* and the sketches done in England.[69] By contrast with his approach to paintings and drawings, Basilius Amerbach did not confine himself to his own part of the world in his collection of prints - which numbered almost four thousand copper engravings and woodcuts - and illustrated books; Italian, Dutch and Flemish artists are richly represented in addition to German ones. Attached to the collection, and in fact the cornerstone of the Amerbach Kabinett, was the large library of almost 10,000 volumes and manuscripts, which was a major attraction when the Amerbach estate was purchased by the Basel Council on behalf of the University.

The Amerbach Kabinett is fundamentally different from the collections of art and curios accumulated by 16th century German princes. These were intended partly to display the collector's wealth by means of curiosities and valuables such as magnificent objects wrought in gold, and partly to provide an image of the known universe by combining, usually without any kind of system, examples of the esoteric, strange and exotic together with artistic objects. Basilius Amerbach's collection was quite different for, although affluent, he possessed neither the wealth nor the power of a princely collector. Moreover, as has been shown, his collecting interests were consistently directed at a number of specific fields; curios and rarities occupied an extremely modest, rather incidental, place in his collection.

In order to overcome the shortage of space created by his large-scale purchases during the plague years of 1576-78 and to provide suitable accommodation in which his greatly expanded collection could be arranged in an orderly manner, Basilius Amerbach had a spacious gallery built, which was known as the "nüwe Cammer" (the new Chamber). This building - the actual Amerbach Kabinett[70] - was erected between 1578 and 1582 on the site of the family property "Zum Kaiserstuhl" by none less than the Basel master builder and sculptor Daniel Heintz, under whose direction the magnificent vaulting over the nave was erected in Berne Cathedral from 1571-75 as was the rood-screen, and who in 1581 was also responsible for the elaborate spiral staircase in the anteroom to the Council Chamber in Basel City Hall. The cabinet-maker Mathys Giger was commissioned to make the furniture for the gallery. In accordance with the collector's precise wishes, he made two large chests-of-drawers for keeping the drawings and prints, and also various chests, shelves, tables and stools. Basilius Amerbach already owned a coin cabinet, which still exists today, with 120 shallow drawers and three niches on the front to display small sculptures.[71]

At the same time as Basilius Amerbach commissioned this new building he also compiled the first inventory of his collection, in which 4,103 objects were listed.[72] When in the winter of 1580/81 he started to arrange his collection in the "nüwe Cammer", he drew up another list describing the contents of the numerous drawers of the pieces of furniture in which the collection was kept.[73] The most important, although never completed, inventory was the one compiled, probably from 1585 to 1587, as an appendix to his will. This, for the first time, also lists the pictures that hung or stood along the walls of the art gallery, and the collector usually named both the artist and the subject of the picture, sometimes with colourful descriptions, as when he noted "with thunder and lightning" against Niklaus Manuel's *The Beheading of John the Baptist* (*Die Enthauptung Johannis des Täufers.* Ill.28, p.51).[74]

Basilius Amerbach died on 25 April 1591. The Amerbach Kabinett remained in its place in the house "Zum Kaiserstuhl" and for two generations was respectfully preserved by Basilius' heirs, the descendants of his sister, Faustina Iselin. The collection was not expanded but it was at least kept intact. Its reputation must soon have spread beyond the boundaries of the city.[75] Thomas Howard, the Earl of Arundel (1585-1646), who was the first man in England to collect Greek antiquities and Renaissance works of art, clearly possessed information about the Amerbach Kabinett and wanted to buy parts of the collection. On his behalf his son contacted the Rev. William Petty in August 1637: "...My lord desires that you should endeavor in and about Bassill to gette things of Holben, especially in a house which beelonged to Amore Bacchus; there beeing a rare dead Christ at length, in oyle, with diverse heads and drawings of Holben and other masters, all now to bee sould. My lord desires that you would buy them and bring them away, or at least the drawings..."[76] It is not surprising that the Earl of Arundel particularly wanted to have the drawings, for he at one time owned the Holbein drawings that are now in the Royal Collection in Windsor Castle.[77] It is not known whether the heirs were actually interested in selling in 1637, and there is no record of further negotiations by the Earl of Arundel.

In 1648 the danger of a sale again became acute with the death of Basilius Iselin, the only child of Basilius Amerbach's nephew and heir, Ludwig Iselin. Johann Rudolf Wettstein (1614-1684), the Professor of Theology and later Librarian of the University Library, now concerned himself with preserving the Amerbach Kabinett intact. The son of the Basel mayor and statesman of the same name, who in 1648 negotiated the formal secession of the Swiss Confederation from the Holy Roman Empire at the Congress of Westphalia, Wettstein wanted to ensure that even if the collection could not remain in Basel, it should at least remain in Switzerland. To this end he wrote to friends in Zürich in 1650, pointing out what a disgrace it would be if the collection were to be sold to a foreign buyer. Meanwhile, another highly placed person known as a passionate collector, Queen Christina of Sweden (1626-1689), was interested in the collection, and even sent a secretary on a visit of inspection to Basel. At the time the citizens of Basel were primarily concerned about the library, and they seem to have been prepared, if necessary, to forego the collection of art and antiquities in order to keep the books. However, this was prevented, partly because of Wettstein's reminder that the collection was that of the heirs of Erasmus and that it would be disgraceful to break up the Amerbach heritage, but above all because the heirs themselves wanted to sell it intact so that they could share out the proceeds equally among themselves.

Then, in 1661, an offer of 9,500 Imperial talers was made for the collection from Amsterdam, which was the centre of the European art trade at the time, by a certain Dr. Martin Bürren, about whom nothing further is known. This reawakened interest in Basel in the preservation of the irreplaceable Amerbach art collection and library. Now even the former mayor Johann Rudolf Wettstein (1594-1666) intervened with the Basel Government to save the collection. On 20 November 1661 the Basel Council decided that, in order to prevent the Amerbach Kabinett's fragmentation, the City would buy it, together with the library belonging to it, for the enormous sum of 9,000 Imperial talers, which was to be paid in three yearly instalments. The University, which was to receive and administer the collection and the library, was asked to contribute to the cost of their purchase.

Basilius Amerbach was not the only art collector of his time in Basel. His friends and university colleagues of about the same age, Theodor Zwinger (1533-1588) and Felix Platter (1536-1614), who helped the medical faculty attain great eminence, also created significant "Cabinets", but these shared the fate of most non-princely collections and were later sold off and scattered. Hans Bock the Elder's *Portrait of Theodor Zwinger* (*Bildnis des Theodor Zwinger*. Ill.52, p.70), the polymath, Hellenist and physician, with the motif of the fall of Bellerophon - a warning against presumptuous human endeavour - was acquired not later than 1587 by Basilius Amerbach, who was also his friend's brother-in-law. Zwinger's collecting passion, which was fed by the spirit of humanism, was mainly concerned with Roman antiquities. Felix Platter was Professor for Practical Medicine and was also the City Physician; during his lifetime his collection in the house "Zum Samson" was more famous than the Amerbach Kabinett and, with 88 works, Platter's collection of paintings was much larger than that of Basilius Amerbach. Like Basilius, Platter also collected coins, but his primary interest was in the natural sciences: Platter's collection of natural history specimens and his garden with its exotic plants by the Petersplatz were considered sights worth seeing.

The tradition started by Amerbach, Platter and Zwinger found a worthy continuation in the 17th century in the collection of the legal scholar Remigius Faesch (1595-1667). The "Faesch Museum" that he created in his house on the Petersplatz enjoyed a reputation that extended far beyond the City.[78] His grandfather, the mayor Remigius Faesch (1541-1610), was married to a granddaughter of the mayor Jakob Meyer zum Hasen, and owned not only the double portrait of Meyer zum Hasen and his wife Dorothea Kannengiesser (Ill.36, p.57) which the mayor commissioned Holbein to paint in 1516 - as well as the two silver point sketches for it - but also the *Darmstadt Madonna*, which Meyer zum Hasen commissioned Holbein to paint in 1526 for the chapel in his home, and which is now named after its present location. Mayor Remigius Faesch sold this altar panel to Lukas Iselin for 100 guilders in 1606 and the latter's heirs sold it in around 1633 to the Amsterdam art dealer Michel Le Blond. He in turn sold it to the Dowager Queen Maria di Medici for 1,000 Imperial guilders. In the autumn of 1947 the *Madonna of Mayor Jakob Meyer zum Hasen* temporarily returned to Basel and for sixteen years hung in the Holbein Room of the Kunstmuseum on loan from the Prince and Princess von Hessen und bei Rhein.

The double portrait and the drawings of Hans Holbein the Younger that he inherited provided the legal scholar Remigius Faesch with a starting point for his own collection. His main interest was in works of German and Swiss 16th century masters, that is, of a period in the past whose art he clearly valued more highly than that of his own time. Unfortunately, no reliable information is available regarding the pictures he owned, but they must have included the six pictures from the *Life of Mary* by Hans Fries (*Marienleben*. Ills.16-19, pp.42-43), as well as the life-like *Portrait of the Squire Bernhard Meyer zum Pfeil* (*Bildnis des Junkers Bernhard Meyer zum Pfeil*. Ill.14, p.40) painted in 1513 by a Basel master, and the two small panels *Death and the Maiden* and *Death and the Matron* (Ills.26-27, p.50) by Hans Baldung. However, it was drawings - he collected some 220 to 230 sheets - and particularly prints that were his special love. In 1641 and 1648 Remigius Faesch drew up two inventories listing the copper engravings and woodcuts he had collected. The later one lists 648 sheets, among them 191 prints by Dürer, 200 by Italian and 257 by German, Dutch and Flemish engravers. Faesch was also passionately interested in numismatics - the inventory of 1648 mentions the impressive figure of about 2,600 coins - and Roman antiquities.

In 1653 Remigius Faesch moved into the magnificent house on the Petersplatz that had been acquired earlier by his father, and he installed his library on the ground floor and his art collection on the first floor. Joachim von Sandrart said in its praise: "The interior of his dwelling resembles a palace rather than a burgher's house, being unusually beautifully decorated with splendid paintings and sculptures, an excellent library and all kinds of other rarities, as though Minerva herself had taken up residence here."[79] From then, Faesch liked to sign his letters "ex Musaeo".

Remigius Faesch never married. He was, as he wrote in 1667 only a few days before his death, concerned that the "Museo or Cabinet containing my library and other valuable things, which I have collected with great trouble, care and expense over thirty and more years, should be preserved".[80] He laid down that his collection had to be kept intact and could not be sold, and he further stipulated that only a male heir with a doctorate in law was eligible to administer it. If ever this condition were no longer fulfilled, the museum together with the library should go to Basel University. This situation occurred with the death of Hans Rudolf Faesch (1758-1817). After the settlement of the legal disputes that arose with the heirs, the Faesch Museum was taken over by the Öffentliche Kunstsammlung in 1823.

Some of Remigius Faesch's heirs had not only conscientiously administered the collection but had also expanded it. Sebastian Faesch (1647-1712), the nephew of the museum's founder, increased the collection of coins and antiquities, while Johann Rudolf Faesch, the museum's last administrator, added to the holdings of prints by Dürer and his German contemporaries. Moreover, in July 1808, he acquired the panel *Esther before Ahasuerus* (*Esther vor Ahasver*. Ill.5, p.34), which was later identified as being by Konrad Witz, as well as sixteen other pictures at the auction in the Markgräfler Hof at which works from the picture gallery of the Basel residence of the Margraves of Baden-Durlach were sold.

Not just this one panel by Konrad Witz (c. 1400-1444/46) was sold at the auction in the Markgräfler Hof, but twelve of them, which must originally have been part of an *Altarpiece of the Redemption*, probably made for the parish church of St. Leonhard in Basel. They seem to have been acquired by the Margrave Carl William of Baden between 1707 and 1712 in Basel for the picture gallery of his residence there. In addition to Johann Rudolf Faesch, other Basel collectors acquired panels from this altarpiece in July 1808, thus saving this precious cultural treasure for Basel. Johann Konrad Dienast (1741-1824) bought *Saint Bartholomew* (*Der hl. Bartholomäus*. Ill.3, p. 33) and *Abishai before David* (*Abisai vor David*. Ill.6, p.34); both panels entered the Öffentliche Kunstsammlung in 1860 as gifts of his granddaughter Emilie Linder. Councillor Peter Vischer-Sarasin (1751-1823) acquired four panels from the alterpiece: *The Angel of the Annunciation* (*Der Engel der Verkündigung*), *The Ecclesia* (*Die Ecclesia*), *The Synagogue* (*Die Synagoge*) and *Antipater before Julius Caesar* (*Antipater vor Julius Caesar*. Ill.4, p.34).[81] His son Peter Vischer-Passavant donated the last two to the Basel Museum in 1843, while the first two were acquired by it in 1928. Furthermore, in 1864 and 1865 the panels *Abraham before Melchisedec* (*Abraham vor Melchisedek*) and *Sibbechai and Benaiah* (*Sibbechai und Benaja*.Ill.7, p.34) became the property of the Öffentliche Kunstsammlung. Today it possesses eleven out of the total of twenty preserved works by this contemporary of Jan van Eyck and pioneer in the precise observation of reality. Konrad Witz, whose time in Basel coincided with the glorious period of the Church Council of 1431-1448, was rediscovered and identified in 1901 by the Basel art historian Daniel Burckhardt-Werthemann, who was the curator of the Öffentliche Kunstsammlung from 1887 to 1901. In the spring of 1917, taking the opportunity presented by the completion of the restoration in Basel of the altar panels Konrad Witz had created around 1444 for the Cathedral of St. Pierre in Geneva, Paul Ganz, Dr. Burckhardt-Werthemann's successor, organised a unique Konrad Witz exhibition in the Museum in the Augustinergasse, at which the Geneva altar and the Basel works were displayed side by side.

The various Konrad Witz panels donated to the Painting Gallery were the most important Old Masters added to it in the course of the 19th century. All the same, two purchases, which were made possible in the 1860s thanks to the funds set up by Mayor Felix Sarasin-Brunner (1797-1862) and the painter Samuel Birmann (1793-1847), also deserve mention. In May 1813 the University authorities, which at the time were responsible for acquisitions, had turned down *Portrait of the Merchant Georg Gisze* (*Bildnis des Kaufmanns Georg Gisze*. Gemäldegalerie, Berlin-

Dahlem) by Hans Holbein the Younger, which was offered by the bookseller Wilhelm Haas and which had been owned by the Basel art dealer Christian von Mechel, because the price of about 200 doubloons seemed too high. However, in October 1862 the Kunstkommission, with the help of the Felix Sarasin Fund, was able to buy the small *Portrait of an Englishman (?)* ([*Bildnis eines Engländers (?)*]. Ill.44, p.65) from the Basel art dealer Rudolf Lang for 3,000 Swiss francs, thus adding to the collection its only painting from the time when Holbein worked in England.[82] The purchase was made at the urging of Jacob Burckhardt who, in a letter addressed to the Kunstkommission, expressed the conviction - "much or little weight as it might carry" - that "this picture is by H. Holbein the Younger and can only be by him". And he went on: "There was at that time no one in the whole world but Holbein who could have painted this portrait, or who would have painted it precisely this way."[83] Another significant purchase followed in 1864, when Tobias Stimmer's pair of portraits of the Zürich Banneret Jacob Schwytzer and his wife Elsbeth Lochmann (Ills.46-47, p.67), which count among his best work, were purchased from a Munich owner for 1,000 Swiss francs, using the resources of the Birmann Fund.[84]

In our century, too, it has from time to time been possible to extend and enhance the core of the collection of Old Masters that dates back to the Amerbach Kabinett and the Faesch Museum by acquiring one work or another. Again, mention should be made of two particularly precious accessions: *Judgment of Paris* (*Das Urteil des Paris.* Ill.23, p.47) painted by Lukas Cranach the Elder in 1528, which came into the collection in 1977 as a gift of Martha and Robert von Hirsch[85], and also *Portrait of a Man with a Fur Hat* by Hans Holbein the Elder (*Bildnis eines Herrn mit Pelzmütze.* Ill.15, p.41), which was bought from Count Lanckoronski's former collection in 1981 with a special grant from the City of Basel.[86]

3   Konrad Witz (c. 1400-1444/46)
Saint Bartholomew (Der hl. Bartholomäus). Outside panel
from the right wing of the Altarpiece of the Redemption. c. 1435
Tempera on canvas laid down on oak, varnished, 99.5 x 69.5 cm
Inv. no. 639
Gift of Emilie Linder (Dienast Collection), 1860

4/5   Konrad Witz (c. 1400-1444/46)
Antipater before Julius Caesar (Antipater vor Julius Caesar)
Esther before Ahasuerus (Esther vor Ahasver)
Inside panels from the left wing of the Altarpiece
of the Redemption. c. 1435
Tempera on canvas laid down on oak, varnished
Left 85.5 x 69.5 cm, right 85.5 x 79.5 cm.
Left inv. no. 642. Gift of Peter Vischer-Passavant, 1843
Right inv. no. 643. Faesch Museum, 1823

6/7   Konrad Witz (c. 1400-1444/6)
Abishai before David (Abishai vor David)
Sibbechai and Benaiah (Sibbechai und Benaja)
Inside panels from the right wing of the Altarpiece
of the Redemption. c. 1435
Tempera on canvas laid down on oak, varnished
Left 101.5 x 81 cm, right 97.5 x 70 cm.
Left inv. no. 641. Gift of Emile Linder (Dienast Collection), 1860
Right inv. no. 642. Gift of Wilhelm Vischer-Bilfinger, 1865

8   Konrad Witz (c. 1400-1444/46)
Joachim and Anna by the Golden Gate
(Joachim und Anna an der Goldenen Pforte)
Tempera on canvas laid down on pine, varnished 156 x 120.5 cm
Inv. no. 647. Gift of Louise
Bachofen-Burckhardt, 1894

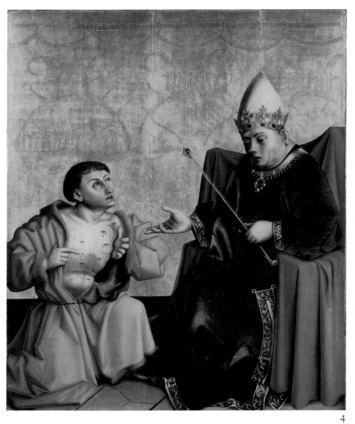

4

5

6

7

10   Master from Basel, 1487
Portrait of Hieronymus Tschekkenbürlin (1461-1536)
(Bildnis des Hieronymus Tschekkenbürlin). 1487
Diptych. The painting of death was produced later (mid 16th century?)
Tempera on limewood, varnished, left 40 x 28.5 cm, right 41 x 29.5 cm
Inv. no. 33. Permanent loan of the Basel Orphanage, 1907

9   Hans Pleydenwurff (c. 1420-1472)
Man of Sorrows (Christus als Schmerzensmann)
Tempera on limewood, varnished, 31 x 23 cm
Inv. no. 1651. Gift of the Amerbach Foundation, 1978

11 Hans Holbein the Elder (c. 1465-1524)
Death of the Virgin (Der Tod Mariae). 1490
Inside panel from the left wing
of the Saint Afra Altarpiece
Tempera on canvas laid down on pine,
varnished, 137 x 71 cm
Inv. no. 300. Purchase, 1865

12 Hans Holbein the Elder (c. 1465-1524). *Death of the Virgin (Der Tod Mariae).* 1500-1501
Part of the former high altar of the Dominican Church in Frankfurt am Main. Tempera on pine, varnished, 165 x 152 cm
Inv. no. 301. Acquired with contributions from the Birmann Fund, the Jacob Burckhardt Foundation,
the Freiwilliger Museumsverein and the Felix Sarasin Fund, 1903

13 Hans Holbein the Elder (c. 1465-1524)
Portrait of Jörg Fischer's Wife at the Age of 34
(Bildnis der Gattin des Jörg Fischer im Alter von 34 Jahren). 1512
Tempera on limewood, varnished, 35 x 26.5 cm
Inv. no. G 1958.7. Gift of J.R. Geigy AG, Basel, on their
200th anniversary, 1958

14 Master from Basel, 1513
Portrait of the Squire Bernhard Meyer zum Pfeil (1488-1558)
(Bildnis des Junkers Bernhard Meyer zum Pfeil). 1513
Tempera on limewood, varnished
40.5 x 35 cm
Inv. no. 22. Faesch Museum, 1823

15 Hans Holbein the Elder (c. 1465-1524). *Portrait of a Man with a Fur Hat (Bildnis eines Herrn mit Pelzmütze)*.1513 Tempera on limewood,
varnished 41.5 x 29.5 cm. Inv. no. G 1981.1. Acquired with a special grant from the City of Basel and private contributions, 1981

16/17   Hans Fries (c. 1465-c. 1523)
Joachim and Anna by the Golden Gate (Joachim und Anna an der Goldenen Pforte)
Birth of the Virgin (Die Geburt Mariae)
Lower outside panels from the left wing of Our Lady's Altarpiece. 1512
Tempera on canvas laid down on pine, varnished, left 107 x 58 cm, right 107 x 64.5 cm
Inv. no. 231 and 230. Faesch Museum, 1823

18/ 19 Hans Fries (c. 1465-c.1523)
The Return from Egypt (Die Rückkehr aus Ägypten)
The Dispute in the Temple (Der zwölfjährige Jesus im Tempel)
Lower inside panels from the left wing of Our Lady's Altarpiece. 1512
Tempera on canvas laid down on pine, varnished, left 107.5 x 65 cm,
right 107 x 57.5 cm. Inv. no. 230 and 231. Faesch Museum, 1823

21 Lucas Cranach the Elder (1472-1553)
Roundel Portraits of Martin Luther and his Wife Katharina von Bora
(Bildnisse des Martin Luther und seiner Gattin Katharina von Bora). 1525
Tempera on beechwood, varnished, diameter 10 cm each
Inv. no. 177 and 177a. Gift of Prof. Johann Rudolf Thurneysen-Faesch, 1762

20 Mathias Grünewald (c. 1480-1531/32)
The Crucifixion (Die Kreuzigung Christi)
Tempera on limewood, varnished, 73 x 52.2 cm
Inv. no. 269. Acquired before 1775

22   Lucas Cranach
the Elder (1472-1553)
*The Virgin and Child
Holding a Piece of Bread
(Maria mit dem ein Brot-
stück haltenden Kind)*
1529
Tempera on limewood,
varnished 84 x 58 cm
Inv. no. 1227
Prof. J.J. Bachofen-
Burckhardt Foundation,
1920

23 Lucas Cranach the Elder
(1472-1553)
*The Judgment of Paris
(Das Urteil des Paris).* 1528
Oil on limewood
85 x 57 cm
Inv. no. G 1977.37. Gift of
Martha and Robert von
Hirsch, 1977

25   Hans Baldung, called Grien (1484/85-1545)
The Crucified Christ with Saints (Christus am Kreuz mit Heiligen). 1512
Tempera on canvas laid down on limewood, varnished, 138 x 140 cm
Inv. no. 17.Gift of the heirs of Anna Katharina Werthemann-Burckhardt, 1860

24   Hans Baldung, called Grien (1484/85-1545). *The Holy Trinity Between the Sorrowing Mother and Saint Giles*
(Die hl. Dreifaltigkeit zwischen der Schmerzensmutter und dem hl. Aegidius)
Tempera on limewood, varnished, 59 x 47.5 cm. Inv. no. 20. Gift of Emilie Linder (Dienast Collection), 1860

26 Hans Baldung, called Grien (1484/85—1545)
Death and the Maiden (Der Tod und das Mädchen). 1517
Tempera on limewood, varnished, 30 x 14.5 cm
Inv. no. 18. Faesch Museum, 1823

27 Hans Baldung, called Grien (1484/85-1545)
Death and the Matron (Der Tod und die Frau)
Tempera on limewood, varnished, 29.5 x 17.5 cm
Inv. no. 19. Faesch Museum, 1823

28 Niklaus Manuel, called Deutsch (c. 1484-1530). *The Beheading of John the Baptist (Die Enthauptung Johannis des Täufers).* c. 1517
Tempera on pine, varnished, 32.5 x 26 cm. Inv. no. 424. Amerbach Kabinett, 1662

29 Niklaus Manuel, called Deutsch (c. 1484 -1530)
Death as a Mercenary Embraces a Young Woman
(Der Tod als Kriegsknecht umfaßt ein junges Weib). 1517
Tempera and pen on pine, varnished, 38 x 29 cm
Inv. no. 419. Amerbach Kabinett, 1662

30 Niklaus Manuel, called Deutsch (c. 1484-1530)
Lucretia. 1517
Tempera and pen on pine, varnished
32. 5 x 26 cm
Inv. no. 420. Amerbach Kabinett, 1662

31 Niklaus Manuel, called Deutsch (c. 1484-1530). *The Judgment of Paris (Das Urteil des Paris)*. 1517-1518
Tempera on canvas, unvarnished, 223 x 165 cm. Inv. no. 422. Amerbach Kabinett, 1662

32   Conrad Apotheker,
called Schnitt? (d. 1541)
*Saint Onuphrius in the
Wilderness
(Der hl. Onuphrius in
der Wildnis)*. 1519
Tempera on canvas,
unvarnished
57 x 38 cm
Inv. no. 672. Amerbach
Kabinett, 1662

33   Ambrosius Holbein
(1494?-1519?)
*The Intercession of
Christ to God the
Father (Christus bei
Gottvater Fürbitte
einlegend)*. c. 1514-1515
Tempera on limewood,
varnished, 36.5 x 30.5 cm
Inv. no. 292. Amerbach
Kabinett, 1662

34   Ambrosius Holbein (1494?-1519?)
Portrait of a Boy with Brown Hair
(Bildnis eines Knaben mit braunem Haar). c. 1516
Tempera on pine, varnished, 33.5 x 28 cm
Inv. no. 295. Amerbach Kabinett, 1662

35   Ambrosius Holbein (1494?-1519?)
Portrait of a Boy with Blond Hair
(Bildnis eines Knaben mit blondem Haar). c. 1516
Tempera on pine, varnished, 33.5 x 27 cm
Inv. no. 294. Amerbach Kabinett, 1662

36   Hans Holbein the Younger (1497/98-1543)
Double Portrait of Jakob Meyer zum Hasen (1482-1531),
Mayor of Basel and his Wife Dorothea Kannengiesser
(Doppelbildnis des Basler Bürgermeisters Jakob Meyer zum Hasen
und seiner Gattin Dorothea Kannengiesser). 1516
Tempera on limewood, varnished, each 38.5 x 31 cm
Inv. no. 312. Faesch Museum, 1823

37   Hans Holbein the Younger (1497/98-1543)
Eight Scenes from the Passion of Christ (Acht Bilder aus der Passion Christi). 1524-1525
Outside panels of a winged altarpiece. Tempera on limewood, varnished, 149.5 x 148.5 cm.
Inv. no. 315. Gift of the City of Basel, 1770

39   Hans Holbein the Younger (1497/98-1543)
Adam and Eve (Adam und Eva). 1517
Tempera on paper laid down on pine, varnished
30 x 35. 5 cm
Inv. no. 313. Amerbach Kabinett, 1662

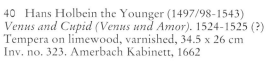

40 Hans Holbein the Younger (1497/98-1543)
Venus and Cupid (Venus und Amor). 1524-1525 (?)
Tempera on limewood, varnished, 34.5 x 26 cm
Inv. no. 323. Amerbach Kabinett, 1662

41 Hans Holbein the Younger (1497/98-1543)
Laïs of Corinth (Laïs von Korinth). 1526
Tempera on limewood, varnished, 34 x 27 cm
Inv. no. 322. Amerbach Kabinett, 1662

42

42 Hans Holbein the Younger (1497/98-1543)
*Portrait of the Artist's Wife and her
Two Oldest Children
(Bildnis von Holbeins Frau mit
den beiden älteren Kindern).* 152(8?)
Tempera on paper, varnished, cut out and laid
down on limewood, 77 x 64 cm
Inv. no. 325. Amerbach Kabinett, 1662

43 Hans Holbein the Younger (1497/98-1543)
*Roundel Portrait of Erasmus of Rotterdam
(Bildnis des Erasmus von Rotterdam im Rund).* c. 1532
Tempera on beechwood, varnished, diameter 10 cm
Inv. no. 324. Amerbach Kabinett, 1662

44 Hans Holbein the Younger (1497/98-1543)
*Portrait of an Englishman (?)
(Bildnis eines Engländers [?]).* c. 1540
Tempera on oak, varnished, 32.5 x 26 cm
Inv. no. 327. Felix Sarasin Fund, 1862

43

45 Unknown Frisian Master
*Portrait of David Joris (1501-1556).
(Bildnis des David Joris).* c. 1550-1555
Tempera on oak, varnished, 89 x 68.5 cm
Inv. no. 561. Gift of the City of Basel, 1714

46 Tobias Stimmer (1539-1584)
*Portrait of Jacob Schwytzer (1512-1581),
Zürich Banneret
(Bildnis des Zürcher Pannervorträgers
Jacob Schwytzer).* 1564
Tempera on limewood, varnished, 191 x 66.5 cm
Inv. no. 577. Birmann Fund, 1864

47 Tobias Stimmer (1539-1584)
*Portrait of Elsbeth Lochmann,
Wife of Jacob Schwytzer
(Bildnis von Elsbeth Lochmann,
der Gattin des Jacob Schwytzer).* 1564
Tempera on limewood, varnished. 191 x 67.5 cm
Inv. no. 578. Birmann Fund, 1864

44

46

47

48   Hans Bock the Elder (c. 1550-1624)
Portrait of Melchior Hornlocher (1539-1619), City Councillor of Basel
(Bildnis des Basler Ratsherrn Melchior Hornlocher). 1577
Tempera on oak, varnished, 86 x 70 cm
Inv. no. 80. Gift of Melchior Nörbel,
bequest of Helene Müller-Hornlocher, 1823

49   Hans Bock the Elder (c. 1550-1624)
Portrait of Katharina Äder (1545-1629), Wife of Melchior Hornlocher
(Bildnis von Katharina Äder, der Gattin des Melchior Hornlocher). 1577
Tempera on oak, unvarnished, 86 x 70 cm
Inv. no. 81. Gift of Melchior Nörbel,
bequest of Helene Müller-Hornlocher, 1823

50   Hans Bock the Elder (c. 1550-1624)
Allegory of Day (Allegorie des Tages). 1586
Tempera on limewood, varnished, 81 x 82 cm
Inv. no. 85. Amerbach Kabinett, 1662

51   Hans Bock the Elder (c. 1550-1624)
Allegory of Night (Allegorie der Nacht). 1586
Tempera on limewood, varnished, 79.5 x 81.5 cm
Inv. no. 86. Amerbach Kabinett, 1662

52   Hans Bock the Elder (c. 1550-1624)
Portrait of Theodor Zwinger (1533-1588)
(Bildnis des Theodor Zwinger)
Tempera on oak, varnished, 67.5 x 53 cm
Inv. no. 1877.
Amerbach
Kabinett, 1662

Troops and Generals

53   Hendrick Goltzius (1588-1617)
Allegory (Allegorie). 1611
Oil on canvas, 180 x 256 cm
Inv. no. 252. Birmann Collection, 1847

In her last will she expressly forebade obituaries[87] and the announcement of her death carried the message: "No flowers".[88] However, the chairman of the Kunstkommission and the curator of the Öffentliche Kunstsammlung did not comply with this instruction and they laid on her grave "a wreath costing 80 Swiss francs with the inscription 'To a generous benefactress from the Kunstkommission' ".[89] Louise Elisabeth Bachofen-Burckhardt, the widow of the famous Basel legal scholar and mythologist Johann Jakob Bachofen-Burckhardt (1815-1887), who rediscovered matriarchy, "passed away after a brief serious illness"[90] on the evening of Saturday 21 February 1920. On 25 November 1904 the deceased had informed the Basel Government that, in her husband's memory, she had donated the collection of paintings in her possession to a foundation to be called the "Professor Johann Jakob Bachofen-Burckhardt Foundation", which was intended to expand and complement the Öffentliche Kunstsammlung. She made it a condition that she should be able to keep the paintings in her care during her lifetime. She had already donated several works to the Museum, for example the panel with *Joachim and Anna by the Golden Gate* (*Joachim and Anna an der Goldenen Pforte*. Ill.8, p.35)by Konrad Witz in 1894. The City acquired the Bachofen House, which had been built at Münsterplatz No. 2 between 1841 and 1845 on the model of Italo-Tuscan Renaissance palaces and which in memory of the previous building on the site bears the name "Zur St. Johanns-Capelle", but it did not enjoy the right to use it until Louise Bachofen-Burckhardt's death. Mrs. Bachofen's bequest was challenged by her heirs; the legal dispute ended in June 1921 when the pictures were finally declared the property of the Museum.[91]

When in March 1905 the contents of the deed establishing the Foundation were revealed "in strict confidence" to the Kunstkommission, the collection of paintings comprised 237 items. The benefactress intended to continue building up her collection of works of art, for it had become the main purpose and pleasure of her life. Indeed, the Committee of the Foundation reported to the Kunstkommission practically every year on further gifts enriching the collection. Thus on 19 March 1908 they learned of the purchase of the panel *The Birth of Saint Nicholas* (*Die Geburt des Hl. Nikolaus*) by Pietro di Giovanni d'Ambrogio, on 30 April 1909 of the acquisition of *Ships on the Sea* by Simon de Vlieger (*Schiffe auf See*. Ill.63, p.84), on 20 May 1910 of that of three paintings, among them the lowland landscape by A. van der Croos (Ill.65, p.85), and on 23 January 1912 of the accession of Pieter Lastman's *Christ and the Samaritan Woman* (*Christus und die Samariterin*.Ill.59, p.81). As early as 1907 a lavish catalogue of the Bachofen Foundation had appeared, written by Rudolf Friedrich Burckhardt; it by then numbered 248 paintings from the 15th to the 19th centuries.[92] In the Annual Report of the Öffentliche Kunstsammlung for 1913, Paul Ganz, the curator at the time, included a further appreciation of the Foundation, which he followed by a list of the 293 works it by then comprised.[93]

There were good reasons why it should have been in 1913 that the general public was informed about the Foundation. In April of that year the Basel Parliament debated a proposal concerning museum buildings. As a series of articles in the *Basler Nachrichten* noted on that occasion, "the extension of the premises has become all the more pressing...for the future growth of the collection, because the magnificent foundation, which Mrs. Bachofen has established for the benefit of the art collection in the name of her husband, Mr. J.J. Bachofen-Burckhardt, promises a considerable and extremely valuable increase".[94] Yet at the very moment when, with Mrs. Bachofen's death, the Foundation created by her was due to be integrated into the Öffentliche Kunstsammlung, the project of a new museum building on the Schützenmatte was finally buried.

The Basel Government then decided to place the Bachofen House at the disposal of the Öffentliche Kunstsammlung as a branch gallery. Basel art from Konrad Witz to Holbein, and Swiss painting from the second half of the 19th century to the present stayed in the old Museum in the Augustinergasse, while the Bachofen House accommodated all the rest, such as the Bachofen collection, the bequest of Hans Vonder Mühll and the Emilie Linder Foundation. The house was first opened to the general public on 10 September 1922. The opportunity to view the Bachofen collection "which enjoyed a reputation in Basel and beyond" had, in particular, been awaited "with a certain impatience".[95] The official inauguration took place on 4 November.[96]

The Bachofen House was originally a private house, and now the pictures that were brought together there were above all ones collected in the 18th and 19th centuries for private houses, which had later come into the Öffentliche Kunstsammlung as donations and bequests. The intimacy of the rooms set off 17th century Netherlandish paintings to particular advantage. "It is especially perceptible in this part of the collection that it was originally intended for the embellishment of private houses, and that in the happier examples the selection has indeed been guided by a fine taste for intimate charm, but not by a passionate obsession which even the great innovators would barely have satisfied", observed the curator at the time, Heinrich Alfred Schmid. Most of all he criticised the absence of the "principal masters of the southern and northern Netherlands, Rubens and van Dyck, Frans Hals, Rembrandt and Vermeer van Delft. What has been donated under those names does not live up to the attribution in a public gallery." He explained: "As our knowledge of European art has grown and our methods of examination have become more refined, many a work that was once highly esteemed has been put into storage as an obvious copy or forgery. But new donations have been added and out of the mass that has been handed down there has now crystallised a small but valuable collection of originals."[97]

The catalogue of the Öffentliche Kunstsammlung that was published in 1849 to mark the inauguration of the Museum in the Augustinergasse lists only a small number of works by Dutch and Flemish masters: *The Holy Family with John as a Boy* (*Die hl. Familie mit dem Johannesknaben*) by Herri met de Bles and *David and Abigail in a Roman Landscape* (*David und Abigail in römischer Landschaft*) by Lambert van Noort came from the Amerbach Kabinett and others, but likewise nothing of particular merit, from the Faesch collection. The *Portrait of David Joris* (*Bildnis des David Joris*. Ill.45, p.66) - which used to be attributed to Jan van Scorel but which might in fact be a self-portrait of the heretical Anabaptist, who lived unrecognised in Basel under a pseudonym from 1544 until his death in 1556 - was confiscated by the Basel Council from his family in 1559 after his identity had been revealed. It then remained in the City Hall until 1714, when the Basel Government transferred it to the art collection. *Hunting Fleas* - the catalogue specifies *By Candlelight* - by the Caravaggist Gerrit van Honthorst (*Flohjagd im Kerzenschein*. Ill.55, p.78) and *Four Church Fathers* from the school of Jordaens had been presented to the Öffentliche Kunstsammlung in 1833 by the heirs of Mayor Christoph Ehinger-Burckhardt (1755-1833). To mark the new Museum's inauguration, Emilie Linder donated *Saint Ambrose* and *Saint Gregory* by Matthias Stomer (*Der hl. Ambrosius. Der hl. Gregor*. Ills.57-58, p.80) from her collection; at that time the two works were attributed to the Spanish school, but they were reattributed to the school of Rubens in the 1852 catalogue. In 1850 Emilie Linder donated a dozen panels and paintings by 15th to 18th century Netherlandish masters from the collection of her grandfather, Johann Konrad Dienast, but they unfortunately contained little of any note. The number of Flemish and Dutch paintings in the collection was increased substantially in 1859 when 28 paintings were acquired through the Birmann bequest. The large-size *Allegory* (Ill.53, p.72) by Goltzius was hung without ceremony over the door leading to the antiquities collection.[98]

The number of Flemish and Dutch paintings in the public collection seems relatively modest when compared with what was privately owned in Basel at the time. Some idea of this is conveyed by the catalogues of three exhibitions of paintings owned privately in Basel which the Kunsthalle organised in the 1870s and in 1891. In the "Exhibition of Paintings by Old and Modern Masters in Local Private Ownership" with which the Kunsthalle celebrated its inauguration in 1872, 46 per cent of the works exhibited were by Flemish and Dutch masters. In the "Exhibition of Privately Owned Paintings in Honour of the Swiss Kunstverein Celebration" held in the summer of 1875, works by Flemish and Dutch masters accounted for 53 per cent of the total, while in 1891, in the "Second Exhibition of Paintings by Old Masters in Private Ownership in Basel", they accounted for 51 per cent. These figures clearly indicate a predilection for the Flemish and Dutch schools of the 17th century. The catalogues of the three exhibitions permit a somewhat more exact identification of the preferences among wealthy Basel merchants and industrialists. The inaugural exhibition of 1872 arranged the "Belgian and Dutch Masters" into groups such as "Rubens and the Brabant School" and "Rembrandt and his School", but "Dutch Little Masters" were the best represented, accounting for 98 out of a total of 163 paintings. The most popular artists, with eight exhibits each, were Pieter Brueghel the Elder (although they were probably works of his school or copies) and the painter of peasant genre scenes, David Teniers the Younger, followed by the landscape painters Jan van Goyen and Jacob van Ruisdael. In the exhibition of 1875, which classified the 66 paintings by "Belgian and Dutch Masters" into "Landscapes" and works by "Painters of Sea-pieces and Marine Landscapes", "Painters of Pasture Landscapes and Cattle" and "Painters of Fowl and Hunting Scenes", there was usually only one work per artist to be found, although there were occasionally two, as in the case of Adriaen Brouwer and Adriaen van Ostade. Only Teniers was represented by three pictures. An analysis of the 1891 exhibition gives a similar result: out of the total of 150 works exhibited in the section "School of the Netherlands and Holland", five were by Teniers and two more by his imitators. Teniers' art was still esteemed in conservative Basel, whereas elsewhere, with the rise of modern painting in the 19th century, his glory had dramatically faded. Against this background, one can understand the criticism expressed by the Basel painter Hans Sandreuter who, on the occasion of the "Second Exhibition of Paintings by Old Masters in Private Ownership in Basel", lamented: "I feel that never has so much thought been given to art in Basel and so little to artists as at the present time. Two exhibitions of Old Masters within six months and a host of other trashy exhibitions."[99]

The figures quoted give no information about the quality of what had been collected. The catalogue of the 1872 exhibition lists no fewer than four Rembrandt pictures. Two of these, *Young Man (Junger Mann)* from the collection of Mrs. Burckhardt-Werthemann and *Portrait of Mayor Mappe of Amsterdam (Bildnis des Bürgermeisters Mappe von Amsterdam)* from the collection of Mr. W. Burckhardt-Sarasin, were again displayed in the Kunsthalle in 1875. However, all the 1891 catalogue contained was two examples of the Rembrandt school, which was probably closer to the truth. The picture from the Burckhardt-Sarasin collection was presumably *Half-length Portrait of a Man in a Cap with a Feather (Brustbild eines Mannes mit Federbarett)*, which is today attributed to a pupil of Rembrandt from his Leiden period.[100] No better fate was reserved for *Old Man Reading (Lesender alter Mann)* from Mrs. Bachofen's collection: this was identified as a copy of *Hermit Reading (Lesender Eremit)* in the Louvre, which is itself no longer attributed to Rembrandt.[101] Mrs. Bachofen was advised on her acquisitions by none less than the director of the Berlin museums, Wilhelm von Bode (1845-1929), but this obviously did not prevent such mistakes.

Five paintings in the section "Netherlandish and Dutch School" in the 1891 exhibition belonged to Hans Vonder Mühll. Two of them - *Carousing Peasants (Zechende Bauern)* by Joost Cornelisz Droochsloot and *Distinguished Hunting Party (Vornehme Jagdgesellschaft)* by Jan van Huchtenburgh - were bequeathed by him to the Öffentliche Kunstsammlung in 1914, together with 25 other paintings by Dutch and Flemish masters. Hans Vonder Mühll (1846-1914) trained as a businessman in Geneva and Leeds, and after returning to Basel he entered the business of his uncles Wilhelm and Karl Ryhiner. After a few years he went into partnership with his brother Albert, with whom he founded a ribbon-making company, Gesellschaft für Bandfabrikation AG. Vonder Mühll, who never married, retired early from business in order to live quietly. He had depressive tendencies and became quite melancholic in the final decade of his life. He found solace in his activities as a collector and in his interest in fine arts. In the early 1880s he began to collect works of 17th century Netherlandish artists exclusively, having a clear preference for their landscapes and genre paintings. Mainly through the mediation of Consul Hermann Wirz (1832-1907)[102], who also acted as an art dealer - the Basel Museum purchased Böcklin's *Odysseus and Calypso (Odysseus und Kalypso.* Ill.111, p.132) from him in 1895 - he acquired several paintings which had long been in private collections in Basel, for instance *Peasants Wedding (Bauernhochzeit)* from 1652 by Jan Victor, a pupil of Rembrandt, which had been exhibited in the Kunsthalle in 1872 on loan from the Hindermann-Merian collection, and *Peasants' Meal (Bauernmahlzeit)*, attributed to Adriaen Brouwer, which Martin Bachofen-Heitz (1727-1814), the builder of the Ebenrain, had bought in 1772 from the Basel engraver and art dealer Christian van Mechel (1737-1817) and which had featured in the Kunsthalle exhibition of 1875 as a loan from Hermann Wirz.[103]

The basis of Mrs. Bachofen's collection was likewise provided by pictures that had long been in private ownership in Basel, since several paintings came from the collection that had been built up by her husband's grandfather, Johann Jakob Bachofen-Burckhardt (1755-1828), the owner of the "Weisses Haus", and his son Johann Jakob Burckhardt-Merian (1788-1876). At the beginning of the 1850s, as evidence of his expertise, the latter published an impressive catalogue, illustrated with lithographed copies drawn by G. Wolf of the forty most important paintings in the collection - *Partie des Tableaux de la Collection de Mr. Bacofen (sic) Basle rue fossé St. Alban*. This includes the charming *Sledge Trip* (*Schlittenfahrt*. Ill.67, p.86) by Nicolaes Berchem, *The Baptism of the Chamberlain* (*Die Taufe des Kämmerers*. Ill.62, p.83), which has recently been attributed to Dirck Bleker[104], and *Landscape with Waterfall (Landschaft mit Wasserfall)*, which is sometimes attributed to Allaert van Everdingen and sometimes to Jacob van Ruisdael, and which Johann Jakob Bachofen-Merian loaned to the Kunsthalle in 1872, together with a few other pictures in his possession, for its inaugural exhibition.

The inclusion of the Professor Johann Jakob Bachofen-Burckhardt Foundation in 1921 increased the number of paintings in the Öffentliche Kunstsammlung by one quarter. It could not, however, realise the wish of the curator Heinrich Alfred Schmid, "that the troops should be joined by a general, i.e., that a few works embodying the pioneering innovations of their epoch should enter the Bachofen House alongside the many charming pictures by old Dutch and Flemish painters".[105] The realisation of this wish had to await the bequest of Max Geldner (1875-1958).

Max Geldner was the son of Carl Geldner (1841-1920), the founder of a coal merchant's, Kohlenunion AG. He entered his father's firm at the age of twenty-five.[106] A keen footballer, he was one of the initiators and founders of the Basel Football Club in 1893. He was also very fond of rowing and remained a passionate skier until an advanced age. In the first decade of the century he began to collect Netherlandish Little Masters, following in his father's footsteps in this respect too. Carl Geldner had been amongst those who lent works for the "Exhibition of Paintings by Old Masters in Private Ownership in Basel" held in the Kunsthalle in 1891, and in around 1905 he published privately a catalogue of his collection, which at that time comprised 127 paintings by Italian, French, German and especially Netherlandish artists. In 1910 Max Geldner became a partner in the family firm. He now also turned his attention to modern Swiss painting, acquiring pictures by Hodler, Albert Welti, Cuno Amiet and Edouard Vallet. Many works that ceased to satisfy his increasingly refined criteria and growing knowledge were sold by him or exchanged for items of higher quality. He kept a meticulous record of his purchases and sales, so that the date and provenance of his acquisitions are usually precisely documented.

In 1920, upon his father's death, Max Geldner took over the management of the family firm as chairman of the Board of Directors. He now became even more active as a collector; he had considerably more money at his disposal, all the more so because, as a bachelor, he did not have to provide for a family. From then on, apart from a few rare exceptions, he made no further purchases of pictures by modern Swiss artists. The eighteen pictures by Netherlandish masters he acquired in the 1920s include some of his collection's best works such as *Wooded Marsh Landscape with Dead Tree (Waldige Sumpflandschaft mit abgestorbenem Baum*. Ill.66, p.85) by Jacob van Ruisdael and the Amsterdam vedutà by Jan van der Heyden (Ill.73, p.90). In 1935 Max Geldner retired from active professional life so as to devote himself entirely to his personal interests. He made nine purchases in 1937, and eight in both 1938 and 1939. Geldner had a knowledgeable adviser in his neighbour Dr. Hans Schneider-Christ (1888-1953), the founder and director of the Rijksbureau voor kunsthistorische documentatie (National Bureau for Art History Documentation) in The Hague. Max Geldner's acquisitions reached a high point in 1939 with the brilliant early work by Rembrandt *David before King Saul Presenting the Head of Goliath (David übergibt Goliaths Haupt dem König Saul*. Ill.60, p.82), which was bought for 60,000 guilders or 142,000 Swiss francs. "For the sake of this single picture alone, we can now confidently send our visitors to see our Netherlandish rooms, too!" wrote Georg Schmidt in the foreword to the catalogue that presented the 32 works by 16th and 17th century Netherlandish masters and the 24 modern pictures which entered the Öffentliche Kunstsammlung in 1958 as the "Max Geldner

Bequest".[107] The financial support of the "Max Geldner Foundation" established by the collector also enables the Kunstmuseum to make further purchases for its collection. The most important of these to date are the pastel *Breakfast upon Leaving the Bath* (*La tasse de chocolat*. Ill.162, p.183) by Degas - "this bold 'resurrection' in sulphur yellow"[108] - and the two paintings *The Footbridge over the Water Lily Pond* (*La passerelle sur le bassin aux nymphéas*. Ill.164, p.184) by Monet and *View of the Jungfrau from the Isenfluh* (*Die Jungfrau, von der Isenfluh aus gesehen*. Ill.119, p.140) by Hodler.[109]

The Netherlandish section of the Öffentliche Kunstsammlung in Basel today comprises 374 paintings.[110] Of these, only a mere half-dozen have been purchased by the Museum while the remainder all stem from donations and bequests from private benefactors. In 1971 an anonymous art-lover set up a "Foundation for the Advancement of Netherlandish Art in Basel", which, on behalf of the Kunstmuseum, acquires works by Netherlandish painters from early times up to and including the 18th century, and then makes them available to the Kunstmuseum on long-term loan. With the Foundation's acquisition in 1988 of the oil sketch for Rubens' *The Trinity* (*Die Dreifaltigkeit*. Ill.76, p.92), which had long been privately owned in England, another "general" joined the "troops" in the Netherlandish section.[111]

54 Willem Cornelisz. Duyster (1598/99-1635)
Two Officers Being Shown Jewels and Precious Gifts
(Zwei Offiziere lassen sich Schmuck
und kostbare Geräte zeigen).
Tempera on oak, varnished, 49 x 40.5 cm
Inv. no. 1340. J.J. Bachofen-Burckhardt Foundation, 1920

55 Gerrit van Honthorst (1590-1656)
Hunting Fleas by Candlelight (Flohjagd im Kerzenschein)
Oil on canvas, 105 x 136 cm
Inv. no. 362. Gift of the heirs of Mayor
Christoph Ehinger-Burckhardt, 1833

56 Hendrick ter Brugghen (1588-1629)
Ballad Singer (Bänkelsängerin). 1628
Oil on canvas, 78.5 x 65.5 cm
Inv. no. 611. Acquired by the Freiwilliger Museumsverein
from the bequest of Gustav R.M. Stehlin, 1902

57 Matthias Stomer
(1600-after 1649)
Saint Ambrose
(Der hl. Ambrosius)
Oil on canvas, 89 x 115 cm
Inv. no. 186. Gift of Emilie
Linder, 1849

58 Matthias Stomer
(1600-after 1649)
Saint Gregory
(Der hl. Gregor)
Oil on canvas, 89 x 115 cm
Inv. no. 187. Gift of Emilie
Linder, 1849

59 Pieter Pietersz. Lastman (1583-1633). *Christ and the Samaritan Woman (Christus und die Samariterin)*
Oil on oak, 73.5 x 67.5 cm
Inv. no. 1365. Prof. J.J. Bachofen-Burckhardt Foundation, 1920

60   Rembrandt Harmensz. van Rijn (1606-1669)
David before King Saul Presenting the Head of Goliath (David übergibt Goliaths Haupt dem König Saul). 1627
Oil on oak, 27.5 x 39.5 cm
Inv. no. G 1958.37. Bequest of Max Geldner, 1958

61   Jan Steen (1625/26-1679)
The Dispute in the Temple
(Der zwölfjährige Jesus im Tempel).
1659-1660
Oil on canvas, 83.5 x 101 cm
Inv. no. 906. Bequest of Hans
Vonder Mühll, 1914

62   Dirck Bleker (?) (1622-1672)
The Baptism of the Chamberlain
(Die Taufe des Kämmerers). 1630-1635
Oil on oak, 78.5 x 89 cm
Inv. no. 1157. Prof. J.J. Bachofen-
Burckhardt Foundation, 1920

63 Simon Jacobsz. de Vlieger
(1601-1653)
Ships on the Sea
(Schiffe auf See)
Oil on oak, 34 x 41 cm
Inv. no. 1354. Prof. J.J.
Bachofen-Burckhardt
Foundation, 1920

64 Jan Josephsz. van Goyen
(1596-1656)
River Scene with Anglers
(Flußlandschaft mit Anglern). 1635
Oil on oak, 37 x 47.5 cm
Inv. no. 925. Bequest of Hans
Vonder Mühll, 1914

65   Anthonie Jansz. van der Croos
(1606/07-1662/63)
*Extensive Landscape with River
(Ebene mit Fluß)*. 1654
Oil on oak, 32 x 37 cm
Inv. no. 1360. Prof. J.J. Bachofen-
Burckhardt Foundation, 1920

66   Jacob Issacksz. van Ruisdael
(1628/29-1682)
*Wooded Marsh Landscape with
Dead Tree (Waldige Sumpflandschaft
mit abgestorbenem Baum)*
Oil on canvas, 60.5 x 74.5 cm
Inv. no. G 1958.38. Bequest of
Max Geldner, 1958

67   Nicolaes Berchem
(1620-1683)
*Sledge Trip
(Schlittenfahrt)*. 1660-1670
Oil on oak, 24.5 x 31.5 cm
Inv. no. 1143. Prof. J.J. Bachofen-
Burckhardt Foundation, 1920

68   Philips Wouwermans
(1619-1668)
Battle Scene (Reiterschlacht)
Oil on oak, 52.5 x 67 cm
Inv. no. 1317. Prof. J.J.
Bachofen-Burckhardt
Foundation, 1920

69   Johannes Lingelbach
(1623/24-1674)
*River with Bathing Gypsies
Near an Italian City
(Fluß mit badenden Zigeunern
bei italienischer Stadt)*
Oil on canvas, 82 x 72.5 cm
Inv. no. 1148. Prof. J. J.
Bachofen-Burckhardt
Foundation, 1920

71 Pieter van den Bosch (c. 1613- after 1663)
The Young Cook
(Die junge Köchin) Oil on oak, 57 x 45.5 cm
Inv. no. 919. Bequest of Hans Vonder Mühll, 1914

72 Frans van Mieris the Elder (1635-1681)
Young Woman with a Feather Fan
(Junge Dame mit Federfächer). 1660-1663
Oil on oak, 20 x 16 cm
Inv. no. G 1958.27. Bequest of Max Geldner, 1958

70 Pieter de Hooch (1629- after 1683)
Woman with a Basket in the Vegetable Garden (Frau mit Bohnenkorb im Gemüsegarten). 1661(?)
Oil on canvas, 69.5 x 59 cm. Inv. no. G 1958.22. Bequest of Max Geldner, 1958

73   Jan van der Heyden (1637-1712)
The Dam in Amsterdam with the Town Hall and the Nieuwe Kerk
(Der Dam in Amsterdam gegen Rathaus und Nieuwe Kerk. After 1669
Oil on oak, 43.5 x 54 cm. Inv. no. G 1958.21. Bequest of Max Geldner, 1958

74   Willem van Aelst (1625/26-c. 1683)
Breakfast (Das Frühstück). 1679
Oil on canvas, 58.5 x 46 cm
Inv. no. 3. Birmann Collection, 1847

75   Jan van de Velde III (c. 1620-1662)
*Still-Life with Wine Glass and Sliced Lemon
(Weinglas und angeschnittene Zitrone)*. 1649
Oil on oak, 31 x 14.5 cm
Inv. no. G 1958.40. Bequest of Max Geldner, 1958

76   Peter Paul Rubens (1577-1640). *The Trinity (Die Dreifaltigkeit)* Oil on oak, 64 x 46.5 cm
Inv. no. G 1988.24. Permanent loan of the Foundation for the Advancement of Netherlandish Art in Basel, 1988

The Pious Art of the High-minded Spinster

77 Master of the "Hausbuch"
(active 1460 - 1490)
Three Hovering Angels (Drei schwebende Engel)
Tempera on pine, varnished
29.5 x 38 cm
Inv. no. 431. Gift of Emilie Linder, 1862

When the tenth Congress of Philologists met in Basel from 29 September to 2 October 1847, "the galleries of the new Museum were opened to visitors" as an exceptional measure on the afternoon of Friday 1 October, "although of them only the Mexican Room had actually been fitted out". The official inauguration of Melchior Berri's building in the Augustinergasse was not to take place until two years later, on 26 Novem-ber 1849. However, even at the time of the Congress, the *Allgemeines Intelligenzblatt der Stadt Basel* announced to its readers: "It will be noted with pleasure what marvellous lighting awaits the painting collection in these high, light rooms, but at the same time there will be fears that our small collection could get lost in their spaciousness." (Similar reservations were incidentally also expressed eighty years later, before the opening of the Kunstmuseum in the St. Alban-Graben.) The reporter was also able to announce: "There is all the more cause for gratification and gratitude over the gift of three cartoons by Cornelius from the cycle in the Ludwigskirche in Munich made in the last few days by a noble art-lover, who, despite her distant place of residence, takes a very warm interest in her native city and its artistic life. These cartoons will be exhibited in the galleries and among them the lofty figure of God the Father will deservedly be greeted with admiration. At the same time as this extremely valuable gift, the noble benefactress has donated to the public collection an equally valuable cartoon by Schnorr from the Niebelungen cycle and two oil paintings from the new Munich school, a mediaeval town by Ahlborn and Neher's Visit of the Three Angels to Abraham, which were previously kept on the premises of the Kunstverein. May this generous support coming to our art collection from outside awaken the same spirit and the same love for it within our city itself."[112]

The donation referred to here was the first that Emilie Linder (1797-1867) made to the Basel Museum from her personal collection during her lifetime. The paintings *Heyday of the Middle Ages* (*Blütezeit des Mittelalters*. 1829) by August Wilhelm Julius Ahlborn[113] and *Visit of the Angels to Abraham* (*Besuch der Engel bei Abraham*. 1830) by Bernhard Neher, the three cartoons for ceiling frescoes (1838) by Peter von Cornelius[114] and the cartoon *Kriemhilde Finds Siegfried's Corpse* (*Kriemhilde findet Siegfrieds Leiche*. Around 1833)[115] by Julius Schnorr von Carolsfeld were the first works by contemporary foreign artists to enter the Öffentliche Kunstsammlung, whose own collecting activity was exclusively limited to national and local art until the beginning of the 20th century. Emilie Linder followed up this first donation with a second one in 1849 to mark the new Museum's inauguration. In addition to *Landscape with Macbeth and the Witches* (*Landschaft mit Macbeth und den Hexen*. Ill.80, p.99) by the Austrian painter Joseph Anton Koch, who worked in Rome, this included a pair of paintings by a 17th century Dutch master: the portrayals of the church fathers *Saint Ambrose* and *Saint Gregory* (*Der hl. Ambrosius. Der hl. Gregor*. Ills.57-58, p.80) by Matthias Stomer[116]. Emilie Linder was principally interested in those contemporary German artists with whom she was on good terms personally, but this interest was not exclusive and she also possessed some paintings by masters of earlier schools. There are occasional views of Italian landscapes among the pictures and drawings by the Nazarenes, but the works collected by Emilie Linder - both the later and the earlier ones - mainly have a religious content. To this extent, there is certainly a connection between the theme of *Three Hovering Angels* (*Drei schwebende Engel*. Ill.77, p. 94) by an unnamed Late Gothic master (known as the "Hausbuchmeister") and the pair of small pictures *Two Hovering Angels* (*Zwei schwebende Engel*. Ills.86-87, p.104) by Johann von Schraudolph (1808-1879).

Emilie Linder, who was born on 11 October 1797 in Basel and who lost both her parents by the age of fifteen, grew up in the house of her maternal grandparents. Her grandfather, Johann Konrad Dienast (1741-1824), a jurist and steward of the church of St. Peter, helped to found the Basel Künstlergesellschaft in 1812. Through his "quite unusual savings" he established an art collection, which he hoped would not, after his death, be "broken up in a manner that art-lovers and connoisseurs would find unseemly".[117] After the early death of his daughter, who was to have inherited his art collection, Dienast bequeathed it to his granddaughter Emilie Linder in 1816. She moved to Munich after her grandfather's death to train as a painter at the Academy which Peter Cornelius headed there. However, she gave up her studies at the Academy after only a few weeks and became a private pupil of Joseph Schlotthauer. As an obituary put it in 1867, Emilie Linder practised "her art in the most modest manner, by dedicating her paintings solely to poor chapels or churches". Although wealthy through her inherited share of her parents' fortune and her grandfather's legacy, she lived "in the most simple seclusion and modesty" and, as the obituary went on to say: "The notable collection of the most beautiful works of art that embellished her home was probably the only enjoyment she allowed herself."

Emilie Linder was less a collector than a supporter and patron of artists. A period of study in Rome had brought her into contact with Friedrich Overbeck, the founder of the Brotherhood of St. Luke, and with the Nazarenes in general, as well as with Joseph Anton Koch. When she acquired or commissioned pictures and above all drawings, she did so less with the idea of increasing her art collection than in order to provide financial help and support for her artist friends. In Munich she got to know Clemens von Brentano (1778-1842) - "a name that is not in good repute everywhere, but that has nonetheless attained a certain fame through his original poetry".[118] The poet soon became passionately attached to Emilie, who was almost two decades younger than he. Following their first meeting in October 1833, Brentano described her as "a woman dressed in black of about 35, of medium stature, with a slim figure, intelligent appearance, black hair, a yellow straw hat and a white veil - courteous and friendly". And he further observed: "she is calm and steady in everything she does; she is thorough, reads nothing but serious, indeed learned, Catholic books - she even has private instruction in Catholic philosophy from one of the most profound thinkers who has ever lived, and she reads a lot of St. Augustine".[119]

Brentano tried to convert Emilie Linder to Catholicism. Quoting the example of the work of the young Catholic painter Edward von Steinle (1810-1886), a pupil of Friedrich Overbeck, he sought to persuade her "that if she were Catholic she would paint better; it would come quite easily to her."[120] At Christmas 1838 Emilie Linder did indeed buy a picture by Steinle - *Saint Luke Painting the Madonna and Child* (*Der hl. Lukas malt Maria mit dem Kinde.* Ill.81, p.100), the theme of which is "Art as the handmaiden of religion" - but she did not yield to her poet friend's urging and cajoling. It was not until after his death, and then on her own initiative, that she converted to Catholicism.

The picture by Steinle entered the collection of the Basel Museum in 1862, as part of a third donation, which was acknowledged thus in the *Basler Nachrichten* of 4 October: "Our Öffentliche Kunstsammlung has long found a principal source of its enrichment in the active public spiritedness of its citizens. Earlier on, when its means were more limited, it was almost entirely dependent on this. And even now, when it enjoys the magnificent bequest of Mr. Samuel Birmann, continued help of every kind is still highly desirable - indeed one might say essential - since the income from the foundation referred to may be spent only on works of art of Swiss origin. Therefore we owe very special thanks to Miss Emilie Linder in Munich, that noble-minded citizen of Basel, who, just as in previous years and equally unceasingly in the last few years, has now once again presented the collection with valuable gifts of all kinds and from the most different fields, so that the shelves are increasingly being filled with art books, the folders with engravings, woodcuts and drawings, and the walls of the Painting Gallery with works by the leading masters of Italy, Germany and the Low Countries. Visitors to the Painting Gallery as from next Sunday will notice with pleasure all the new accessions which one section after another owes to the noble donor. We would simply mention the *Death of St. Joseph* by Overbeck, *Luke the Evangelist Painting the Holy Virgin* by Steinle, the *Repentant Magdalene*, possibly by Correggio, the *Holy Family* in the style of Luini, the male half-length portrait from the school of Raphael, the female one that may be a Cranach, the attractive landscapes, sea-pieces and genre paintings by Netherlandish and other artists. It is no trifling matter when someone who is a passionate art-lover and connoisseur nevertheless gradually surrenders a distinguished collection from which she has derived pleasure for many years solely in order that the pleasure may be enjoyed in still wider circles, and that the educative influence exerted by a major work of art may benefit all fellow citizens. It is only from this point of view that we can fully appreciate how much Miss Emilie Linder has done for our art collection for years and is doing again now."[121]

Of the works mentioned in this donation that were not by contemporary German painters not all had been acquired by Emilie Linder herself. For the most part they came from the collection inherited from her grandfather Johann Konrad Dienast. In 1850, 1860 and then in 1862 she donated these to the Öffentliche Kunstsammlung. Under a provision in Emilie Linder's will, the remaining paintings and drawings that she kept in her Munich home - among them three landscapes by J.A. Koch (Ills.78-79,p.98) and the two little pictures with hovering angels (Ills.86-87,p.104) acquired from her last teacher Johann von Schraudolph in 1865 - were bequeathed to the Museum upon her death in 1867. Emilie Linder's collection, which presents the development of German Romantic, particularly religious, painting from the beginning of the 19th century to the 1860s, and which documents the work of both the Nazarenes and the Munich school in over two hundred pictures and drawings, is unique in Switzerland. Appreciation of this collection has, however, always been coloured by current tastes.[122]

78

79

80 Joseph Anton Koch (1768-1839)
Landscape with Macbeth and the Witches.
(Landschaft mit Macbeth und den Hexen). 1829-1830
Oil on canvas, 115 x 155.5 cm
Inv. no. 393. Gift of Emilie Linder, 1849

78 Joseph Anton Koch (1768-1839). *A Tiber Landscape with Merry Peasants (Tiberlandschaft mit fröhlichen Landleuten).* 1818
Oil on canvas, 74.5 x 105 cm. Inv. no. 394. Bequest of Emilie Linder, 1867

79 Joseph Anton Koch (1768-1839). *Landscape Near Olevano with Peasants Dancing*
(Landschaft bei Olevano mit tanzenden Landleuten). c. 1823-1824
Oil on canvas, 58.5 x 82.5 cm. Inv. no. 395. Bequest of Emilie Linder, 1867

81   Johann Edward von Steinle (1810-1886)
Saint Luke Painting The Madonna and Child
(Der hl. Lukas malt Maria mit dem Kinde). 1838
Oil on canvas, 87 x 133 cm
Inv. no. 575. Gift of Emilie Linder, 1862

82   Friedrich Overbeck (1789-1869). *Portrait of the Painter Franz von Rohden (1817-1903) (Bildnis des Malers Franz von Rohden)*
Oil on canvas, 47 x 37.5 cm. Inv. no. 1966. Purchase, 1946

83 Johann Heinrich Ferdinand Olivier (1785-1841)
The Spies of Canaan (Die Kundschafter von Kanaan)
Oil on canvas, 34.8 x 27 cm
Inv. no. 476. Bequest of Emilie Linder, 1867

84 Johann von Schraudolph (1808-1879)
The Annunciation (Die Verkündigung an Maria). 1828
Oil on pine, 34.5 x 26 cm
Inv. no. 548. Bequest of Emilie Linder, 1867

85 Friedrich Overbeck (1789-1869). *The Death of Joseph (Der Tod des hl. Joseph)*. 1832-1836
Oil on canvas, 100.5 x 75.5 cm. Inv. no. 482. Gift of Emilie Linder, 1862

86   Johann von Schraudolph (1808-1879)
Two Hovering Angels
(Zwei schwebende Engel). 1865
Oil on canvas, 29 x 24.6 cm
Inv. no. 549. Bequest of Emilie Linder, 1867

87   Johann von Schraudolph (1808-1879)
Two Hovering Angels
(Zwei schwebende Engel). 1865
Oil on canvas, 29.3 x 24.7 cm
Inv. no. 852. Bequest of Emilie Linder, 1867

88 Caspar Wolf
(1735-1783)
*Snow Bridge and Rainbow
in Gadmental
(Schneebrücke und
Regenbogen im Gadmental).*
1778
Oil on canvas, 82 x 54 cm
Inv. no. G 1960.10.
Purchase, 1960

Samuel Birmann is sometimes called "the real founder of the Öffentliche Kunstsammlung in Basel". It was his bequest that enabled the Basel Museum "to create, alongside the existing collection of Old Masters, a modern Swiss art collection such as did not then exist anywhere in Switzerland".[123] Samuel Birmann was born in Basel in1793, the elder son of the landscape painter and art dealer Peter Birmann (1758-1844). He, too, trained as a painter and at an early age executed paintings, watercolours and drawings showing views of his native city and its immediate and more distant surroundings. In 1815 he travelled to Rome with two painter friends, Jakob Christoph Bischoff (1793-1825) and Friedrich Salathé (1793-1858), who were the same age as he. When he returned to Basel after having studied in Italy for two years, Samuel Birmann had to take over the artistic direction of his father's business, which was not only an art dealer's but also printed and published etchings and aquatints of popular views recorded on journeys throughout Switzerland. The death in 1830 of his younger son Wilhelm caused Peter Birmann to give up his business. In 1836 Samuel Birmann showed the first signs of a mental illness inherited from his mother. He sought relief by visiting health resorts, and distraction by going on lengthy journeys, which took him to the great art galleries, exhibitions and artists' studios. His travels also made him aware of the importance of modern means of transport and led him to discover a gift for speculative investment in railway and steamship lines. Samuel Birmann died by his own hand in September 1847.

In his will drawn up in 1844 Samuel Birmann left the Öffentliche Kunstsammlung his and his father's artistic works, his own art collection and the one inherited from his father, as well as half of his fortune, or over 200,000 Swiss francs. The number of objects in the Museum's collection was doubled by this bequest. However, its importance does not lie principally in the ninety-five pictures from the Birmann painting collection, whose quality is generally unremarkable, even though the twenty-eight paintings by Netherlandish masters include the beautiful still-life by Willem van Aelst *Breakfast* (*Das Frühstück*. Ill.74, p.91) and the extraordinary *Allegory* (Ill.53, p.72) by Goltzius. What was of incomparably greater value - and remains so today - was the "Birmann Fund". By virtue of this, the Öffentliche Kunstsammlung became "an autonomous, vital institution which was no longer reliant only on chance gifts as it had been before, but which could itself decide how to expand its collection".[124]

The Kunstkommission was thereby confronted with a new task: it now had not only to supervise and administer, but also to build up the collection through the selection and purchase of works of art. Samuel Birmann's bequest made it possible for the Kunstkommission to appoint a curator for the Öffentliche Kunstsammlung. In 1848, contrary to the custom of the time, the position was offered to an academic, the art scholar and historian Jacob Burckhardt (1818-1897). However, he never took up his duties, and even before the new Museum in the Augustinergasse was inaugurated he relinquished the position in order to devote himself entirely to academic activities. The curator's post did not carry any authority or responsibility, but was limited to looking after visitors, giving guided tours and, if any time was left over, to producing a catalogue. All matters of significance were decided through instructions issued by the Kunstkommission and its chairman. Jacob Burckhardt could therefore much more effectively influence the expansion of the Museum's collection as a member of the Kunstkommission, to which he belonged from 1859 to 1882. And indeed a large number of the purchases made in this period can be traced back to proposals made by him.[125]

The last will and testament of Samuel Birmann came into force at the beginning of 1859, after the death of his widow, who had enjoyed the right of use. But even before that, efforts were made to build up a collection of modern Swiss art. The Museum received generous help in the beginning from the Basel Kunstverein[126], which had been founded in 1839 for the "dissemination in Basel of a love and understanding of art", and also from the Freiwilliger Museumsverein, which had been established in 1850 to support the university collections. Three main sources can be identified for the acquisitions that were made. In the 1850s and early 1860s the Kunstkommission commissioned some of the best living Swiss artists to paint pictures for the Basel Museum, or selected existing paintings from their studios. Secondly, ideas for purchases also came from temporary exhibitions, which were then still rather rare and which, before the Kunsthalle was inaugurated in May 1872, were held at the Lesegesellschaft or in the Stadtcasino (City social rooms). The "Turnus", the Swiss art exhibitions organised by the Swiss Kunstverein that were held in rotation in different towns, were a particularly important market for works of art. Thirdly, the Basel art dealer Johann Rudolf Lang (1822-1874) - who was also a member of the Basel Parliament - must count as having been the Museum's most important supplier of paintings from Holbein to Böcklin during a period of almost two decades. Rudolf Lang, who had "long done a great deal to advance artistic interests", as was acknowledged in a short obituary in the *Basler Nachrichten*[127], had founded an art dealer's in the house "Zum rothen Fahnen" at 43 Freie Strasse in 1852. Two years later, his younger brother Heinrich Lang-Schäublin (1834-1911)[128] entered the business, which he took over after its founder's death and ran on his own until 1910. The Lang brothers dealt with the most important Swiss artists of their time, for instance Calame, Anker, Koller, Steffan and especially with Böcklin. They also had close personal links with Jacob Burckhardt, who gladly advised them.

It was inevitable that the Kunstkommission should frequently provoke violent criticism over its purchasing policy. For example, in April 1870 a reader's letter in the *Basler Nachrichten* headed "Reprimand" complained: "No guild or local government, no electoral college or any kind of democratic institution can match their overweening arrogance. The new acquisitions for our art collection are founded on oracular infallibility."[129]

In June 1853, in its first commission, the Kunstkommission requested the internationally famous Geneva painter Alexandre Calame (1810-1864) to paint a large-size Swiss landscape for the Basel Museum.[130] The choice of subject was left to the painter but it was admitted that a painting similar to the one acquired by Peter Vischer-Passavant in 1849 *By the Lake of Uri* (*Am Urnersee*. Ill.91, p.116) - which was to enter the Kunstmuseum's collection in 1950 as the gift of his descendants - would be welcome. A price of between 6,000 and 8,000 Swiss francs was proposed, but in the end it amounted to 10,000 Swiss francs. The view of Lake Uri executed for Peter Vischer ranks among the most important of the painter's pictures, and was even then famous well beyond Basel. In the event, Calame preferred not to try to match his masterpiece, and in 1856 he delivered a landscape composition of more dramatic character: *The Rosenlaui Valley with the Wetterhorn* (*Das Rosenlauital mit dem Wetterhorn*. Ill.92, p.117).[131]

In January 1856 the painting *Messenger's Carriage in a Sunken Road* (*Botenwagen im Hohlweg*. Ill. 98, p.122) that had been commissioned the previous year from the Zürich landscape and animal painter Rudolf Koller (1828-1905) was delivered to the Öffentliche Kunstsammlung.[132] As with Calame and most of the other artists who were given commissions, further purchases were to follow. In July 1868 a second painting, *The Evening* (*Der Abend*. Ill.100, p.123), which Koller had exhibited at the Paris "Salon" in the spring of that year, was acquired by the Museum from the artist for 8,000 Swiss francs, this time using interest from the Birmann Fund.[133] In January 1872 the Museum, following a proposal from Jacob Burckhardt, who was personally acquainted with the artist, secured *Cows on the Bank of a Lake* (*Kühe am Seeufer*. Ill.99, p.122) from the art dealer Rudolf Lang for 5,000 Swiss francs - "although we have some already", as the distinguished Kunstkommission member knew full well.[134]

In December 1859 the Kunstkommission approached Charles Gleyre (1806-1874) to see if he would be willing to paint a picture for the Basel Museum. The choice of subject was left to the artist, but the price was not to exceed 10,000 Swiss francs.[135] Gleyre must have decided very soon on the theme of *Pentheus pursued by the Maenads* (*Pentheus von den Maenaden verfolgt*. Ill.93, p.118). He did a large-size charcoal sketch for the composition, and in November 1860 the engraver Friedrich Weber (1813-1882), who was a friend of Gleyre, brought a photograph of it back to Basel from Paris to submit to the Kunstkommission. This met with satisfaction and the artist was commissioned to execute the painting.[136] There was then some considerable delay: Gleyre did not begin the picture for Basel until 1863, where it finally arrived in February 1865, five years after it had been commissioned.[137]

In June 1860 the Basel Kunstverein acquired a major work by the Lucerne artist Robert Zünd, *The Harvest* (*Die Ernte*. Ill.97, p.121), for 2,000 Swiss francs from the Swiss Art Exhibition, which was being held at that time in the Stadtcasino, and placed the picture with the Museum on long-term loan.[138] Zünd had apparently completed *The Harvest* the previous year and had also exhibited it at the Paris "Salon".[139] In 1874 the Öffentliche Kunstsammlung acquired the work from the Kunstverein with the help of the Birmann Fund[140] and also bought another of the painter's pictures, *Biblical Landscape (The Prodigal Son)* (*Biblische Landschaft [Der verlorene Sohn]*). Ill.95, p.120), for 3,100 Swiss francs from the art dealer Rudolf Lang.[141] The latter work had been shown seven years earlier at the Swiss Art Exhibition in the Stadtcasino and the *Basler Nachrichten* critic had praised it at the time as being "the most significant landscape and possibly even the best picture in the whole exhibition".[142] In 1869, too, the critic considered the "large wooded landscape in the evening sun, with biblical *staffage* by Zünd" that was displayed at the Swiss Art Exhibition to be "the finest picture in this genre that we have seen by this painter and indeed one of the best he has ever painted". He was glad that the picture - the work in question was *The Rest on the Flight into Egypt* (*Die Ruhe auf der Flucht nach Egypten*. Ill.96, p.120) - had been acquired by a Basel collector, the former chairman of the Kunstverein, Colonel Rudolf Merian-Iselin, although "he would have preferred it to have been bought by our Museum, which does not yet possess a picture by this painter".[143] In the same year the Museum had bought a picture by the Vaudois artist François Bocion, *Unloading Hay at Ouchy* (*Le déchargement du foin à Ouchy*. Ill.104, p.126), at the Swiss Art Exhibition.[144]

In the spring of 1869 Charles Gleyre's painting *The Charmer* (*La Charmeuse*. Ill. 94, p.119) was also shown at the Swiss Art Exhibition as a loan from the art dealer Rudolf Lang.[145] "The picture is delicately and finely painted, pure and chaste in its meaning, soft and complete in its modelling: it will attract the most visitors", prophesied the critic from the *Basler Nachrichten*.[146] Arnold Böcklin disagreed: he called Gleyre "philistine and antiquarian", and was extremely disparaging about his composition *Hercules at the feet of Omphale* (*Hercule aux pieds d'Omphale*. 1863) - a picture that Jacob Burckhardt would have liked to see in the Museum's collection[147] - saying that it "looked like a junk shop in which he wanted to display all his knowledge of antiquity". In Böcklin's view: "The elaborate execution of a picture is by no means to be condemned, and there is a special charm if the eye can follow the details with interest, only these have to be introduced cleverly and artistically."[148]

"Anyone who appreciates only the kind of painting that neatly and meticulously delineates every minute detail and nothing but detail may pass straight by this work", a critic advised the readers of the *Basler Nachrichten* in November 1862, when the first picture by Böcklin - *Diana's Hunt* (*Die Jagd der Diana*. Ill.106, p.128) - was purchased by the Öffentliche Kunstsammlung and was then exhibited in the Museum. It must have attracted attention by virtue of its size alone since, being 188.5 cm high and 345 cm wide, it was larger even than the *Allegory* by Goltzius (Ill.53, p.72) from the Birmann collection, which measures 180 by 256 cm. In addition: "Böcklin as a landscapist (and for the time being we consider landscape his real territory) is, like all true masters of this style, no mere copier of nature, no mere portraitist of well-known places. His creative inspiration is derived from a poetic feeling within him, and he uses nature's forms and colours only as a means to express different moods, so that those moods find their echo in the beholder."[149] Böcklin, who had been teaching landscape painting for a year and a half at the Weimar Art Academy, submitted an oil sketch to the Basel Kunstkommission in February 1862, expressing the wish to be allowed to execute a corresponding painting for the Museum of his native city. The sketch was not liked, but Böcklin was invited, at his convenience, to send in a landscape sketch for examination. Instead of doing so, Böcklin proposed in a letter to the Kunstkommission that it "choose between two large, predominantly landscape paintings on which he is currently working, one depicting Diana's Hunt and the other showing Cain and Abel". However, the Kunstkommission was not so easily deflected from its position and decided that "regardless of Mr. Böcklin's refusal, it has to insist on the principle that when it is commissioning paintings, an outline of the picture has to be submitted to it by the artist, whether in a photograph, a drawing or any other form".[150] It was only then that Böcklin sent in a pen and ink study for the painting *Diana's Hunt*. This received the Kunstkommission's approval, and it decided to order the large-size painting, but not without having haggled with the artist until he reduced his price from 10,000 to 9,000 Swiss francs.[151]

When a second picture by Böcklin, *Viola* (1866), was purchased for the Museum's collection from the art dealer Rudolf Lang for 2,500 Swiss francs in June 1866, the *Basler Nachrichten* prophesied: "There will certainly be no lack of philistines who will turn up their noses and shrug as they go past the picture - let them if they want. An artist like Böcklin is well advised not to bother about such reactions but to go his own way regardless."[152] Indeed, no other painter can have provoked more explosive debate in Basel's art circles than Böcklin. He returned to Basel from Italy in September 1866 together with his family. The committee of the Kunstverein organised a banquet in his honour at which the hope was expressed that Böcklin "will stay here for a considerable time and that his native city will provide him with a suitable setting for joyful artistic creativity".[153] Within the Kunstkommission his friends and supporters Jacob Burckhardt and the engraver Friedrich Weber especially argued that more of his pictures should find a permanent home in Basel. In January 1868 they spoke in favour of purchasing the painting *The Magdalene's Sorrow over the Body of Christ* (*Trauer der Maria Magdalena an der Leiche Christi*. Ill.108, p.129), which is worlds away from Overbeck's *The Death of Joseph* (*Der Tod des hl. Joseph*. Ill.85, p.103) painted three decades earlier. In February Böcklin asked the Kunstkommission for permission to exhibit this new accession at the "Salon" in Paris - for which Colonel Rudolf Merian-Iselin also lent *Petrarch at the Source of the Vaucluse* (*Petrarca an der Quelle von Vaucluse*. Ill.107, p.128).[154]

Jacob Burckhardt then ensured that Böcklin was commissioned to paint the walls beside the staircase of the Museum in the Augustinergasse. The large cartoons by Peter Cornelius and Schnorr von Carolsfeld which Emilie Linder had donated to the Museum in 1847 had been hanging there ever since the inauguration of Melchior Berri's building. They must have been an eyesore for Jacob Burckhardt, who was strongly opposed to the Nazarene movement in art.[155] The three frescoes that Böcklin designed and executed between November 1868 and January 1870 did not, however, meet with the unanimous approval of those who had commissioned them. The first mural representing *Magna mater* was accepted without criticism, but "more charm" was demanded in the figures in *Flora*.[156] Finally, the judgment on the third fresco, *Apollo with the Quadriga (Apollo mit dem Viergespann)*, was scathing: the Kunstkommission went so far as to recommend the artist - "also in his own interest" - to replace the mural "by another composition"[157]. An open disagreement could no longer be avoided. At the end of June 1870 Böcklin left Basel and moved with his family to Munich.[158] These differences over the frescoes beside the staircase also put a temporary halt to the Museum's purchases of pictures by Böcklin.

On 29 November 1871 the morning edition of the *Basler Nachrichten* carried the message: "We have the pleasure of informing art-lovers that Mr. Franz Buchser, who has returned from America after five years, is staying in our city for a few days. Anyone looking at the pictures and the numerous sketches that the artist has brought back will agree that he has not wasted his time, that he has not only made perceptible progress himself but has also conquered new territory for art ... One painting, 'Abnegation', which was much acclaimed at the recent Paris World's Fair[159], is on exhibition at the art dealer's Mr. R. Lang. Art-lovers interested in other things can look at them every morning in the Three Kings inn, where the artist is in personal attendance and shows the greatest courteousness."[160] At the suggestion of Jacob Burckhardt, the Museum acquired the large composition mentioned, which is better known under the title *Asceticism and the Joy of Living* (*Askese und Lebenslust*. Ill.101, p.124), for 6,000 Swiss francs.[161]

In December 1872 pictures by Buchser were again to be seen in Basel, this time in the "Permanent Exhibition" at the Kunsthalle, which was inaugurated the same year. These were *The Song of Mary Blane*, *The Volunteer's Return*, a version of the *Rapids of Ste. Marie*, and presumably also *Old Virginia* and *Bathers in the Emme* (*Badende in der Emme*). The *Basler Nachrichten* reported on the event in detail.[162] The critic concluded his descriptions of the pictures which Buchser had painted in the United States between 1866 and 1871 with the following reflections: "If it is true that the alien and foreign has a particular charm for us, while the familiar often seems dull and ordinary, then how much more must our attention be excited by a scene that in such an original manner displays before us the life of a race of human beings which is so distant from our cultural conceptions and yet has come so close to us in scarcely a decade. How interested we were years ago in Harriet Beecher Stowe's negro stories! It seems to us that our interest in the African race, downtrodden and yet with cultural potential as it is, must definitely be more highly developed when we see pictures in which extremely odd and remarkable members of it are represented in a way that is so true to nature and so humane. Franz Buchser has dedicated himself with great skill to the task of presenting the life of negroes in North America, and some of the fame won by that major American authoress might be transferred to this illustrator of negro life. Buchser's brush has also written a page in the cultural history of North America, and it may not be the least of his achievements." The Öffentliche Kunstsammlung acquired *The Volunteer's Return* (Ill.103, p.125) with the help of the Birmann Fund - the *Basler Nachrichten* criticised the similarity between this group of three people and *Oath of the Three Confederates* (*Schwur der drei Eidgenossen*. 1833) by Jean-Léonard Lugardon - as well as *The Rapids of Sault Ste. Marie, Canada* (*Die Stromschnellen von Sault Ste-Marie, in Kanada*. Ill.102, p.124).[163]

At the Vienna World's Fair of 1873, Böcklin's *Battle of the Centaurs* (*Kentaurenkampf*. Ill.109, p.130) caused a great stir and brought the artist the distinction of a bronze medal. However, the Kunstkommission - again following a recommendation from Jacob Burckhardt - decided to acquire another picture exhibited there in the section "Fine Art of the Present": Charles Gleyre's *The Charmer* (Ill.94, p.119)[164]. The people of Basel were already familiar with this from the Swiss Art Exhibition of 1869. (*Battle of the Centaurs* was ultimately acquired by the Öffentliche Kunstsammlung, at the urging of Jacob Burckhardt, three years later when it was exhibited in the Kunsthalle in June 1876.) In October 1880, too, the work of another artist was given preference over a picture by Böcklin exhibited in the Kunsthalle at the time, when Albert Anker's *The Children's Breakfast* (*Kinderfrühstück*. Ill.114, p.135), which was particularly liked by the art-lovers in Rudolf Lang's art dealer's, was purchased by the Museum.[165] "This purchase will certainly provoke less controversy than several other acquisitions of recent years", the *Basler Nachrichten* prophesied on that occasion.[166]

In 1877 Friedrich Weber had already offered to find out whether Albert Anker had a picture suitable for Basel.[167] In October 1879 his efforts resulted in the purchase of *The Quack* (*Der Quacksalber*. Ill.113, p.134) for 3,000 Swiss francs. The picture had not yet been completed at the time, and the artist also wanted to exhibit it the following May at the Paris "Salon".[168] Under the title *Le mège*, and glossed in the catalogue with the explanation *Charlatan illegally practising medicine*, this picture was singled out for praise in the review that the Marquis de Chennevières devoted to the "Salon" in the *Gazette des Beaux-Arts*, being described as "one of the most attractive genre paintings in the entire Salon". The critic felt that: "The tonality of *Le Mège* by Anker is, as always, unfortunately too red, but the scene is excellently arranged and both very innocently and very delicately expressed." He noted that it was particularly foreigners who excelled in genre pictures: "They bring to them an ingenuity of composition and a meticulous execution, essential qualities for works of this kind, which are all too often beyond the range of our native impatience, which does not like the discipline of detail."[169] (It will be recalled that Edouard Manet's *Chez le Père Lathuille* was the main centre of interest at this "Salon".) As Anker confessed to a friend, he was glad to have finally sold a picture to Basel: "Are they afraid of drowning in a glass of water! and of putting beside their Holbeins pictures that they might not think perfect?" he mocked.[170]

"Our Basel Museum cannot compete with the great picture galleries", an anonymous correspondent remarked in the *Basler Nachrichten* on 15 December 1885: "The only way it can attain eminence is by cultivating specialities. Hans Holbein is one such speciality; on the other hand, we have no Rubens at all, so an alternative should be sought in the Rubens of the 19th century" - by whom Arnold Böcklin was obviously meant.[171] At the end of that month another letter appeared in the paper on the subject "The Öffentliche Kunstsammlung, its financial resources and its aims". The correspondent observed: "A kindly providence has passed down to us, as the nucleus of our collection, a series of first-rate masterpieces; a munificent bequest gives us the means to add contemporary works to this nucleus, and the financial resources at our disposal are sufficient to permit acquisitions that are in keeping with this noble nucleus". He felt that the money available from the Birmann Fund for the acquisition of Swiss works of art, which came to about 10,000 Swiss francs annually, should be concentrated "on the significant and the unusual", on works that exceeded "the scope of the individual enthusiast". And yet: "How many pictures now in the collection have been selected not out of deep admiration but because of the well-meaning idea that they are well or reasonably well painted, are by a Swiss painter who also deserves consideration, by whom we should also have something, etc.; in fact because of the attitude that a well-meaning building authority might adopt in allocating carpentry jobs to various local contractors." On the subject of acquisitions during the years 1871 to 1883, the writer reached the conclusion: "Of course there are some treasures among them in which we can rejoice, but there is also so much that is insignificant, from Anker's muslin-clad children drinking coffee to Schwegler's boring fur merchant[172]! Looking at the one letter B, we find that the 13 years yield 3 Buchsers, 3 Barzaghis, 2 Böcklins." And he expressed the view: "How much richer we should be in the letter B if we had 3 Buchsers and 2 Barzaghis fewer and perhaps 2 or 3 Böcklins more." The correspondent was particularly angered by the fact that in 1879 the Museum had paid 10,000 Swiss francs for the *Scene from Schiller's Fiesco* (*Scene aus Schillers Fiesco*) by Antonio Barzaghi-Cattaneo (1837-1922),[173] who was so highly valued by Jacob Burckhardt - and by whom only the ceiling paintings in the ambulatory of the Federal Parliament in Berne building can be seen today - whereas its most recently acquired Böcklin, *The Sacred Grove* (*Der heilige Hain*. Ill.110, p.131), had cost only 8,400 Swiss francs. For he considered it "Basel's solemn duty to ensure that as much of Böcklin's immortal legacy as possible finds a permanent home in the museum of his native city; a solemn duty, let it be understood, not towards Böcklin but *towards ourselves*". And he warned against an omission in the present that could not be repaired in the future: "With what blushes will the educated 20th century citizen of Basel follow the traces of Böcklin abroad, how embarrassed he will be to think that the richest spectrum of this extraordinary genius cannot be encountered at home, where it would naturally have belonged and where it could have gone. It would be painful enough for that future citizen to think that we were simply poor and small, and could not compete with rich collectors and great picture galleries; how much more bitter will be the thought that what we lacked to compete successfully was not the means but simply the will."[174]

After Böcklin's fame had spread and the business-like Berlin art dealers Fritz Gurlitt and Carl Steinbach had started representing him, the prices for his pictures rose considerably. *Naiads at Play* (*Das Spiel der Najaden*. Ill.112, p.133) cost the Museum 20,000 Swiss francs in the autumn of 1886. In December 1888 the artist reduced his price for *Vita somnium breve* (1888) from the 25,000 Swiss francs originally set to 20,000 Swiss francs. The purchase of *Odysseus and Calypso* (*Odysseus und Kalypso*. Ill.111, p.132) almost fell through in the autumn of 1895 because of the price of more than 35,000 Swiss francs that was asked. The maximum available from the Birmann Fund was 20,000 Swiss francs, and it was only thanks to the intervention of private patrons and the Freiwilliger Museumsverein that it proved possible, almost at the last minute, finally to obtain the masterly work for Basel. The pessimistic vision of the letter quoted above was fortunately not realised. In the course of time Böcklin's native city became the home of the largest and most important collection of his pictures, sculptures and drawings to be found anywhere.[175]

"No one will assert that Hodler...has enjoyed the esteem in Basel that his importance merits", wrote the correspondent of the *Basler Nachrichten* in the autumn of 1911 when a more comprehensive overview of the work of Ferdinand Hodler (1853-1918) was finally offered through his first one-man exhibition in the Kunsthalle: "Our Museum has made praiseworthy attempts in this direction. But the prices for Hodler pictures are shooting up, and it would be very sad if for this reason our descendants were one day to say scornfully that we missed one of the great innovators."[176] Wilhelm Barth, the curator of the Basel Kunsthalle from 1904 to 1934, delivered an even more cutting judgment when, after the artist's death, he lamented the "monumental lack of understanding" that Basel's art authorities had shown towards Hodler. Basel had "passed by Hodler and his work, had neglected to secure for its Museum one of the great paintings in which the master's style and striving are concentrated, and the artist had been quite sensitive about this".[177]

The first public purchase in Switzerland of a painting by Hodler had been made by the Berne Kunstgesellschaft (Art Society) in 1887, when it ventured to acquire the self-portrait *The Angry Man* (*Der Zornige*. 1880/81). In 1901 a stir was caused by the Government of the Canton of Berne when, despite fierce opposition, it purchased four of the painter's major works: *Night* (*Die Nacht*. 1890), *The Disillusioned* (*Die Enttäuschten*. 1892), *Eurhythmy* (*Eurhythmie*. 1895) and *Day* (*Der Tag*. 1899/1900). Paul Klee commented in a letter: "Our museum has gained so much through the acquisition of these pictures that in Switzerland only the Holbein collection in Basel can be put alongside it."[178] Zürich came by its first Hodler picture in 1896, when the Confederation placed the second version of *Wrestlers' Procession* (*Schwingerumzug*. 1882/87) on long-term loan with the Künstlerhaus, the forerunner of the Kunsthaus. In 1903 the Zürich Kunstgesellschaft acquired the portrait *Girl with Cornflowers* (*Mädchen mit Kornblumen*. Around 1894). In Basel only three of Hodler's paintings found their way into the Öffentliche Kunstsammlung during his life-time: *The Battle of Näfels* (*Die Schlacht bei Näfels*. Ill.117, p.138) in 1901, *Lake Geneva Seen from Chexbres* (*Der Genfersee von Chexbres aus*. Ill.120, p.141) in 1905 and *Communion with Infinity* (*Aufgehen im All*. Ill.115, p.136) in 1910. Was it mere coincidence that the first work by the Berne artist to enter the Basel Museum's collection, the design for a mosaic on the courtyard façade of the Swiss Landesmuseum in Zürich, was acquired in the very same year as Arnold Böcklin died?

The appreciation of Hodler's work in Basel was from the very beginning overshadowed by the controversy surrounding Böcklin.[179] This could already be seen in November 1883 when three of Hodler's pictures, among them *Craftsman Reading* (*Lesender Handwerker*. c.1881) were included in the exhibition of Swiss artists held in Basel. The Basel press took no notice of Hodler's works, but had eyes only for Arnold Böcklin's *Ruin by the Sea* (*Ruine am Meer*). The critic from *Schweizerischer Volksfreund* enthused, "in this picture he once again parades before our eyes the whole of his colour magic"[180].

"There is no rush because Hodler will hardly become fashionable like Böcklin", was the opinion expressed by the art historian Professor Paul Schubring as late as December 1909 in a meeting of the Kunstkommission at which he informed its members that the Philosophy Faculty proposed to award Hodler an honorary doctorate in commemoration of Basel University's 450th anniversary.[181] The proposal did not go unopposed in the Faculty, and the Rector at the time, Karl Vonder Mühll, expressed certain reservations, "because Hodler is not from Basel"[182]. All the same, it was hoped "he may then donate a picture"[183]. The eulogy ran: "For Ferdinand Hodler from Berne, in honour of the discipline and courage with which he has sought his own course, and in recognition of the painter's successes in his struggle to find a style for monumental murals."[184] Hodler was not present in person at the ceremony held in the Museum's auditorium on 24 June 1910 at which he was awarded the distinction of an honorary doctorate. Instead he telegraphed his thanks by return from Geneva: "I am sincerely grateful for the honour bestowed on me."[185] He did not, however, donate a picture.

Basel's interest in collecting works by Hodler intensified remarkably in the spring of 1910, presumably in anticipation of his honorary degree. On 13 April the Kunstkommission unanimously decided to purchase the picture *Communion with Infinity* (Ill.115, p.136) which was offered by the Galerie Heinemann of Munich for 12,000 marks. The Basel Kunstverein also acquired a picture from Hodler's earlier period: *Disappointed Soul* (*Enttäuschte Seele*. Ill.116, p.137), also known as *A Poor Soul*, which from 17 May onwards was exhibited in Louis La Roche-Ringwald's painting gallery under the title *Beggar*.[186] In 1927, in fulfilment of an agreement between the Basel Kunstverein and the Basel Government, the Öffentliche Kunstsammlung acquired permanent possession of the latter picture, together with thirteen others, including Hodler's *Craftsman Reading* and *View into Infinity* (*Blick in die Unendlichkeit*. Ill.123, pp.144-145).

In 1910 the Basel textile manufacturer Louis La Roche-Ringwald (1844-1921), the owner of one of the most important collections of modern German and Swiss art, sold his villa with its adjoining painting gallery at 23 Steinenring and liquidated his art collection at sales held in Basel and Berlin. At the same time the Basel businessman Max Geldner (1875-1958) was making the first purchases for what subsequently became an extensive Hodler collection, from which the Öffentliche Kunstsammlung acquired thirteen paintings under his bequest. Geldner's first acquisition of a Hodler work - the single-figure version of the composition *Sacred Hour* (*Heilige Stunde*. Ill.122,p.143) - was entered in his "Accessions Book" in the spring of 1910. In December of the same year Geldner bought three more pictures, again direct from the artist. When he asked for a few drawings to be included for good measure, Hodler refused and informed the young collector: "In any case, the pictures you have acquired are an investment, not an expenditure."[187] Geldner's next purchases were made in January and February 1911 from art dealers and collectors in Geneva; they included *Halberdier in Retreat from Marignano* (*Hellebardier aus Rückzug bei Marignano*. Ill.118, p.139), which the collector loaned to the Basel Museum for two years, until February 1913.[188]

In April 1916 Max Geldner lent six pictures by Hodler, among them *Sacred Hour*, to the "Exhibition of Modern Art in Private Ownership in Basel", together with works by other artists. Another Basel collector, Dr. Paul Linder (1871-1941), lent a total of fourteen of Hodler's pictures from his extensive collection for the occasion, among them the painting *Mountain Summit. The Niesen* (*Der Niesen*. Ill.121, p.141) - to use the title current today - was again loaned by Dr. Paul Linder for the Hodler Memorial Exhibition held in Berne in the late summer and autumn of 1921, although it was marked in the catalogue as being for sale.[189] In April 1922 the Kunstkommission purchased the picture for the Basel Museum with money from the Birmann Fund. As can be read in the Annual Report, the purchase was made "against the curator's advice", for Heinrich Alfred Schmid, who was known equally well as the biographer of Grünewald and Böcklin and as a Holbein expert, made no secret of the fact that he had no time for modern art.[190] *The Niesen* was one of two pictures by Ferdinand Hodler with which the Swiss artist was represented in the legendary "Armory Show" held in New York in February and March 1913. The "International Exhibition of Modern Art" organised in the former armoury of the 69th Regiment was the first at which the latest European art tendencies were displayed in the United States, first in New York and thereafter in Chicago and Boston.[191]

89   Caspar Wolf (1735-1783). *Storm on Lake Thun (Sturm auf dem Thunersee).* 1776
Oil on canvas, 54 x 82 cm. Inv. no. G 1985.20. Gift of Edith Raeber-Züst, 1985

90   Caspar Wolf (1735-1783). *The Lauteraar Glacier (Der Lauteraargletscher).* 1776
Oil on canvas, 55 x 82.5 cm. Inv. no. 1586. Purchase, 1932

91   Alexandre Calame (1810-1864)
By the Lake of Uri (Am Urnersee). 1849
Oil on canvas, 194 x 260.5 cm
Inv. no. 2243. Gift of the heirs of Marie Vischer-d'Assonleville, 1950

92   Alexandre Calame (1810-1864)
The Rosenlaui Valley with the Wetterhorn (Das Rosenlauital mit dem Wetterhorn). 1856
Oil on canvas, 173.5 x 239 cm
Inv. no. 161. Gift of the Freiwilliger Museumsverein, 1856

93   Charles Gleyre (1806-1874)
Pentheus Pursued by the Maenads
(Pentheus von den Maenaden verfolgt). 1864
Oil on canvas, 121 x 201 cm
Inv. no. 249. Birmann Fund, 1865

94   Charles Gleyre (1806-1874)
The Charmer (La Charmeuse). 1868
Oil on canvas, 82.5 x 50.5 cm
Inv. no. 250. Birmann Fund, 1873

95 Robert Zünd
(1827-1909)
*Biblical Landscape
(The Prodigal Son)
(Biblische Landschaft
[Der verlorene Sohn]).* 1867
Oil on canvas, 120 x 158 cm
Inv. no. 661.
Birmann Fund, 1874

96 Robert Zünd
(1827-1909)
*The Rest on the Flight
into Egypt
(Die Ruhe auf der
Flucht nach Ägypten).* 1869
Oil on canvas, 119 x 159 cm
Inv. no. 664. Bequest
of Mrs. Rudolf Merian-Iselin,
1901

97   Robert Zünd (1827-1909)
The Harvest (Die Ernte). 1859
Oil on canvas, 112 x 156.5 cm
Inv. no. 660. Birmann Fund, 1874

98 Rudolf Koller (1828-1905)
*Messenger's Carriage in a
Sunken Road
(Botenwagen im Hohlweg)*. 1855
Oil on canvas, 102.5 x 123.5 cm
Inv. no. 398. Gift of the
Kunstverein, the Freiwilliger
Museumsverein and an
anonymous patron, 1856

99 Rudolf Koller (1828-1905)
*Cows on the Bank of a Lake
(Kühe am Seeufer)*. 1871
Oil on canvas, 114.5 x 141.5 cm
Inv. no. 402. Birmann Fund, 1872

100   Rudolf Koller (1828-1905)
The Evening (Der Abend). 1868
Oil on canvas, 137 x 204 cm
Inv. no. 400. Birmann Fund, 1868

101

102

101   Frank Buchser (1828-1890)
*Asceticism and the Joy of Living
(Abnegation)
(Askese und Lebenslust
[Abnegation]).* 1865
Oil on canvas, 102 x 153 cm
Inv. no. 148. Birmann Fund, 1871

102   Frank Buchser (1828-1890)
*The Rapids of Sault Ste. Marie, Canada
(Die Stromschnellen von Sault Ste. Marie,
in Kanada).* 1868
Oil on canvas, 58 x 114.5 cm
Inv. no. 142. Birmann Fund, 1872

103   Frank Buchser (1828-1890)
The Volunteer's Return. 1867
Oil on canvas, 97 x 77 cm
Inv. no. 146. Birmann Fund, 1872

104   François Bocion (1828-1890)
Unloading Hay at Ouchy
(Le déchargement du foin à Ouchy). 1867
Oil on canvas, 51 x 125 cm
Inv. no. 79. Birmann Fund, 1869

105   Arnold Böcklin (1827-1901). *Idealised Portrait of Angela Böcklin as a Muse (Idealbildnis der Angela Böcklin als Muse)*. 1863
Oil on canvas, 70 x 57.5 cm. Inv. no. 1451. Acquired from the Basel Kunstverein with a special grant from the City of Basel, 1927

106

107

108   Arnold Böcklin (1827-1901)
The Magdalene's Sorrow Over the Body of Christ
(Trauer der Maria Magdalena an der Leiche Christi). 1867
Oil on canvas, 85 x 149 cm
Inv. no. 104. Birmann Fund, 1868

106   Arnold Böcklin (1827-1901)
Diana's Hunt (Die Jagd der Diana). 1862
Oil on canvas, 188.5 x 345 cm
Inv. no. 99. Purchase, 1862

107   Arnold Böcklin (1827-1901)
Petrarch at the Source of the Vaucluse
(Petrarca an der Quelle von Vaucluse). 1867
Oil on canvas, 128 x 192.5 cm
Inv. no. 103. Bequest of Mrs. Rudolf Merian-Iselin, 1901

109   Arnold Böcklin (1827-1901)
Battle of the Centaurs (Kentaurenkampf). 1873
Tempera on canvas, varnished, 105 x 195 cm
Inv. no. 107. Birmann Fund, 1876

110   Arnold Böcklin (1827-1901)
The Sacred Grove (Der heilige Hain). 1882
Tempera on canvas, varnished, 105 x 150.5 cm
Inv. no. 110. Birmann Fund, 1882

111 Arnold Böcklin (1827-1901)
Odysseus and Calypso (Odysseus und Kalypso). 1883
Tempera on mahogany, varnished, 104 x 150 cm
Inv. no. 108. Acquired with contributions from the
Birmann Fund, the Freiwilliger Museumsverein and
art patrons, 1895

112   Arnold Böcklin (1827-1901)
Naiads at Play (Das Spiel der Najaden). 1886
Tempera on canvas, varnished, 151 x 176.5 cm
Inv. no. 111. Birmann Fund, 1886

113 Albert Anker (1831-1910)
The Quack (Der Quacksalber). 1879
Oil on canvas, 80 x 124 cm
Inv. no. 11. Birmann Fund, 1880

114 Albert Anker (1831-1910). *The Children's Breakfast (Kinderfrühstück)*. 1879
Oil on canvas, 81.5 x 65.5 cm. Inv. no. 10. Birmann Fund, 1880

115 Ferdinand Hodler (1853-1918)
*Communion with Infinity
(Aufgehen im All)*. 1892
Oil on canvas, 138 x 78 cm
Inv. no. 859. Birmann Fund, 1910

116   Ferdinand Hodler (1853-1918)
Disappointed Soul (Enttäuschte Seele). 1889
Oil on canvas, 71.5 x 93.5 cm
Inv. no. 1446. Acquired from the Basel Kunstverein
with a special grant from the City of Basel, 1927

117   Ferdinand Hodler (1853-1918)
The Battle of Näfels
(Die Schlacht bei Näfels). 1897
Tempera on paper, 49.5 x 95 cm
Inv. no. 289. Birmann Fund, 1901

118   Ferdinand Hodler (1853-1918)
*Halberdier in Retreat from Marignano
(Hellebardier aus Rückzug bei Marignano).*
1897-1898
Oil on canvas, 204 x 107 cm
Inv. no. G 1958.49. Bequest of Max Geldner, 1958

120 Ferdinand Hodler (1853-1918)
Lake Geneva Seen from Chexbres
(Der Genfersee von Chexbres aus). 1905
Oil on canvas, 82.5 x 104 cm
Inv. no. 290. Birmann Fund, 1905

119 Ferdinand Hodler (1853-1918)
View of the Jungfrau from the Isenfluh
(Die Jungfrau, von der Isenfluh aus gesehen). 1902
Oil on canvas, 75 x 56 cm
Inv. no. G 1982.30. Gift of the Max Geldner Foundation, 1982

121 Ferdinand Hodler (1853-1918)
The Niesen (Der Niesen). 1910
Oil on canvas, 83 x 105.5 cm
Inv. no. 1385. Birmann Fund, 1922

122   Ferdinand Hodler (1853-1918)
Sacred Hour (Heilige Stunde). 1910
Version with one figure
Oil on canvas, 180 x 89.5 cm
Inv. no. G 1958.53. Bequest of Max Geldner, 1958

123 Ferdinand Hodler (1853-1918). *View into Infinity (Blick in die Unendlichkeit).* 1915
First monumental version. Oil on canvas, 446 x 895 cm. Inv. no. 1445
Acquired from the Basel Kunstverein with a special grant from the City of Basel, 1927

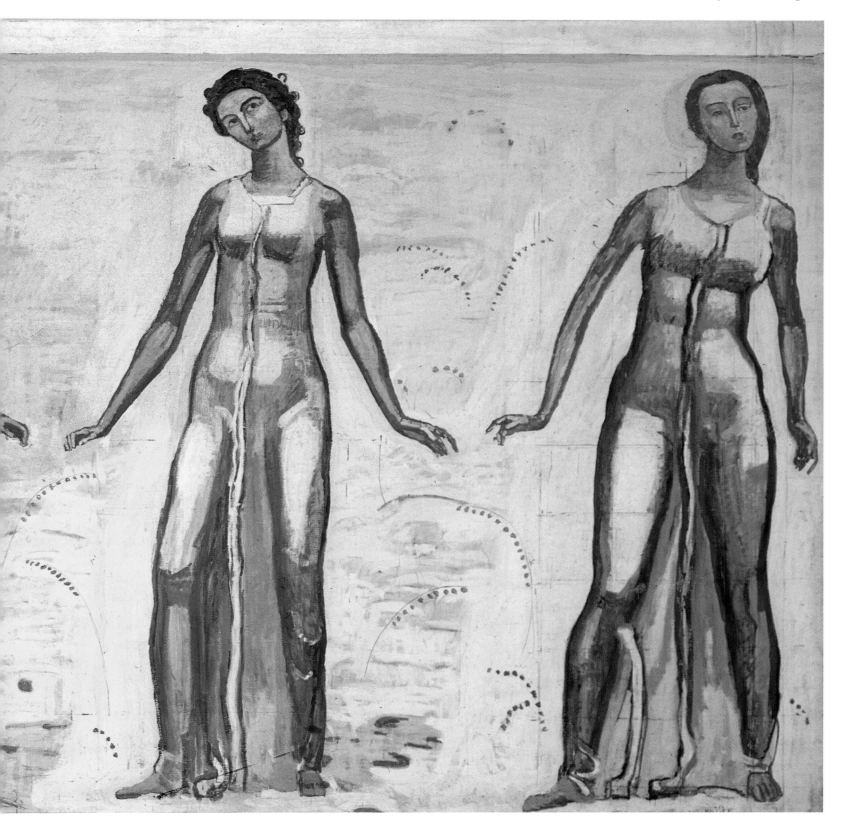

124 Félix Vallotton (1865-1925). *The Old Concierge (Le vieux concierge)*.1893
Oil on canvas, 73 x 115 cm. Inv. no. G 1968.13. Gift of Helene Ras-Weidmann
and Dr. Max Ras-Junghans in memory of Max Ras-Weidmann, 1968

125 Félix Vallotton (1865-1925). *Three Women and a Young Girl Frolicking
in the Water (Trois femmes et une petite fille jouant dans l'eau)*. 1907
Oil on canvas, 130.5 x 195.5 cm. Inv. no. G 1957.2. Birmann Fund, 1957

124

125

I n the summer of 1889 Claude Monet launched a subscription among his friends and acquaintances to acquire Edouard Manet's controversial *Olympia* from the artist's widow and to present it to the French State, so that the Musée du Luxembourg should at last open its portals to Impressionism.[192] In Basel, too, the Museum was to acquire its first picture by a French Impressionist through a collection organised by three artists.

An exhibition in the Kunsthalle in January 1912 provided the first fairly comprehensive survey in Basel of the work of the Impressionists. A number of artists and art-lovers sent a petition to the Öffentliche Kunstsammlung urging it to purchase one of the pictures exhibited. The idea of a petition originated with the painters Paul Burckhardt (1890-1961) and Hermann Meyer (1878-1961), and the sculptor Carl Burckhardt (1878-1923), Paul Burckhardt's older brother.[193] Meyer and Carl Burckhardt were pupils of Fritz Schider (1846-1907). A native of Salzburg, Schider discovered the painting of the Barbizon School and the work of Gustave Courbet while he was studying in Munich, during which time he also became a friend of Wilhelm Leibl (1844-1900), whose niece Lina Kirchdorffer he married. Courbet's art had a formative influence on Schider but subsequently - as is shown by his masterpiece *The Chinese Tower in the English Garden in Munich (Der Chinesische Turm im Englischen Garten in München.* Ill.126, p.148) - he moved very close to Manet and the Impressionists. In 1876 Schider was given a teaching post at the Allgemeine Gewerbeschule (School of Arts and Crafts) in Basel, where he opened his pupils' eyes to the new French painting.

In its response to the petition, the Kunstkommission noted that it did not have the 15,000 to 20,000 Swiss francs at its disposal that would have been needed to purchase a major work by Monet or Sisley. However, it informed the petitioners that the donation of a picture would be accepted very readily if the necessary funds could be raised privately. Paul Burckhardt and Hermann Meyer thereupon went from door to door soliciting contributions from well-to-do citizens of Basel for the purchase of Pissarro's *L'Hermitage, Pontoise* (Ill.141, p.166).[194] In this way, 5,200 Swiss francs was collected. The Kunstkommission was hesitant about contributing the remaining 800 Swiss francs and the view was, in fact, expressed that "the picture is not a good one and the Kunstkommission should have nothing to do with its purchase".[195] In the end, the Basel Government contributed the amount still outstanding. In April 1912 the Pissarro picture was presented to the Öffentliche Kunstsammlung as a gift. On 12 May the *Basler Nachrichten* reported that the Modern Room now contained the *Landscape near Pontoise,* "which had been presented to the gallery as a gift by Basel art-lovers. With this high quality, finely toned picture, the Impressionism of the seventies of the last century is now also represented here. That this example should be by Camille Pissarro, this artist of Jewish origin, full of spontaneous temperament, full of the sensitivity peculiar to his race, will be especially welcomed by every connoisseur of Impressionism."[196] *L'Hermitage, Pontoise* was not only the first Impressionist picture to enter the collection of the Basel Museum, it was also the first to be acquired by a museum anywhere in Switzerland. In June of the same year the Musée d'art et d'histoire in Geneva also acquired an Impressionist painting: *The Barrage of the Loing at Saint-Mammès (Le barrage du Loing à Saint-Mammès.* 1885) by Sisley.[197]

Six years earlier an "Exhibition of French Art" had already presented a cross-section of modern French painting in Basel.[198] With a small selection of works by Degas, Monet and Renoir, who were then still alive, the exhibition had introduced French Impressionism in Switzerland for the first time. Hermann Kienzle complained: "All the rooms of the Kunsthalle are crammed full; neither in the way the pictures are hung nor in the setting has the much-praised French taste had an effect. On a closer look it must be said that the banal and the insipid one comes across in all art exhibitions is very much present and, what is more, sets the tone."[199] Paul Klee, who travelled to Basel on 23 March 1906 for a concert by the Joachim Quartet, paid little attention to this, but noted in his diary: "A happy coincidence introduced me to some good French Impressionist pictures. Simon, Carrière, 5 Renoirs, 4 Monets,

126 Fritz Schider (1846-1907)
The Chinese Tower in the English Garden in Munich (Der Chinesische Turm im Englischen Garten in München). 1872
Oil on canvas, 140 x 111 cm. Inv. no. 542. Birmann Fund, 1904

one Degas, etc. and a Rodin room."[200] Six years later, on the occasion of a Renoir exhibition in Heinrich Thannhauser's Moderne Galerie in Munich, Klee was still to recall the group of Renoir works - which comprised two landscapes, *Cabaret of Mother Antony* (*Le cabaret de la mère Antony*. 1866), the *Portrait of Rapha* (1871) and the portrait of Madame Victor Chocquet (1875).[201]

Hermann Kienzle (1876-1946), who was later the principal of the Allgemeine Gewerbeschule and director of the Gewerbemuseum (Museum of Arts and Crafts) and who was also a member of the Kunstkommission of the Öffentliche Kunstsammlung from 1918 to 1925, argued in a newspaper article that one of the Basel institutions that collected sculpture should buy a work by Rodin[202] from the "Exhibition of French Art" - the sculptor was the chairman of the exhibition committee in Paris - expressing the view that: "Some of the portrait busts are at least the equal of antique works in the greatness of their conception, and of Florentine busts of the Quattrocento in the intensity of their characterisation, and they would be an extremely welcome addition to the small collection of portraits which the Sculpture Hall already possesses...A tireless creator, a bold innovator, a profound human being - thus do we think of Rodin today, and that should be justification enough for him to be represented in a public collection in Basel."[203]

The Kunstkommission had only the day before decided - "after a fairly lengthy discussion", as the minutes of the meeting note - to purchase Rodin's *Heroic Bust of Victor Hugo* (*Buste héroïque de Victor Hugo*. Ill.159, p.180) for 4,000 Swiss francs. This was a happy decision, especially given that the other suggestions put forward for discussion were not any of the pictures by the Impressionists represented in the exhibition - the prices of which would have far exceeded the funds available[204]- but paintings by "Salon" artists who have been more or less forgotten today.

"To judge by the purchases made so far, the things that will remain in Basel will be considerably more pleasing than important," was Hermann Kienzle's view on the purchases made by private collectors from the "Exhibition of French Art".[205] Most people in Basel were to continue to have difficulty in understanding Impressionism because - as Wilhelm Barth (1869-1934) pointed out in the autumn of 1915 - "the basic prerequisite is lacking, the thorough consideration of the consequences of Impressionism and of the trends away from Impressionism found in artists such as Cézanne, van Gogh, Gauguin and Picasso. In brief, even educated people, here as elsewhere, have not really kept up with the artistic development of recent decades, it has never been brought home to them. So they repeatedly find themselves confronted by the same riddles and reject what they do not understand with ridicule or indignation."[206] To counteract this "sorry state of affairs", no fewer than three Impressionist exhibitions were mounted by Barth between 1912 and 1915 at the Kunsthalle, of which he was the curator from 1909 to 1934. Barth considered Impressionism to be the foundation of all modern art. He was also a tireless advocate of French art in the Kunstkommission of the Öffentliche Kunstsammlung, of which he was a member from 1915 to 1923.

From 1915 onwards two other members of the Kunstkommission - the painter Paul Burckhardt, who had initiated the Pissarro collection together with Hermann Meyer (who succeeded him on the Kunstkommission in 1923), and Professor Friedrich Rintelen (1881-1926) - argued that more thought should be given to building up a small collection of French painting for the Museum. And so it happened on occasion that the art historian felt it his duty to remind the Kunstkommission, in its allegiance to Böcklin, "that around the year 1862 Corot and Delacroix solved problems of colour that were more important for international developments" than did the Basel master in his oil study *Spring* (*Der Frühling*. 1862) which they wanted to acquire.[207]

In the middle of the 1910s there was only one collector in Basel - the lawyer Dr. Paul Linder (1871-1941) - who possessed not only works by 19th century French painters like Courbet, Daumier, Renoir, Cézanne and Gauguin, but also avant-garde pictures by Matisse, Derain and Picasso.[208] In 1917 Rudolf Staechelin (1881-1946), who for three years had been collecting pictures by painters from French-speaking Switzerland, also began to build up a significant collection of Impressionist and Post-Impressionist paintings. In the course of a few months Staechelin put together an impressive number of pictures by Manet, Degas, Monet, Pissarro, Sisley, Renoir, Cézanne, van Gogh, Gauguin and Picasso. It was first shown in September 1920 in the Kunsthalle. Staechelin was elected a member of the Kunstkommission in the autumn of 1923. Looking back, George Schmidt was to praise his achievements in that body with the following remarks: "As a private collector Rudolf Staechelin applied the very highest standards of quality, and because he repeatedly allowed the Kunstkommission to view his own collection, he enabled it to base its judgments on comparisons with originals, and he also forced it to be rigorous in its judgment."[209]

In April 1918 the Kunstverein, in collaboration with the Muséee Rodin in Paris, organised an exhibition of over 80 sculptures and a hundred watercolours and drawings by Rodin. It was the first major retrospective after Rodin's death the year before. The exhibition was an amazing success - there were 18,080 visitors, about ten times the normal number! - and it was subsequently also shown in Zürich and Geneva. While it was still on show in Basel, Wilhelm Barth asked Léonce Bénédite, the curator of the Musée Rodin, whether the larger - than - life plaster cast of *The Walking Man* (*L'homme qui marche*. Ill.160, p.181) was for sale and could be acquired for the Sculpture Hall. This request was repeated on 27 September 1918, shortly before the exhibition closed in Geneva. However, the work was not allowed to remain in Switzerland but returned to Paris before being transported to Basel again in June 1919 to take the place it had occupied a year earlier in the middle of the Kunsthalle's large exhibition room lit by skylights.[210] On 20 June 1919 Dr. Albert Oeri and Carl Burckhardt, on behalf of the Committee for the Sculpture Hall, launched an appeal "To art-loving Basel!" in the daily press, in which they announced a fund-raising campaign to buy *The Walking Man*. The text of the appeal was presumably written by Carl Burckhardt, for the sculptor had installed the Rodin exhibition in the Kunsthalle and had written a piece on the subject *Rodin and the Plastic Problem*, which was not, however, published until 1921.

The fund-raising appeal for *The Walking Man* evokes the figure in the following way: "Decapitated and without arms, it at first glance gave the impression of a chance fragment, of something inchoate, unfinished. Yet the more one looks at this strange figure, the more complete and unified it seems to be. The suggestion of a restrained power, which permeates every form of the statue and which is visible in the vigorous stride only as if in a reflex, grips the viewer more and more. He stands before the statue as if before a living organism that has grown like a tree - that asserts itself self-confidently like securely, simply constructed architecture. This magnificent effect, which is found in only the best of Rodin's works, derives from the inner moulding of the figure - or, to put it more simply: the statue possesses those great qualities which the sculpture of antiquity has kept alive to the present day and which links even the modern approach of a Rodin with the perception of earlier epochs."[211]

The result of the collection at first turned out to be "very disappointing".[212] The work was priced at 6,000 French francs, which was considered justified for an original casting made before Rodin's very eyes. In January 1920 the Kunstkommission decided to raise its intended contribution from 500 to 1,000 Swiss francs but, in return, it required the sculpture to be given to the Museum.[213]

In the 1920s Wilhelm Barth continued with the series of major exhibitions, of which the Rodin retrospective was the first, devoted to individual masters of Impressionism and especially Post-Impressionism. In the spring of 1921 Cézanne's work was shown in the Kunsthalle, in 1924 and 1927 that of Vincent van Gogh, and in 1928 that of Paul Gauguin. These comprehensive presentations had an effect on the Museum's collecting policy. Particularly after the City made more funds available for purchases in 1919, the Kunstkommission contemplated the acquisition of Impressionist pictures more frequently than before. For example, in 1921 it reacted with interest to the news that Julius Dreyfus-Brodsky of Basel was offering Cézanne's still-life *Fruit Bowl and Apples* (*Compotier et pommes*) for sale from his mother-in-law's estate.[214] However, the work was not acquired by the Museum: today it hangs in Oskar Reinhart's collection "Am Römerholz" in Winterthur.

Discussions about purchasing works by Impressionists became more frequent after Friedrich Rintelen succeeded Heinrich Alfred Schmid as the Museum's curator in the summer of 1925. Shortly after taking office Rintelen tried to show visitors to the Museum "once, even if only for a short time, how a wall would look in the collection if it were hung with pictures by French artists"[215]. In order to do so, he borrowed a number of pictures that were privately owned in Basel; three works loaned from the collection of Fritz and Erna Schön were for sale: Courbet's *Asters (Bouquet d'asters)*, Cézanne's *Plate of Apples (Le plat de pommes)*[216], and van Gogh's *L'Arlésienne*[217]. *L'Arlésienne* had been given a place of honour at the van Gogh exhibition in the Kunsthalle the year before, and the Kunstkommission would have liked to acquire it for the Museum's collection. However, this proved to be impossible despite Rudolf Staechelin's willingness to help with the finances. *L'Arlésienne* entered the collection of the Metropolitan Museum of Art in New York in 1951. The Amerbach Foundation was, however, able to acquire Courbet's *Asters* (Ill.136, p.162) and placed it with the Museum in February 1926.

The purchase, which was particularly recommended by Hermann Meyer, of Cézanne's *Bather with Outstretched Arms (Baigneur au bord de l'eau)*, a work from Edgar Degas' collection which the Zürich art dealer and auctioneer Gustav Bollag offered in January 1926 for 40,000 Swiss francs, did not materialise either. The price was judged too high and, as Gustav Bollag was not prepared to go below 32,000 Swiss francs, the picture was not purchased.[218] It was offered to the Kunstmuseum again thirty years later, but by then the price had risen to 142,000 Swiss francs. However, Georg Schmidt opposed its purchase on the grounds that, because of its small size, it was "not a museum picture".[219] In 1989 the small *Bather* was acquired by the American painter Jasper Johns for his private collection.[220]

Friedrich Rintelen died quite unexpectedly in May 1926. During his curatorship, which lasted only a few months, he did not succeed in adding a French Impressionist picture to the collection. Rudolf Staechelin therefore proposed that the small picture *Young Girl Lying on the Grass (Jeune fille couchée sur l'herbe.* Ill.150, p.172) by Renoir - which came from Dr. Paul Linder's collection - should be bought in memory of the deceased.[221]

Rintelen's successor, Otto Fischer (1886-1948), not only laid the foundations for the modern section of the Öffentliche Kunstsammlung but also tried, with expertise and persistence, to enlarge the group of Impressionist works. When in the summer of 1928 the Kunsthalle showed the magnificent Gauguin exhibition, Fischer's first proposal was to purchase the pastel sketch of the main figure in the picture *Words of the Devil (Les paroles du diable.* Ill.156, p.178). A year later he was able to add Gauguin's *Portrait of the Painter Achille Granchi-Taylor (Portrait du peintre Achille Granchi-Taylor.* Ill.146, p.170) which, as he stated in a press communiqué, fits in "happily with the small group of unpretentious but refined French pictures in the Öffentliche Kunstsammlung".[222] However, when in June 1931 a petition signed by 110 artists and art-lovers called on the Kunstkommission to buy Gauguin's *Portrait of the Artist's Mother (Portrait de la mère de l'artiste)*, which was on offer for 80,000 Swiss francs, Fischer felt that the enthusiasm for Gauguin reigning in Basel "was perhaps somewhat exaggerated".[223]

Never before, and never again since, did the art market offer such an abundance of major Impressionist and Post-Impressionist works as during the economic and political crisis that occurred in the first half of the 1930s. The Kunsthalle's two van Gogh exhibitions had strengthened the wish in Basel to own a work by van Gogh. The list of pictures by him offered to the Museum at the time is impressive. In the autumn of 1932 the Kunstkommission considered the purchase of *Portrait of the Postman Roulin (Portrait du facteur Roulin)*, offered for 80,000 marks by Dr. Fritz Nathan of Munich.[224] In 1933 there were as many as seven of the artist's paintings to choose between: *The Auvers Stairs (L'escalier d'Auvers)* for 78,000 Swiss francs[225], *Le Moulin de la Galette* for 50,000 Swiss francs[226], a still-life with faded *Sunflowers (Nature morte aux Tournesols)* for 60,000 Swiss francs[227] and also two pictures from Hugo von Tschudi's estate: *Rain (Paysage sous la pluie)* [228], which the Philadelphia Museum of Art received in 1986 as a bequest from Henry P. McIlhenny, and a *View of Auvers (Vue à Auvers)*[229]. After paying a visit to the brothers Josse and Gaston Bernheim-Jeune in the autumn of 1933 in the company of Rudolf

Staechelin, Otto Fischer suggested to the Kunstkommission that, in addition to pictures by Courbet and Cézanne, it should also buy *Oleanders (Les lauriers roses)* [230] by van Gogh and his *Peasant in a Straw Hat (Paysan en chapeau de paille)*, a portrait of Patience Escalier. It was decided that 75,000 Swiss francs would be offered for the latter, but the seller wanted 125,000 Swiss francs.[231] The Kunstkommission asked for all the pictures being offered for sale to be sent to Basel for a thorough inspection, but in each case the price demanded exceeded the Museum's resources.

Finally, in the autumn of 1934, the portrait of Marguerite Gachet (1869-1949) was secured for the Museum at a price of 300,000 French francs. Van Gogh wrote to his brother Theo on 26 or 27 June 1890 about the creation of *Marguerite Gachet at the Piano (Mademoiselle Gachet au piano.* Ill.151, p.173): "Yesterday and the day before I painted the portrait of Mademoiselle Gachet, which I hope you will soon see. The dress is pink, the wall in the background green with orange dots, the carpet red with green flecks, the piano purple; the size one metre high by 50 cm wide. I painted this figure with pleasure - but it was difficult." Dr. Paul Gachet, who was offering it for sale and who was the subject's brother, was not willing to send the picture to Basel for inspection, so the Kunstkommission dispatched Otto Fischer and Rudolf Staechelin to Paris and Auvers-sur-Oise. They were favourably impressed by the picture and six members of the Kunstkommission consequently accompanied the curator to Paris from 29 September to 1 October 1934. They were in general surprised by the picture's extraordinary state of preservation and strength of colour. In Dr. Gachet's country house in Auvers they then discovered pictures that were even more impressive: van Gogh's *Self-Portrait* from the late summer of 1889, his *Portrait of Dr. Gachet (Portrait du docteur Gachet)*, *The Church at Auvers (Eglise d'Auvers)* and *Thatched Cottages at Cordevilles, at Auvers-sur-Oise (Chaumes de Cordevilles à Auvers-sur-Oise)*. These were not, however, for sale, and between 1949 and 1954 they were donated by Paul and Marguerite Gachet to the French State (today they are in the Musée d'Orsay in Paris). But how right Rudolf Staechelin proved to be when he prophesied of *Marguerite Gachet at the Piano*: "The quieter, finer picture will not disappoint with the passage of time"[232]!

There was a special desire for a major work by Cézanne in addition to one by van Gogh. Here, too, there was no lack of offers. In the spring of 1934 Otto Fischer had the opportunity to call on the artist's son in Paris and to inspect Auguste Pellerin's famous Cézanne collection. Some of the pictures were for sale, albeit for a very high price. "The most important work is the famous large composition of Bathers from the last years, in which the Kunsthaus Zürich is also interested. However, the asking price is 2 million French francs", Fischer reported to the Kunstkommission. He recommended that this possibility should be kept under review but that no action should be taken until the owner brought down his prices.[233] In the summer of 1935 Fischer saw at Vollard's another "composition with Bathers from Cézanne's late period", which might have been a *Study for the Large Bathers (Ebauche des Grandes Baigneuses)*.[234] The price was between 30,000 and 35,000 Swiss francs. The curator did not recommend the work's purchase. Was he still dreaming of *Les Grandes Baigneuses*, which was acquired by the Philadelphia Museum of Art in 1937?

The Museum did not, for the time being, purchase a painting by Cézanne. However, the Kunstkommission made the courageous and far-sighted decision to acquire two lots totalling 148 drawings by the master of Aix for the Kupferstichkabinett in 1934 and 1935.[235] It was fully realised at the time that, despite numerous excellent offers, the funds available to the Museum for acquisitions were too modest for it ever to be able to bring together a correspondingly significant collection of paintings by Cézanne.

In 1934 the Museum could have acquired en bloc a collection of sixty-two paintings and a marble sculpture by Rodin which belonged to Oskar Schmitz, who was Swiss by birth and had previously resided in Dresden, and which was temporarily exhibited in Basel (in 1932/33 it had also been displayed in the Kunsthaus Zürich).[236] But where was the Museum to find the requisite one and a half million Swiss francs? Then in 1936 a smaller first-class private Impressionist collection was placed with the Museum on long-term loan. From this the Öffentliche

Kunstsammlung was to purchase Monet's *Boulevard de Pontoise at Argenteuil* (*Le Boulevard de Pontoise à Argenteuil*. Ill.142, p.167) in 1953 and Renoir's *Woman in a Garden* - also known as *Woman with a Seagull Feather* (*Femme dans un jardin [La femme à la mouette]*. Ill.139, p.165) - in 1988.[237]

When Georg Schmidt succeeded Otto Fischer as curator of the Kunstmuseum in 1939, he summarised the position thus: "The French painters of the 19th century are our most obvious gaps. Our worst deficiencies here are met by loans. Systematic expansion would be quite possible as far as the market is concerned but not financially. We could fill all the gaps at once if we had the necessary funds, but all we can contemplate is to fill them one by one when there is a particularly favourable offer."[238] He especially regretted that there was no picture by Cézanne in the collection. As early as 1921, on the occasion of the first Cézanne exhibition in Basel, which was held in the Kunsthalle from 6 February to 16 March, Schmidt had written: "If these treasures were to remain *permanently* in Basel, then people would visit Basel for their sake, as well as for the Holbeins and Böcklins." However, given the local circumstances then, Schmidt went on to modify his hopes, reducing them to the wish: "If only at least *one* painting would remain in our museum!"[239] It was Georg Schmidt's destiny to fulfill this wish himself - but this occurred much later, in 1955, with the acquisition of *Mont Sainte-Victoire Seen from Les Lauves* (*Le Mont Sainte-Victoire, vu des Lauves*. Ill.155, p.177) and still later, in 1960, with *Five Bathers* (*Cinq Baigneuses*. Ill.152, p.174). Schmidt discovered *Five Bathers* in the Beyeler Gallery at the end of 1959 and considered "this purchase as the crowning achievement of his entire activity at the Museum".[240]

The biggest addition to the Basel Impressionist collection came in the 1970s, thanks to a bequest and a donation. In 1970 twelve paintings by Manet, Monet, Pissarro, Renoir, Sisley, van Gogh, Monticelli and Seurat, and three sculptures by Renoir and Rodin that had been in the collection of Emile Dreyfus (1881-1965) came into the Kunstmuseum as a Foundation. After the death of Robert von Hirsch (1883-1977) - who had already given the Öffentliche Kunstsammlung one of Gauguin's masterpieces, the wonderful *Ta matete (Marketplace)* (*Ta matete [Au marché]*. Ill.157, p.179), in 1941 - the Museum received pictures by Ingres, Daumier, Degas and Cézanne, and also ten drawings by Cézanne, in addition to paintings by Hans Holbein the Elder and Lukas Cranach the Elder.[241] On 26 June 1978, at the auction of von Hirsch's collection at Sotheby's in London, the Kunstmuseum was also able to obtain Cézanne's portrait of the friend of his youth Fortuné Marion (c.1871).[242]

Elsewhere, too, it was above all private collectors who first showed enthusiasm and support for the new French painting, and who then ultimately presented or bequeathed their treasures to the museums of their native cities. Where would the Musée d'Orsay be without the bequests and donations of Gustave Caillebotte, Count Isaac de Camondo and Etienne Moreau-Nélaton; the National Gallery in London without Sir Hugh Lane; the Metropolitan Museum of Art without the Havemeyers, or the Art Institute of Chicago without Potter Palmer?

127   Claude-Joseph Vernet (1714-1789)
Shipwreck (Naufrage). 1780
Oil on canvas, 49.5 x 65 cm
Inv. no. 624. Gift of Mayor Felix Sarasin, 1857

128   Jean-Auguste-Dominique Ingres (1780-1867)
Venus Wounded by Diomedes
(Vénus blessée par Diomède remonte au ciel).
c. 1803
Oil on walnut, 27 x 34 cm.
Inv. no. G 1977. 38. Gift of
Martha and Robert von Hirsch, 1977

129   Jean-Auguste-Dominique Ingres (1780-1867)
Head of Mars (Tête du dieu Mars). 1848-1850
Oil on canvas, 32.5 x 31.5 cm
Inv. no. 1715. Purchase, 1938

130   Théodore Géricault (1791-1824)
The Martyrdom of Saint Peter the Apostle
(after Titian),
(Le Martyr de Saint Pierre
[d'après le Titien]). c . 1814
Oil on canvas, 65 x 54 cm
Inv. no. G 1967.4. Purchase, 1967

130

131 Eugène Delacroix
(1798-1863)
*Mortally Wounded Brigand
(Brigand blessé)*. c. 1825
Oil on canvas, 33 x 41 cm
Inv. no. 1726. Purchase, 1939

132 Eugène Delacroix
(1798-1863)
*The Witches' Sabbath
(Scène de Sabbat)*. 1831-1833
Oil on canvas, 32.5 x 41 cm
Inv. no. G 1988.5 . Purchase, 1988

133 Eugène Delacroix
(1798-1863)
*Nereid (after Rubens)
(Néréide [d'après Rubens])*.
c. 1822
Oil on canvas, 46.5 x 38 cm
Inv. no. 1602 . Gift of friends of
Prof. Friedrich Rintelen, given in
his memory, 1933

135   Honoré Daumier (1808-1879)
Don Quixote's Vigil
(La veille de Don Quichotte). 1855-1856
Oil on oak, 37 x 46 cm
Inv. no. G 1977.39.
Gift of Martha and Robert von Hirsch, 1977

134 Eugène Delacroix (1798-1863). *The Raising of Lazarus (La résurrection de Lazare).* 1850
Oil on canvas, 61.5 x 50.5 cm. Inv. no. G 1964.2. Gift of Dr. Fritz Hagemann, 1964

136 Gustave Courbet (1819-1877)
Asters (Bouquet d'asters). 1859
Oil on canvas, 46 x 61 cm
Inv. no. 1428. Amerbach Foundation, 1926

137 Jean-Baptiste-Camille Corot (1796-1875). *Italian Girl by a Fountain (Italienne à la fontaine).* 1865-1870
Oil on canvas, 83 x 55 cm. Inv. no. G 1963.28. Acquired with a special grant from the City of Basel, 1963

138 Edgar Degas (1834-1917)
At the Races
(Sur le champ de courses [Les courses]).
1860-1862
Oil on canvas, 43 x 65.5 cm
Inv. no. G 1977.36. Gift of Martha and
Robert von Hirsch, 1977

139 Pierre-Auguste Renoir (1841-1919). *Woman in a Garden (Woman with a Seagull Feather) (Femme dans un jardin [La femme à la mouette]).*
c. 1868. Oil on canvas, 106 x 73.5 cm. Inv. no. G 1988.22. Acquired with a special grant from the City of Basel
and contributions from numerous patrons, 1988

140 Camille Pissarro (1830-1903)
Snow at l'Hermitage
(Effet de neige à l'Hermitage). 1875
Oil on canvas, 54 x 73 cm
Inv. no. G 1991.16. Purchase, 1991

141 Camille Pissarro (1830-1903)
L'Hermitage, Pontoise. 1878
Oil on canvas, 55 x 65.5 cm
Inv. no. 871. Acquired with
contributions from private art
patrons and the City of Basel, 1912

142 Claude Monet (1840-1926)
Boulevard de Pontoise at Argenteuil
(Le Boulevard de Pontoise à Argenteuil). 1875
Oil on canvas, 60.5 x 81.5 cm
Inv. no. 2320. Purchase, 1953

143 Georges Seurat (1859-1891)
Landscape with a Stake
(Paysage au piquet). 1881-1882
Oil on canvas, 38 x 46.5 cm
Inv. no. G 1970.19 . Permanent loan
of the Dr. h.c. Emile Dreyfus Foundation, 1970

144   Vincent van Gogh (1853-1890)
*View of Paris Seen from Montmartre
(Vue de Paris, prise de Montmartre)*. 1886
Oil on canvas, 38.5 x 61.5 cm
Inv. no. 1982. Purchase, 1946

145   Paul Signac (1863-1935)
Square Saint-Pierre, Butte Montmartre. 1883
Oil on canvas, 66.5 x 54 cm
Inv. no. 2049. Gift of Dr. Hans Graber, 1947

146 Paul Gauguin (1848-1903)
Portrait of the Painter Achille Granchi-Taylor
(Portrait du peintre Achille Granchi-Taylor). 1885
Oil on canvas, 46.5 x 55.5 cm
Inv. no. 1551. Purchase, 1930

147 Emile Bernard (1868-1941)
Portrait of Julien Tanguy (1825-1894), called Père Tanguy
(Portrait de Julien Tanguy, dit le Père Tanguy). 1887
Oil on canvas, 36 x 31 cm
Inv. no. 2237. Purchase, 1950

148 Vincent van Gogh (1853-1890)
Self-Portrait with Japanese Woodcut
(Autoportrait à l'estampe japonaise). 1887
Oil on canvas, 43 x 34 cm
Inv. no. G 1970.7. Permanent loan of the
Dr.h.c. Emile Dreyfus Foundation, 1970

149 Camille Pissarro (1830-1903)
The Gleaners (Les glaneuses). 1887-1889
Oil on canvas, 65.5 x 81 cm
Inv. no. G 1970 .14. Permanent loan of the
Dr.h.c. Emile Dreyfus Foundation, 1970

150 Pierre-Auguste Renoir (1841-1919)
Young Girl Lying on the Grass
(Jeune fille couchée sur l'herbe)
Oil on canvas, 20.5 x 31.5 cm
Inv. no. 1433. Purchase, 1926

151 Vincent van Gogh (1853-1890)
*Marguerite Gachet at the Piano
(Mademoiselle Gachet au piano).* 1890
Oil on canvas, 102.5 x 50 cm
Inv. no. 1635. Purchase, 1934

152   Paul Cézanne (1839-1906)
Five Bathers (Cinq Baigneuses). c. 1885
Oil on canvas, 65.5 x 65.5 cm
Inv. no. G 1960.1. Acquired with contributions from the City of Basel,
the Max Geldner Foundation and from private art patrons, 1960

153 Paul Cézanne (1839-1906)
The Pigeon Tower at Bellevue (Pigeonnier de Bellevue). c. 1890
Tempera on canvas, 54.5 x 81.5 cm
Inv. no. G 1977.35. Gift of Martha and Robert von Hirsch, 1977

155   Paul Cézanne (1839-1906)
Mont Sainte-Victoire Seen from Les Lauves
(Le Mont Sainte-Victoire, vu des Lauves). 1904-1906
Oil on canvas, 60 x 72 cm
Inv. no. G 1955.12. Acquired with contributions
from the City of Basel, the Department of Education,
Ciba AG, J.R. Geigy AG and Sandoz AG, 1955

154   Edgar Degas (1834-1917). *Fallen Jockey (Jockey blessé)*. 1896-1898
Oil on canvas, 181 x 151 cm. Inv. no. G 1963. 29. Acquired with a special grant from the City of Basel, 1963

156   Paul Gauguin (1848-1903)
Words of the Devil (Les paroles du diable). 1892
Pastel on paper, 76.5 x 34.5 cm
Kupferstichkabinett inv. no. 1928.17. Purchase, 1928

157 Paul Gauguin (1848-1903)
Ta matete (Marketplace) (Ta matete [Au marché]). 1892
Oil on canvas, 73 x 91.5 cm
Inv. no. 1849. Gift of Dr.h.c. Robert von Hirsch, 1941

158 Auguste Rodin (1840-1917)
Bust of the Sculptor Jules Dalou (1838-1902)
(Buste du sculpteur Jules Dalou). 1883
Foundry mark Alexis Rudier, Fondeur, Paris. 52 x 42.5 x 25.2 cm
Inv. no. G 1970.18. Permanent loan of the Dr.h.c. Emile Dreyfus
Foundation, 1970

159 Auguste Rodin (1840-1917)
Heroic Bust of Victor Hugo (1802-1885)
(Buste héroïque de Victor Hugo). 1897
Bronze, 70.5 x 58.5 x 57 cm
Inv. no. P 15. Purchase, 1906

161 Odilon Redon (1840-1916). *Portrait of Jeanne Chaîne (Portrait de Jeanne Chaîne)*. 190:
Pastel on paper, 79.5 x 69 cm. Inv. no. G 1955.4. Purchase, 1955

162 Edgar Degas (1834-1917). *Breakfast upon Leaving the Bath (La tasse de chocolat)*. 1900-1
Pastel on paper, 93 x 79 cm. Inv. no. G 1979.43. Gift of the Max Geldner Foundation, 1979

163 Claude Monet (1840-1926). *Chrysanthemums (Massif de chrysanthèmes)*. 1897
Oil on canvas, 82 x 100.5 cm. Inv. no. G 1970.11. Permanent loan of the
Dr.h.c. Emile Dreyfus Foundation, 1970

164 Claude Monet (1840-1926). *The Footbridge over the Water Lily Pond*
(La passerelle sur le bassin aux nymphéas). 1919
Oil on canvas, 66 x 107.5 cm Inv. no. G 1986 .15 . Acquired with contributions from
the City of Basel and the Max Geldner Foundation, 1986

160 Auguste Rodin
(1840-1917)
*The Walking Man
(L'homme qui
marche)*. 1907
Plaster cast,
214.5 x 123 x 148.5 cm
Inv. no. P 49.
Purchase, 1920

163

164

Dance Halls for Music of the Future

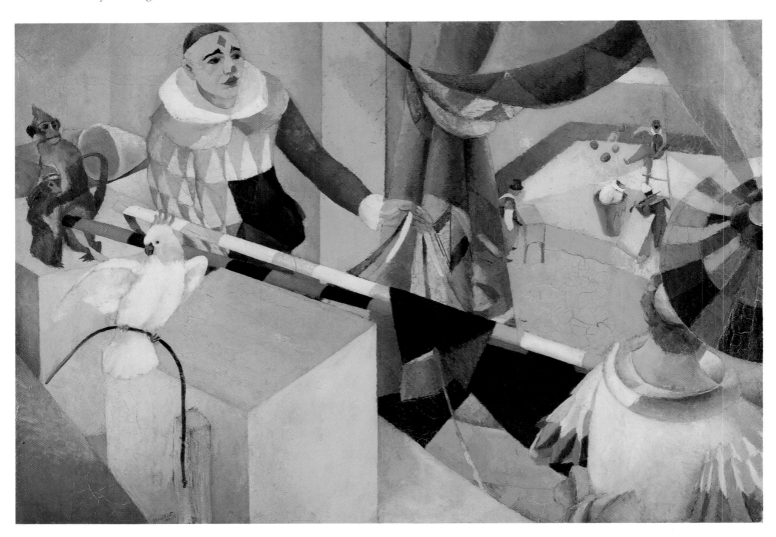

165 Louis Moilliet (1880-1962)
At the Circus (Im Zirkus). 1914-1915
Oil on canvas, 140 x 200 cm
Inv. no. 942. Birmann Fund, 1915

W hen in 1926 the planning of a new museum for the Öffentliche Kunstsammlung was given a fresh impetus by the acquisition of the Württembergerhof, it was not only special rooms to accommodate the collection of Old Masters that were demanded, but also a gallery for modern art. However, this modern collection had still to be created.

A press communiqué issued at the end of January 1916 indicates what was then on show in the "Modern Art Room" of the old Museum in the Augustinergasse. There was nothing but pictures by Swiss painters: *At the Watering Place* (*An der Tränke*. 1888) by Segantini (acquired in 1904), Hodler's study for *The Battle of Näfels* (*Schlacht bei Näfels*. Ill.117, p.138; acquired in 1901) and his *Lake Geneva Seen from Chexbres* (*Der Genfersee von Chexbres aus*. Ill.120, p.141; acquired in 1905), Max Buri's *The Village Politicians* (*Die Dorfpolitiker*. 1904; received in 1905 as a long-term loan of the Swiss Confederation), Giovanni Giacometti's *The Bread* (*Das Brot*. Painted and acquired in 1914) and also Cuno Amiet's *Farmers' Garden* (*Bauerngarten*. Painted and acquired in 1914). Finally three new acquisitions added to the collection the previous year were exhibited for the first time: Numa Donzé's *Liberation* (*Befreiung*. 1906), *The Fig Tree* (*Der Ficus*. 1915) by Heinrich Müller and *At the Circus* (*Im Zirkus*. Ill.165, p.186) by Louis Moilliet.[243] Moilliet's circus picture of 1914/15 had been included in November 1915 in the exhibition "Painters from the French-speaking part of Switzerland" in the Kunsthalle and had caused "considerable controversy" there, as Wilhelm Barth, the head of the Kunsthalle, noted: "Its effect on our public was at first like a double punch, with its apparently eccentric, bizarre and confused forms and with its brightness of colour that pushed astonishment to the point of horror and disgust."[244] In the Museum's Modern Room, too, *At the Circus* must have seemed an audaciously revolutionary work compared with the other pictures on display. In respect of its composition, style and colours, it was the first truly modern picture in the Basel Museum's collection, and was to remain so for over a decade.[245]

In 1927 Otto Fischer was appointed the new curator of the Öffentliche Kunstsammlung, and he took up his post on 1 November of that year. Fischer was a committed champion of modern art who had been the director of the Staatliche Gemäldegalerie in Stuttgart since 1921. His championship of modern art in Stuttgart had reached a high point in the summer of 1924 with the "Exhibition of Recent German Art". This survey of the modern, since the turn of the century, comprised 400 works by German and Swiss painters and sculptors such as Beckmann, Bissier, Campendonk, Dix, Feininger, Felixmüller, Hermann Haller, Heckel, Hodler, Hofer, Klee, Paula Modersohn-Becker - among the works by her that were displayed was the *Self-Portrait* (*Selbstbildnis*. Ill.177, p.202) which Georg Schmidt acquired for Basel in 1939 - Munch, Nolde, Pechstein, Rohlfs, Hermann Scherer, Schlemmer, Schmidt-Rottluff and several others. The exhibition provoked a storm of indignation and the term "degenerate art" was heard in the debates about it. Given the circumstances, Otto Fischer must have been particularly pleased by the invitation to become the curator of the Öffentliche Kunstsammlung.

Only a few weeks before Fischer took up his post in Basel, the Kunstkommission had decided, through the mediation of one of its members, the painter Alfred Heinrich Pellegrini, to purchase two paintings by Edvard Munch, *Portrait of Käte Perls* (*Bildnis Käte Perls*. Ill.174, p.200) and *Large Coastal Landscape* (*Große Küsten-landschaft*. Ill.175, p.200), and thus ventured "a foray into leading contemporary art beyond the limitations of Swiss territory", as the Öffentliche Kunstsammlung's Annual Report put it.[246]

Further progress in the expansion of the modern collection came only hesitantly. In 1930 Otto Fischer acquired Emil Nolde's *Blue Irises* (*Blaue Iris*. Ill.178, p.203), thus throwing "a bridge to what we possess by Munch and some of the young Basel artists (Hermann Scherer and Albert Müller)". In a letter to Nolde of 11 February 1930, Fischer said: "It is incidentally the first picture by a living modern German painter to come into our gallery, so let us hope that it will soon find itself in good company." The newly acquired picture by Nolde was hung temporarily between Albert Müller's *Large Tessin Landscape* (*Große Tessinerlandschaft*. 1925) and Hermann Scherer's *Villa Loverciana with Trees in Bloom* (*Villa Loverciana mit blühenden Bäumen*. Ill.200, p.221). "It causes surprise between these, too, through the great power and inner fullness of its colours. What one senses with special force is the way the plants grow upwards, how from the depth of their roots they send up the thick clumps of their blue-green sword-like leaves, and find their magnificent, extravagant fulfilment in the riot of abundant blossoms so saturated in colour. It is not merely fullness of colour but also fullness of life that the artist has created here."[247]

In the same year Fischer was also able to buy *The Blue Flask* (*Le flacon bleu.* Ill. 193, p.216) by James Ensor. And then at the beginning of 1931 came the first picture by Paul Klee: *Senecio* (Ill.190, p.213) of 1922. This painting had already been shown in 1924 in the "Exhibition of Recent German Art" that Fischer had organised for Stuttgart and had also been displayed in Basel in the spring of 1929 in the exhibition the Kunsthalle had devoted to the Bauhaus in Dessau. In September 1930 Otto Fischer had approached the artist with a request for help over the acquisition of one of his pictures: "From what I hear, you still have many acquaintances and admirers in Basel, and you will certainly be familiar with our museum. So you might perhaps be pleased if we can permanently display something really good from among your works" was the hope Fischer expressed in his letter of 19 September 1930.[248]

In the summer of 1931 Fischer added a third picture by Munch, *Scene from Ibsen's Ghosts* (*Szene aus Ibsens Gespenstern*), to the two already in the Museum. Munch's work possessed a special relevance for the younger generation of Basel artists - as indeed did that of Ernst Ludwig Kirchner - and it therefore seemed particularly desirable that Munch should be well represented in the Museum's collection. Nevertheless, the offer of another, excellent picture by the Norwegian *Country Road in Aasgaardstrand* (*Landstraße [Straße in Aasgaardstrand].* Ill.176, p.201) - was turned down by the Kunstkommission in December 1933. *Country Road* had been given to the Karlsruhe Kunsthalle in 1929 by the art historian Curt Glaser (1872-1944). In the spring of 1933 the picture was included in the exhibition "Government Art 1918 to 1933", which the painter Professor Hans Adolf Bühler, who was brought in as director of the Karlsruhe Kunsthalle shortly after Hitler's seizure of power, organised with the intention of discrediting the works of modern art acquired by his predecessors and exposing them to ridicule. The event acted as a kind of signal and in 1937 led to the "Degenerate Art" exhibition held in Munich.[249] On Otto Fischer's recommendation, *Country Road* was then acquired by the Basel collector Consul Fritz Schwarz von Spreckelsen; in 1978 his widow and daughter gave the painting to the Öffentliche Kunstsammlung.

In 1932, at the suggestion and with the financial support of the Basel collector Emanuel Hoffmann-Stehlin (1896-1932), a picture by the Flemish Expressionist Frits van den Berghe, *La Lys* (Ill.194, p.216), and a major work by Max Ernst, *The Big Forest* (*La grande forêt.* Ill.207, p.227) were bought at the auction in Brussels of the Walter Schwarzenberg collection.[250] These were, however, modest beginnings for a collection of modern art. Otto Fischer warned in relation to the project for the construction of the Kunstmuseum: "Our moderns would not even fill the large entrance hall. The other rooms are dance halls for music of the future."[251]

A guide to the Kunstmuseum in the St. Alban-Graben, which was opened on 29 August 1936, provides a room-by-room list of the works of art exhibited and reveals how Otto Fischer arranged the modern section on the second floor. The visitor was greeted in the entrance hall by Ferdinand Hodler's monumental painting *View into Infinity* (*Blick in die Unendlichkeit.* Ill.123, pp.144-145).[252] In addition to other paintings by Hodler, the two pictures by Edvard Munch acquired in 1927 were also hung there. The gallery proper began with a large room and a small room with paintings by Arnold Böcklin. The next rooms were exclusively devoted to 19th and 20th century Swiss and Basel painting. Then came a French room and and a small Impressionist room, in which the Museum's own paintings were clearly outnumbered by loans. A "Contemporary Room" where, in addition to Moilliet's *At the Circus*, there were pictures by representatives of the "Red-Blue" group of artists and by a few other younger Basel painters, as well as Klee's *Senecio*, Nolde's *Blue Irises*, Max Ernst's *The Big Forest* and van den Berghe's *La Lys*, brought the visitor back to the entrance hall.

After the inauguration of the Kunstmuseum, Fischer continued his purchasing programme for the modern section by acquiring Lovis Corinth's *Portrait of Reich President Friedrich Ebert (Bildnis des Reichspräsidenten Friedrich Ebert.* Ill.196, p.218), two sculptures by Maillol *Chained Action (Action enchaînée.* 1906) and *The Cyclist (Le cycliste.* 1907/08) - and Wilhelm Lehmbruck's *Woman's Torso (Frauentorso.* 1910). The Ebert portrait had been exhibited at the Kunsthalle in the spring of 1936 in the Corinth retrospective. The funds available to the museum for acquisitions were not sufficient to purchase the picture, which was on offer from the artist's widow. The Social Democratic City Councillor Fritz Hauser, who was Director of the Education Department, therefore promised to try to find a solution and he did, in fact, succeed in raising contributions from the Basel trade unions and the City's Government.

Overall, the initial purchases of works by international modern artists may at first sight seem to have been rather modest, but it is important to remember that not only were the available funds extremely limited but also that the accessions in question did not go unopposed at the time in the Kunstkommission. Moreover, Otto Fischer had to build up other parts of the collection during the same period. The Kunstmuseum owes to him its first purchases of Post-Impressionist works: the pastel *Words of the Devil (Les paroles du diable.* Ill.156, p.178) and *Portrait of the Painter Achille Granchi-Taylor* (Ill. 146, p.170) by Paul Gauguin and also van Gogh's *Marguerite Gachet at the Piano (Mademoiselle Gachet au piano.* Ill.151, p.173).

Georg Schmidt (1896-1965), who succeeded Otto Fischer as curator of the Öffentliche Kunstsammlung on 1 March 1939, came up against the "noticeable contradiction between architectural lavishness and artistic content" as he remarked in the spring of 1939 in a letter addressed to the Basel Government[253] , in which he requested a special credit for the purchase of works of "degenerate art". Shortly after taking office he found out that the Lucerne art dealer Theodor Fischer was going to auction on behalf of the German Ministry of Enlightenment and Propaganda 120 works of art that had been removed from German museums by the new rulers in a veritable "iconoclasm". Schmidt applied to the Basel Government for funds so that, both at the auction in Lucerne on 30 June 1939 and also direct in Berlin, he would be able to buy pictures and sculptures by artists who had been banned by the National Socialists as "degenerate". "For the City of Basel and for the Kunstmuseum this is a unique opportunity to attain international status overnight, and in an area in which we have so far been totally inadequate", Schmidt argued: "One can only compare this opportunity with the selling-off of the private collections of the French aristocracy after the French Revolution. Basel *must not* fail to respond."[254] The Government subsequently granted the Kunstmuseum a special credit not of 100,000 Swiss francs as requested, but of only 50,000 Swiss francs. Schmidt was certainly not able to acquire any paintings by van Gogh or Picasso with that amount, but it did permit him, in both Lucerne and Berlin, to purchase nineteen paintings, a gouache and a sculpture that had previously been displayed in German museums. Thus Corinth's *Ecce Homo* (Ill.197, p.219) and Georg Schrimpf's *Girl at the Window (Mädchen am Fenster)* had once belonged to the Berlin Nationalgalerie; *Head for the War Memorial in Güstrow (Kopf zum Krieger-Ehrenmal in Güstrow)* by Ernst Barlach, *Calvary (Le calvaire)* by André Derain and *Five Figures in Space (Roman) (Fünf Figuren im Raum [Römisches].* Ill.205, p.226) by Oskar Schlemmer had belonged to the Folkwang Museum in Essen; Max Beckmann's park landscape *Nice in Frankfurt am Main (Nizza in Frankfurt am Main.* Ill.195, p.215), Marc Chagall's gouache *Winter* and also Klee's *Villa R.* (Ill.189, p.212) had belonged to the Städtische Galerie in Frankfurt am Main; Franz Marc's *Fate of the Animals (Tierschicksale.* Ill.182, p.206) had belonged to the Moritzburger Museum in Halle; *The Tempest (Die Windsbraut.* Ill.180, p.205) by Kokoschka had belonged to the Hamburg Kunsthalle; Derain's *Vineyard (Vignoble)*, Nolde's *Marshy Landscape (Marschlandschaft)* and Schlemmer's *Women's Staircase (Frauentreppe.* Ill.206, p.226) had belonged to the Mannheim Kunsthalle; and Otto Dix's *The Artist's Parents (Die Eltern des Künstlers.* Ill.191, p.214) and the *Old Peasant Woman (Alte Bäuerin)* by Paula Modersohn-Becker had belonged to the Wallraf-Richartz Museum in Cologne. The Nazis' action in confiscating "degenerate" works of art thus enabled the Basel Kunstmuseum to profit from the pioneering achievements of certain German museums and from their readiness to collect contemporary art, and gave it an unusual opportunity to catch up in this area.

Several of the pictures bought in 1939 had been shown in Basel only a few years earlier in various exhibitions. This is true, for instance, of Derain's *View from the Window (Calvary)*, which was shown in June 1935 as a loan from the Folkwang Museum in the Derain retrospective organised by the Kunsthalle, and of *Boy with Cat* (*Knabe mit Katze*. c. 1900), which the City of Hanover lent in February and March 1936 for the Kunsthalle exhibition devoted to Paula Modersohn. From 1921 to 1938 Georg Schmidt was the art critic of the Basel newspaper *National-Zeitung*. His exhibition reviews reveal the judgment he had formed earlier of some of the pictures he acquired for the Kunstmuseum in 1939.

In his review of the Max Beckmann exhibition held in the Kunsthalle in August 1930, where the painting *Nice in Frankfurt am Main* was to be seen as a loan of the Städel Kunstinstitut in Frankfurt, Georg Schmidt wrote: "The pictures from the years 1919-23 all have a certain petit bourgeois narrowness and cosiness. The still-lifes, portraits and landscapes (above all 'Nice in Frankfurt') show strong similarities with the petit bourgeois 'New Objectivity'. But for Beckmann this attitude is absolutely genuine. Indeed, the works of that period, because of their human warmth, are perhaps the most appealing in the whole of Beckmann's previous development. They are warmer than the works of painters of the New Objectivity proper: Dix, Scholz, Stöcklin. And in their artistic technique they have more of the qualities that correspond to warmth - painterly sensitivity and musicality - than do those named. The pictures of that period have a delicacy and richness of colour not found in Beckmann's work of any other time. And it is above all through these pictures that Beckmann has established a clear identity in the art world."[255]

The Lovis Corinth exhibition that was shown by the Kunsthalle in April 1936 included *Large Still-Life with Figure of a Girl* (*Großes Stilleben mit Mädchenfigur*. Loan of the Nassau Landesmuseum Wiesbaden) and *Ecce Homo* (loan of the Nationalgalerie Berlin) as well as the *Portrait of Reich President Friedrich Ebert* subsequently acquired by Otto Fischer for the Kunstmuseum's collection. In his review Schmidt went into detail over the great *Ecce Homo*: "In this picture we first see the full consequences of the late change in Corinth's art. His overcoming of the last vestiges of naturalism liberates him from the contradiction between naive realism and spiritual claims from which most of his earlier compositions suffered. The intensification of his realism to the point of systematically anti-naturalistic expressiveness makes him able to present a spiritual event such as 'Ecce Homo'. The bleeding arms are just as expressive as is the face. Perhaps in the long run they may be even more expressive in human terms."[256]

The list of works that Georg Schmidt hoped to buy at the auction in June 1939 in Lucerne also included Henri Matisse's *The River Bank* (*La berge*. Ill.166, p.193). In the late summer of 1931 it had been lent by the Folkwang Museum in Essen to the Kunsthalle in Basel for its major Matisse exhibition. However, a Swiss private collector forestalled Schmidt at the Lucerne auction and secured the picture for 5,100 Swiss francs. In the spring of 1953 this Collioure landscape was again offered for sale, this time in an exhibition of French painting in the Château d'Art Gallery in Basel, which later became the Beyeler Gallery. Georg Schmidt was then able to buy it for the Kunstmuseum for 60,000 Swiss francs.

Thanks to the purchases made in 1939, German and Austrian Expressionism in particular were now represented in the Basel Kunstmuseum with an impressive series of major works - "except for Kirchner and we must acquire one of his Swiss landscapes some time", as Georg Schmidt stated in the autumn of 1939 in a discussion of future purchasing plans: "Basel would have owed him that during his lifetime, and still does after his death."[257] An exhibition of Ernst Ludwig Kirchner in the Kunsthalle in June 1923 had left a lasting impression on a number of young Basel artists, for instance Albert Müller (1897-1926), Hermann Scherer (1893-1927), Paul Camenisch (1893-1970) among others, and led to the foundation of the "Red-Blue" ("Rot-Blau") group of artists on New Year's Eve 1924/25.[258] "None of the Moderns has so far had so many followers", Kirchner himself commented.[259] It therefore grieved him that, although works by these local pupils had been acquired by the Öffentliche Kunstsammlung, he himself was represented by "not a single picture or print in the Basel Museum". "That's the way it always is."[260]

Otto Fischer failed to get the purchase of a Kirchner painting through the Kunstkommission in the spring of 1937, and in June 1939 no possibility of an acquisition materialised at the Lucerne auction. Not until September 1944 was the Öffentliche Kunstsammlung able to buy the summer landscape *Amselfluh* (Ill.198, p.220) from the Kirchner estate as a counterpart to the winter picture *Davos in Winter (Davos Snowed In)* (*Davos im Winter [Davos im Schnee]*. Ill.199, p.220) donated at the same time by the Winterthur collector Georg Reinhart.[262]

Schmidt does not seem to have felt any sense of urgency about making additional purchases of works by 20th century German artists; he added to those obtained in 1939 only in the case of Paul Klee - acquisition of the pictures *Garden City Idyll* (*Gartenstadtidyll*. 1926), *A Page from the Municipal Records* (*Ein Blatt aus dem Städtebuch*. 1928) and *Blue Night* (*Blaue Nacht*. Ill.211, p.231) in 1941 - and Nolde (purchase of the picture *Figure and Mask* [*Figur und Maske*] by the Verein der Freunde des Kunstmuseums in 1944).

On the other hand, the systematic expansion of the collection of works by modern French artists, especially the Cubists Picasso, Braque, Gris and Léger, did seem necessary to him: "So long as they are totally lacking, we should not think of any others". He also considered the Italians Modigliani and de Chirico to be indispensable, as well as the Dutch "Constructivists" Mondrian and van Doesburg.[263] This explains why the inclusion of the Emanuel Hoffmann Foundation, which had been set up in 1933 by Maja Sacher-Stehlin (1896-1989) and had previously been loaned to the Basel Kunstverein, was judged by Schmidt to be "of much greater consequence" for the expansion of the modern art collection than the purchases of the "Degenerates" in the previous year.[264] The inclusion of the Emanuel Hoffmann Foundation in 1940 brought into the Kunstmuseum twenty-one paintings and sculptures by Ensor, Braque, Chagall, Klee, Antoine Pevsner, Mondrian, van Doesburg, Moholy-Nagy, Hans Arp, Sophie Taeuber and Max Ernst. Then during the war years the Foundation purchased pictures by Juan Gris, Picasso, Delaunay, Giorgio de Chirico and Salvador Dalí.[265]

Ultimately, however, it was a series of generous and magnificent donations and bequests, for instance from the collections of Raoul La Roche (1952, 1956 and 1963), Richard Doetsch-Benziger (1960), Oskar and Annie Müller-Widmann (1965) and Marguerite Arp-Hagenbach (1968), that helped the Basel collection of modern art to attain its international reputation.

The donors also included artists, such as Arp and Picasso. In the summer of 1949 Hans Arp loaned a number of pictures from his collection to the Kunstmuseum, and held out the prospect of a legacy, but without making any firm commitment. After the artist's death in 1966, his second wife, Marguerite Arp-Hagenbach, fulfilled this intention and Kandinsky's *Improvisation 35* (Ill.183, p.207), a picture by Theo van Doesburg, two works by Sophier Taeuber-Arp and a sculpture by Max Bill, all of which had been owned by the artist, were transferred to the Öffentliche Kunstsammlung as the "Hans Arp Donation".[266]

During his lifetime Pablo Picasso generously presented numerous museums with gifts of his pictures. Yet no donation took place under such extraordinary circumstances as the one to Basel. In the summer of 1967 the Rudolf Staechelin Family Foundation found itself obliged to sell several paintings as a result of financial difficulties experienced by the collector's son. These included not only van Gogh's *Woman Rocking a Cradle* (*La berceuse*. Today in the Walter H. Annenberg collection), but also two pictures by Picasso - *The Two Brothers* (*Les deux frères*. Ill.167, p.194) and *Seated Harlequin* (*Arlequin assis*. Ill.202, p.223) - which had been exhibited in the Basel Kunstmuseum since 1947 as long-term loans and which were regarded by visitors as belonging to the Museum's collection. In order to keep the two pictures in the Kunstmuseum they were offered for sale to the City of Basel for 8.4 million Swiss francs for the two, despite higher offers from abroad. On 12 October the Government, with astonishingly few opposing votes, approved a special credit of 6 million Swiss francs; the remaining 2.4 million Swiss francs was collected through a large-scale fund-raising campaign, which culminated in an unforgettable "beggars' party". However, the Government's decision was put to a referendum and the Basel electorate had to vote on the credit of 6 million Swiss francs. When the referendum was voted upon on 17 December 1967 - with a turnout of barely 40 per cent - 32,118 citizens approved the government grant and 27,190 rejected it.[267]

This must have been the first time that a community was asked to decide in a referendum about the purchase of modern works of art. Picasso himself felt this public approval to be a tribute he did not receive every day, and he was particularly moved by the commitment of young people. He and his wife Jacqueline demonstrated this by giving the City of Basel three paintings and a pastel study for *Les demoiselles d'Avignon*. The Basel art patron and collector Maja Sacher-Stehlin expressed her joy at the surprising consequence of the referendum by giving the Kunstmuseum a Cubist picture by Picasso, *The Poet* (*Le Poète*. 1912), from her own collection. In 1974, a year after the death of Picasso, who was perhaps the most important artist of the 20th century, the City of Basel honoured him by naming the square behind the Kunstmuseum "Picassoplatz".

166   Henri Matisse (1869-1954). *The River Bank* (*La berge*). 1907
Oil on canvas, 73 x 60.5 cm. Inv. no. 2316. Purchase, 1953

167 Pablo Picasso
(1881-1973)
The Two Brothers
(*Les deux frères*). 1906
Oil on canvas
142 x 97 cm
Inv. no. G 1967.8
Permanent loan
of the City of Basel,
1967

168 Pablo Picasso
(1881-1973)
*Bread and Fruit
Dish on a Table*
(*Pains et compotier
aux fruits sur une
table*). 1908-1909
Oil on canvas
164 x 132.5 cm
Inv. no. 2261
Acquired with a
contribution from
Dr.h.c. Richard
Doetsch-Benziger,
1951

169 Henri Rousseau (1844-1910)
Forest Landscape with Setting Sun
(Negro Attacked by a Jaguar)
(Nègre attaqué par un jaguar). c. 1910
Oil on canvas, 114 x 162.5 cm
Inv. no. 2225. Purchase, 1948

170   Henri Rousseau
(1844-1910)
*The Muse Inspiring
the Poet*
(*La Muse inspirant
le Poète*). 1909
Oil on canvas
146 x 97 cm
Inv. no. 1774
Acquired with contributions
from art patrons, 1940

171 Marc Chagall (1887-1985)
Portrait of my Fiancée with Black Gloves
(*Portrait de ma fiancée en gants noirs*). 1909
Oil on canvas, 88 x 64 cm
Inv. no. 2239. Acquired with a contribution
from Dr. h.c . Richard Doetsch-Benziger, 1950

172 Marc Chagall (1887-1985)
The Cattle Dealer
(*Der Viehhändler*). 1912
Oil on canvas, 97 x 200.5 cm
Inv. no. 2213. Acquired with a
contribution from Dr. h.c.
Richard Doetsch-Benziger, 1948

173 Marc Chagall (1887-1985)
La prisée (Rabbi). 1923-1926
Oil on canvas,
117x 89.5 cm
Inv. no. 1738 . Acquired with
a special grant from the City
of Basel, 1939

171

172

174 Edvard Munch (1863-1944)
Portrait of Käte Perls
(*Bildnis Käte Perls*). 1913
Oil on canvas, 120.5 x 116 cm
Inv. no. 1444. Purchase, 1927

175 Edvard Munch (1863-1944)
Large Coastal Landscape
(*Große Küstenlandschaft*). 1918
Oil on canvas, 121 x 160.5 cm
Inv. no. 1443. Purchase, 1927

176   Edvard Munch (1863-1944)
Country Road in Aasgaardstrand
(*Landstraße [Straße in Aasgaardstrand]*). 1902
Oil on canvas, 88.5 x 114 cm
Inv. no. G 1979.8. Gift of Sigrid Schwarz von
Spreckelsen and Sigrid Katharina Schwarz, 1979

177   Paula Modersohn-Becker (1876-1907). *Self-Portrait (Selbstbildnis)*. 1906
Oil on canvas, 61 x 50 cm. Inv. no. 1748. Acquired with a special grant from the City of Basel, 1939

178 Emil Nolde (1867-1956). *Blue Irises (Blaue Iris)*. 1915
Oil on canvas, 89 x 74 cm. Inv. no. 1550. Purchase, 1930

177

179 Egon Schiele (1890-1918)
Portrait of Erich Lederer (1896-1985)
(Bildnis Erich Lederer). 1912-1913
Tempera and oil on canvas, 140 x 55.5 cm
Inv. no. G 1986.16. Gift of Mrs. Erich Lederer-
von Jacobs in memory of her husband, 1986

180   Oskar Kokoschka (1886-1980)
The Tempest (Die Windsbraut). 1914
Oil on canvas, 181 x 221 cm
Inv. no. 1745. Acquired with a special
grant from the City of Basel, 1939

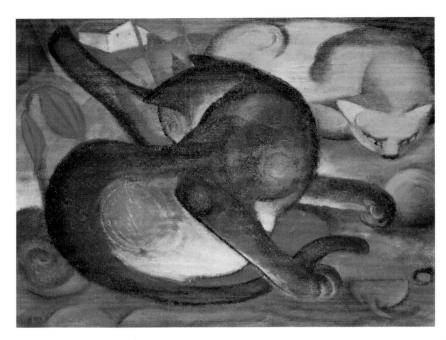

181 Franz Marc (1880-1916)
Two Cats (Zwei Katzen). 1912
Oil on canvas, 74 x 98 cm
Inv. no. 1746. Acquired with a
special grant from the City of
Basel, 1939

182 Franz Marc (1880-1916)
*Fate of the Animals (The Trees Showed
Their Rings, The Animals Their Veins)
(Tierschicksale [Die Bäume zeigten
ihre Ringe, die Tiere ihre Adern])*. 1913
The right side destroyed by fire in 1917;
restored by Paul Klee in 1918
Oil on canvas, 195 x 263.5 cm
Inv. no. 1739. Acquired with a special
grant from the City of Basel, 1939

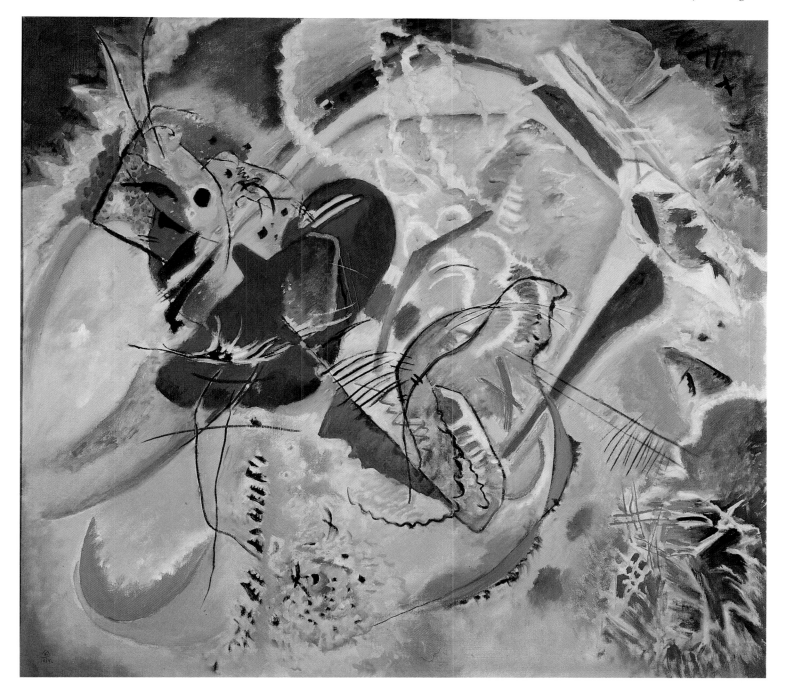

183 Wassily Kandinsky (1866-1944)
Improvisation 35. 1914
Oil on canvas, 110.5 x 120 cm
Inv. no. G 1966.11. Gift of Hans Arp, 1966

184   Robert Delaunay (1885-1941)
Homage to Blériot (Hommage à Blériot). 1914
Tempera on canvas, 250.5 x 251.5 cm
Inv. no. G 1962.6. Purchase, 1962

185 Hans Arp (1886-1966)
Dada Relief. 1916
Wood relief, painted, 24.5 x 18.5 cm
Inv. no. G 1968.28. Gift of
Marguerite Arp-Hagenbach, 1968

186   Theo van Doesburg (1883-1931)
Composition in Dissonance
(Composition en dissonances). 1918
Oil on canvas, 63.5 x 58.5 cm
Inv. no. G 1968.56. Gift of
Marguerite Arp-Hagenbach, 1968

187   Piet Mondrian (1872-1944)
Composition in Pale Shades with Grey Contours
(Composition aux couleurs claires avec contours gris). 1919
Oil on canvas, 49 x 49 cm
Inv. no. G 1968.87.
Gift of Marguerite Arp-Hagenbach, 1968

188   Kurt Schwitters (1887-1948)
Spring Painting (Mz 20B)
(Das Frühlingsbild [Mz 20B]). 1920
Collage, 102.5 x 84 cm
Inv. no. G 1968.102
Gift of Marguerite Arp-Hagenbach, 1968

189 Paul Klee (1879-1940)
Villa R. 1919
Oil on cardboard, 26.5 x 22 cm. Inv. no. 1744.
Acquired with a special grant from the City of Basel, 1939

190 Paul Klee (1879-1940)
Senecio. 1922
Oil on cardboard, 40.5 x 38 cm
Inv. no. 1569. Purchase, 1931

191 Otto Dix (1891-1969)
The Artist's Parents
(Die Eltern des Künstlers). 1921
Oil on canvas, 101 x 115 cm
Inv. no. 1743. Acquired with a
special grant from the City of Basel, 1939

192   Max Beckmann (1884-1950)
Nice in Frankfurt am Main
(*Nizza in Frankfurt am Main*).1921
Oil on canvas, 100.5 x 65 cm
Inv. no. 1737. Acquired with
a special grant from the City
of Basel, 1939

193 James Ensor (1860-1949)
The Blue Flask (Le flacon bleu).
1917
Oil on canvas, 54.5 x 65.5 cm
Inv. no. 1562. Purchase, 1930

194 Frits van den Berghe
(1883-1939)
La Lys. 1923
Oil on canvas, 115 x 147 cm
Inv. no. 1581
Gift of Dr. Emanuel
Hoffmann-Stehlin, 1932

195   Lovis Corinth (1858-1925)
The Artist's Daughter Wilhelmine with Flowers
(Blumen mit Tochter Wilhelmine). 1920
Oil on canvas, 111 x 150 cm
Inv. no. 1741. Acquired with a special
grant from the City of Basel, 1939

196   Lovis Corinth (1858-1925). *Portrait of Reich President Friedrich Ebert (1871-1925) (Bildnis des Reichspräsidenten Friedrich Ebert).* 1924
Oil on canvas, 140 x 100 cm. Inv. no. 1699. Acquired with contributions from the Trade Unions and the Department of Education, 1937

197   Lovis Corinth (1858-1925). *Ecce homo.* 1925
Oil on canvas, 190.5 x 150 cm. Inv. no. 1740. Acquired with a special grant from the City of Basel, 1939

198   Ernst Ludwig
Kirchner (1880-1938)
Amselfluh. 1922
Oil on canvas
120 x 170.5 cm
Inv. no. 1952
Acquired with
contributions from
Dr.h.c. Richard
Doetsch-Benziger
and Max Ras, 1944

199   Ernst Ludwig
Kirchner (1880-1938)
*Davos in Winter
(Davos Snowed In)
(Davos im Winter
[Davos im Schnee])*. 1923
Oil on canvas
121 x 150 cm
Inv. no. 1931
Gift of Georg Reinhart,
Winterthur, 1944

200   Hermann Scherer (1893-1927)
Villa Loverciana with Trees in Bloom (Villa Loverciana mit blühenden Bäumen). 1926
Oil and tempera on canvas. 120.5 x 110.5 cm
Inv. no. 1475. Gift of the heirs of the artist, 1928

201   Ernst Ludwig Kirchner (1880-1938)
Friends (Die Freunde). 1924
Larchwood, painted with tempera, height 175 cm
Inv. no. G 1956.27.
Gift of Mrs. Georg Reinhart, née Olga Schwarzenbach, 1956

202   Pablo Picasso (1881-1973)
Seated Harlequin (Portrait of the Painter Jacinto Salvado)
(Arlequin assis [Bildnis des Malers Jacinto Salvado]). 1923
Tempera on canvas, 130.5 x 97 cm
Inv. no. G 1967. 9. Permanent loan of the City of Basel, 1967

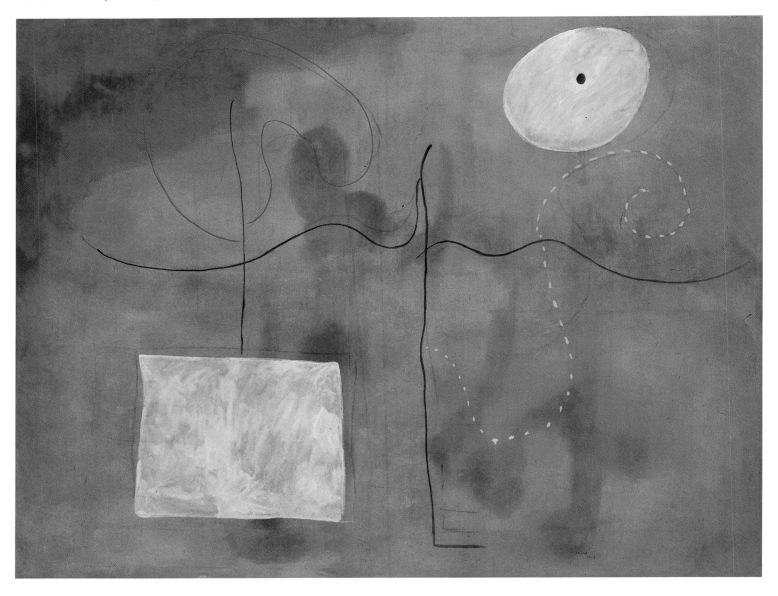

203   Joan Miró (1893-1983)
Painting (*Peinture*). 1925
Oil on canvas, 114.5 x 146 cm
Inv. no. 2315
Acquired with a contribution from
Dr. h.c. Richard Doetsch-Benziger, 1953

204 Joan Miró (1893-1983). *The Gentleman* (*Le gentleman*). 1924
Oil on canvas, 52.5 x 46.5 cm. Inv. no. G 1968.84. Gift of Marguerite Arp-Hagenbach, 1968

205   Oskar Schlemmer (1888-1943)
Five Figures in Space (Roman)
(*Fünf Figuren im Raum [Römisches]*). 1925
Tempera and oil on canvas, 97 x 62 cm
Inv. no. 1752. Acquired with a special
grant from the City of Basel, 1939

206   Oskar Schlemmer (1888-1943)
Women's Staircase (Frauentreppe). 1925
Tempera and oil on canvas, 120.5 x 69 cm
Inv. no. 1753
Acquired with a special grant
from the City of Basel, 1939

207   Max Ernst (1891-1976)
The Big Forest (*La grande forêt*). 1927
Oil on canvas, 114.5 x 146.5 cm
Inv. no. 1580. Acquired with a contribution
from Dr. Emanuel Hoffmann-Stehlin, 1932

208 Piet Mondrian (1872-1944)
Composition. 1929
Oil on canvas, 52.5 x 52.5 cm
Inv. no. G 1968.88. Gift of Marguerite Arp-Hagenbach, 1968

209 Hans Arp (1886-1966)
Arrow of Clouds (Wolkenpfeil). 1932
Wood relief, painted, 110 x 140 cm
Inv. no. G 1965.11. Gift of the Oskar and
Annie Müller-Widmann Collection, 1965

210 Yves Tanguy (1900-1955). *Such Splendour (La splendeur semblable)*. 1930
Oil on canvas, 91.5 x 73 cm. Inv. no. G 1980.51. Gift of Dr. Charles F. Leuthardt, Riehen, 1980

211

212

211   Paul Klee (1879-1940). *Blue Night (Blaue Nacht)*. 1937 Pastel on cotton, 50.5 x 76.5 cm. Inv. no. 1796. Birmann Fund, 1941

212 Paul Klee (1879-1940). *Rich Harbour (Reicher Hafen)*. 1938. Oil on news-paper laid down on jute, 75.5 x 165 cm. Inv. no. 2212. Gift of the heirs of the artist, 1948

213   Henri Matisse (1869-1954)
Still-Life with Oysters
(Nature morte aux huîtres). 1940
Oil on canvas, 65.5 x 81.5 cm
Inv. no. 1881. Purchase, 1942

214   Pablo Picasso (1881-1973). *Woman with a Hat Seated in an Armchair (Femme au chapeau, assise dans un fauteuil)*. 1941-1942
Oil on canvas, 130.5 x 97.5 cm. Inv. no. G 1967.3. Purchase, 1967

214

215 Henri Matisse (1869-1954). *Composition (Les Velours).* 1947
Gouache on paper, collage, 51.5 x 217.5 cm. Inv. no. 2328. Acquired with contributions
from Dr. h.c. Richard Doetsch-Benziger and Marguerite Arp-Hagenbach, 1954

216   Pablo Picasso (1881-1973)
Women on the Banks of the Seine (after Courbet)
(Les Demoiselles des bords de la Seine, d'après Courbet). 1950
Oil on plywood, 100.5 x 201 cm
Inv. no. G 1955.2. Purchase, 1955

Treasure-house of Cubism

217 Georges Braque (1882-1963)
Violin and Pitcher (*Broc et violon*).
1909-1910
Oil on canvas, 117 x 73.5 cm
Inv. no. 2285.
Gift of Raoul La Roche, 1952

In December 1986 George Braque's *Woman Reading* (*Femme lisant*. 1911) was auctioned in London for 6.6 million pounds, or 15.6 million Swiss francs[268] and a year later Pablo Picasso's *Souvenir of Le Havre* (*Souvenir du Havre*. 1912) went for 4.18 million pounds, which at the time corresponded to 10.25 million Swiss francs.[269] Both paintings came from the collection of the Basel banker Raoul La Roche, who had obtained them by auction at the "Kahnweiler Sales" after the First World War. *Souvenir of Le Havre* had cost him 900 French francs at the third auction on 4 July 1922, as against the estimate of 2,000 French francs, while for *Woman Reading*, bought at the fourth auction on 7/8 May 1923, he had paid only 400 French francs. As is often the case with pictures whose subject is difficult to recognise, *Woman Reading* was incorrectly entered in the auction catalogue as *Still-Life*.[270]

With over two dozen paintings and as many drawings and "papiers collés" by Braque, ten or more pictures by Picasso, about twenty-five paintings by Juan Gris, at least twenty pictures by Fernand Léger, fairly large groups of works by Ozenfant and Le Corbusier, and several sculptures by Jacques Lipchitz, the collection of Cubist and Purist art owned by Raoul La Roche was one of the most comprehensive - and perhaps the most outstanding - that existed anywhere. In 1952, 1956 and 1963 La Roche gave the Kunstmuseum ninety works by these artists from his collection. These donations elevated the modern section of the Öffentliche Kunstsammlung to international rank. Thanks to them, the Kunstmuseum today counts among the most important treasure-houses of Cubism, together with the Museum of Modern Art in New York, the Musée national d'art moderne and the Musée Picasso in Paris, and the Hermitage in St. Petersburg.

Raoul La Roche was born in Basel on 23 February 1889, the son of the banker Louis La Roche-Burckhardt. After attending grammar school in Basel and the School of Commerce in Neuchâtel, Raoul La Roche spent some time in Berlin and London before settling in Paris in 1911. He joined the Banque Suisse et Française, which later became the Crédit Commercial de France, where over the years he rose to managerial rank. He also became the chairman and patron of the Société Helvétique de Bienfaisance (Swiss Welfare Society) and the Maison Suisse de Retraite (Swiss Retirement Home).[271]

In 1918 La Roche made the acquaintance of his compatriot and contemporary Charles Edouard Jeanneret (1887-1965) at a "Swiss luncheon" of the Swiss colony. The latter had at the time just turned to painting at the prompting of Amédée Ozenfant (1886-1966) and they had together published the manifesto *Après Cubisme*, in which they laid down the ideas and theories of "Purism". In 1920 the two friends founded the influential periodical *L'Esprit nouveau*, an "Illustrated international review of contemporary activity". In the first issue, published in October 1920, and subsequently, they signed some of their jointly written articles *Le Corbusier-Saugnier*. Under the pseudonym of Le Corbusier, Jeanneret was to become world famous as an architect.

La Roche let himself be infected and inspired by the new spirit propagated by his painter friends, and he began to buy their pictures. The *Still-Life* (1920) by Ozenfant that was reproduced in issue No. 7 (April 1921) of *L'Esprit nouveau* - and which is known today under the title *Flask, Guitar, Glass and Bottles on a Grey Table* (*Flacon, guitare, verre et bouteilles à la table grise)* - is indicated as being from the "Collection La R."; on the other hand, the *Still-Life* (1920) by Jeanneret reproduced in the same issue, which came into the La Roche collection under the title *Composition with Lantern and Guitar* (*Composition à la lanterne et à la guitare*), was at that time, according to its caption, still owned by the Léonce Rosenberg Gallery.

Between June 1921 and May 1923 the stock of the Kahnweiler Gallery and the art dealer's private collection, which had been confiscated by the French authorities during the First World War, were auctioned in four major sales in the Hôtel Drouot. This action was taken because Daniel-Henry Kahnweiler (1884-1979), the champion and promoter of the Cubists Picasso, Braque, Gris and Léger, as well as of the "Fauves" Derain and Vlaminck, was a German national. In a period of just under two years, over 900 works by the artists he represented came under the hammer. "They were unknown painters, or virtually, at that time", Kahnweiler observed later: "apart from

Picasso and Derain, they were not yet in any museum".[272] The interest of collectors in the "Kahnweiler Sales" was correspondingly slight, and the prices - with the possible exception of Derain's pictures - consequently stayed within extremely modest bounds. It was mainly young, open-minded writers and intellectuals - André Breton, Paul Eluard and Tristan Tzara[273] - who profited from the low prices, but Ozenfant and Le Corbusier did so too. They each acquired a still-life by Picasso at the second auction: Le Corbusier *The Bottle of Rum* (*La bouteille de rhum*) from 1911[274] and Ozenfant *Violin, Bottle, Glass* (*Violon, bouteille, verre*) from 1913.[275]

The two painter friends also encouraged Raoul La Roche to buy paintings, "papiers collés" and drawings by Picasso, Braque and Léger at the "Kahnweiler Sales", thereby laying the foundations for his collection of Cubist art. La Roche did not himself appear as a buyer at the four auctions; instead he got Ozenfant and the Russian sculptor Oscar Miestchaninoff (1884-1956) to bid on his behalf. The precise scope of the purchases made by La Roche at the time cannot be established with certainty because no purchase documents or bills seem to have survived. However, he must have secured at least nine works by Picasso and some thirty paintings and "papiers collés" by Braque, as well as two lots of Braque drawings, one with nineteen and one with six works, which were auctioned in the fourth sale. The Braque paintings included major works by the artist such as *Violin and Pitcher* (*Broc et violon*. Ill.217, p.238) and *The Portuguese (The Emigrant)* (*Le Portugais [L'émigrant]* Ill.218, p.245). The first went to Miestchaninoff at the first sale for 3,200 French francs while the second was acquired by Ozenfant at the second sale for 840 French francs. Ozenfant also acquired a *Still-Life*[276] by Léger for La Roche at the third sale.

La Roche is thought to have spent a total of 50,000 French francs on buying Cubist works at the "Kahnweiler Sales".[277] Through these purchases he had, for relatively little money, acquired a sizeable and also significant collection that concentrated mainly on the Cubist works of Picasso and Braque. After the "Kahnweiler Sales", as a token of his gratitude for the help Le Corbusier had given him in building up his collection, Raoul La Roche gave his friend Braque's still-life *Clarinet and Bottle of Rum on a Mantlepiece* (*Clarinette et bouteille de rhum sur une cheminée*. 1911; now in the Tate Gallery, London), which the latter had selected in the final sale. "Unfortunately circumstances did not allow you to take advantage as I did of the exceptional bargains that arose", the collector wrote to Le Corbusier on 21 May 1923, consoling him with the thought "but after all you have the enormous resource of yourself being the creator of works of art of the first order".[278]

La Roche expanded his collection through further purchases on the art market, which must have cost him considerably more than his acquisitions at the "Kahnweiler Sales". For example, Braque's *The Violin (Mozart/Kubelick)* (*Le violon [Mozart/Kubelick]*) of 1912 had been bought by André Breton at the fourth sale in May 1923 for 160 French francs; on 3 October 1925 he sold the still-life for 3,000 French francs to Kahnweiler[279], who then sold it to La Roche. The collector also acquired on the art market several Braque pictures produced after 1914, such as *The Musician* (*La musicienne*. Ill.227, p.252), *Still-Life on a Pedestal Table* (*Nature morte sur un guéridon*) and *Le Radical* (all painted in 1918), as well as *Café-Bar* (Ill.228, p.253) and *The Black Pedestal Table* (*Le guéridon noir*. both painted in 1919). Similarly he rounded off his collection of Picasso works with a later picture, *Still-Life with Stripes* (*Nature morte aux raies*)[280] dating from 29 January 1922. The fact that this still-life was reproduced in a colour plate in issue No. 17 (June 1922) of the periodical *L'Esprit nouveau* indicates how far La Roche was now guided by the Purist aesthetic propagated by Le Corbusier and Ozenfant. Picasso's Cubist masterpiece *The Aficionado* (*L'aficionado [Le Toréro]*. Ill.219, p.246) also came into the La Roche collection through the art market. The reproduction of the picture - under the title *Still-Life* and dated 1908 - in issue No. 13 of *L'Esprit nouveau*, published in December 1921, gave the name of the owner as the art dealer Paul Rosenberg, who at the time was Picasso's agent. If one considers that the Basel collector Rudolf Staechelin paid Paul Rosenberg 100,000 French francs for Picasso's *Seated Harlequin* (*Arlequin assis*. Ill.202, p.223) in June 1924, one understands why La Roche could not afford as many works by Picasso as by other artists.

La Roche did not confine himself to Braque and Picasso in his purchases at the "Kahnweiler Sales", but also obtained a still-life by Fernand Léger. Three other paintings by Léger that were sold at the first and fourth auctions were acquired by La Roche subsequently: *Woman in Blue* (*La femme en bleu*. Ill. 226, p.251), *The Staircase* (*L'escalier*. 1914) and *Houses among Trees* or *Landscape no. 3* (*Les maisons dans les arbres [Paysage no.3]*. Ill.225, p.250). *Woman in Blue* had been bought for 2,150 French francs at the auction in June 1921 by M. Borel on behalf of his brother-in-law, the art dealer Léonce Rosenberg (1879-1947), who also purchased the other two pictures.

Most of the pictures acquired by La Roche that were not bought in the "Kahnweiler Sales" came from Léonce Rosenberg's Galerie de l'Effort moderne; this applies both to the Braque and Léger works he owned and, in particular, to his extensive collection of pictures by Juan Gris. All the pictures by Gris that La Roche owned dated from between 1915 and 1920, which was the period when Rosenberg replaced Kahnweiler as Juan Gris' agent. The only works by Gris in the La Roche collection that came from the Galerie Simon (which is what Kahnweiler's gallery was called when it reopened in the autumn of 1920) were three pictures painted in the autumn and winter of 1920[281].

In the case of Fernand Léger, unlike that of Braque, Picasso and Gris, La Roche continued to add paintings from the 1920s to his collection. This was partly for financial reasons, for Léger's prices remained far below those of the Cubists. (As late as January 1928 Alfred Flechtheim noted in the catalogue of the Léger exhibition organised by his Berlin gallery: "So far no museum has ventured to acquire a work by Léger.") But the more crucial consideration for the collector must have been that in the 1920s the ideals of *L'Esprit nouveau* and Purism, which were oriented towards an industrial aesthetic, were embodied particularly convincingly in Léger's work.

"La Roche, if one owns as fine a collection as you do, one should build a house worthy of it," Le Corbusier now told him, and La Roche replied, "All right, Jeanneret, you build that house for me!"[282] In the spring of 1923 Le Corbusier had sketched the initial designs for a residential project for a site in the Rue du Docteur Blanche in Auteuil, although without any immediate thought of La Roche. In the summer of 1923 the latter decided to buy a plot of land on the site so that Le Corbusier could build a house on it for him. In February 1924 building work began not only on the La Roche villa but also on a second one that was intended for the architect's younger brother, the musician Albert Jeanneret. (At the same time Le Corbusier was building two studio houses in Boulogne for the sculptors Jacques Lipchitz and Miestchaninoff, who were friends of his.) In March 1925 the "Maison de collectionneur", with its plastically shaped gallery, was ready for inauguration.[283]

The client was delighted with the result in spite of several deficiencies, and he was convinced that the building would go down in architectural history.[284] Le Corbusier had created a "poem of walls", was the praise from La Roche; he thought it almost a pity to decorate them with pictures.[285] This issue also led to differences of opinion between Le Corbusier and Ozenfant that eventually put an end to their friendship. La Roche asked the architect to hang the pictures in the house so as to ensure "that their arrangement harmonises with the architecture"[286]. Ozenfant subsequently rearranged the pictures without Le Corbusier's knowledge. The architect protested: "I expressly desire certain parts of the structure to be left absolutely free of pictures so as to create a dual effect of pure architecture on the one hand and painting on the other."[287]

Le Corbusier later designed a storage room so that the pictures would not all have to be hung permanently but could be brought out for occasional viewing. However, no room of this kind was ever installed. Instead, the collector found a solution to his dilemma by entrusting a fairly large group of pictures to the Zürich Kunsthaus on long-term loan. In the autumn of 1932 La Roche lent the Kunsthaus five paintings for its large Picasso exhibition and he left them there after the exhibition came to an end.[288] Two of them were replaced in January 1935 by two still-lifes by Juan Gris and Léger's *Landscape no.3*. These loans remained in the Kunsthaus until March 1950 - the pictures by Gris even until 1952 - when the collector transferred them on long-term loan to the Kunstmuseum in Basel. The Kunsthaus was not left empty handed, however, for in 1933 La Roche had given it the still-life *La viole* (1920)[289] following the retrospective it had organised in memory of Juan Gris.

La Roche generously supported with his loans not only the Zürich Picasso retrospective and the Juan Gris memorial exhibition but also the exhibition that the Kunsthaus devoted to Fernand Léger in the spring of 1933. Elsewhere, too, paintings from his collection were an important component of major exhibitions of Cubism and its masters, e.g. the Braque retrospective oganised by the Basel Kunsthalle in 1933 with the support of Maja Sacher-Stehlin, "The Masters of Independent Art 1895-1937" that was staged in the Petit Palais in Paris from June to October 1937, "Picasso, Braque, Gris, Léger" in the Berne Kunsthalle in the spring of 1939, "Juan Gris, Georges Braque, Pablo Picasso" in the Basel Kunsthalle in March 1948 and the Juan Gris retrospective in the Berne Kunstmuseum in 1955.

In the summer of 1949 the committee of the Basel Kunstmuseum, led by Georg Schmidt, spent several days in Paris visiting museums, private collections and art dealers.[290] They also viewed Raoul La Roche's collection. In March 1950, as a result of this visit, Georg Schmidt was allowed by the collector to select six pictures by Braque and four each by Picasso and Léger - all works of the first order - and to exhibit them, for the time being as "long-term loans"[291], in the Kunstmuseum. *Le guéridon* (1911) by Braque and Picasso's *Still-Life with Stripes* (1922) went back to Paris in October 1952 as gifts to the Musée national d'art moderne from the collector, who on the same occasion also gave the Paris museum Picasso's *The Violin* (*Le violon*.1914), Juan Gris' *Still-Life on a Chair* (*Nature morte sur une chaise*. 1917) and Braque's *Guitar and Fruit Dish* (*Guitare et compotier*.1919). The remaining loans to Zürich made up part of the first donation Raoul La Roche gave to the Öffentliche Kunstsammlung in November 1952. It comprised a total of twenty-four Cubist and Purist masterpieces - four pictures by Picasso, nine by Braque, five by Gris, four by Léger and one each by Le Corbusier and Ozenfant. The Öffentliche Kunstsammlung's report on its activities in 1952 states: "Just as the Raoul La Roche collection is a glorious page in the history of Basel's private collections, so too can the 'Raoul La Roche Donation' be described as one of the greatest pieces of good fortune to befall our art collection in its entire history, which has indeed not been lacking in good fortune."[292]

The modern section of the Kunstmuseum had gained new importance through this unique addition; now the pictures required more space. In the autumn of 1955 it was therefore decided to bring all Böcklin's paintings, some of which were still hanging on the second floor, down to the first floor. The existing holdings were not, however, sufficient to set up a room devoted exclusively to Juan Gris; similarly, it seemed desirable to strengthen the Léger collection. Schmidt turned yet again to Raoul La Roche with a request for additional loans. These were again generously granted: six pictures by Juan Gris and the same number by Léger - among them the two fine, large works *Mechanical elements* (*Eléments mécaniques*. Ill.230, p.255) and *Mother and Child* (*La Mère et l'enfant*. Ill.229, p.254) - entered the Kunstmuseum, initially as "anonymous loans" so that it now stood "in first place so far as Cubist art is concerned", as D.-H. Kahnweiler assured Raoul La Roche after a visit to Basel[293]. In the same year the collector decided also to give this group of works to the museum of his native city.

Once more, Georges Salles, the director of the French National Museums, was allowed to choose a picture from the La Roche collection as a token of thanks for the granting of an export licence for the pictures given to Basel. This time the work selected was Braque's *Woman with a Guitar* (*Femme à la guitare*. 1913). In 1954 La Roche had already given the Musée des Beaux-Arts in Lyons a picture by Braque, *The Violin* (*Le violon*. 1911), in memory of his stay there during the Second World War.

In the spring of 1955 Georg Schmidt learned that Kahnweiler was offering for sale the paraphrase that Picasso had painted in 1950 after Courbet's *Women on the Banks of the Seine* (*Les Demoiselles des bords de la Seine*. Ill.216, p.236). Schmidt had once admired the picture on the occasion of a visit to the artist in Vallauris, and he was convinced that it would make a worthy addition to Basel's Picasso collection. The asking price was 15 million French francs. The Kunstmuseum did not have such an amount available, but then Schmidt remembered that Raoul La Roche had once given him permission, should it be necessary, to sell a painting from his donation in order to finance the purchase of a picture by Braque, Picasso or Léger. The Lucerne art dealer Siegfried Rosengart was prepared to exchange Picasso's *La pointe de la cité* (1911) and Braque's *Still-Life on a Pedestal Table* (*Nature morte sur un guéridon* . 1918) from the 1952 donation for the new Picasso. At Schmidt's urging, La Roche informed the Kunstkommission that he agreed to this arrangement, but he refused to have the newly acquired picture labelled as part of his donation because his collection was exclusively limited to the early period of Cubism.[294]

In December 1960 Schmidt discovered one of Braque's later works - *Guéridon (Le jou)* of 1930 - that seemed to him a desirable addition to the existing group of the artist's works. Once more, the wherewithal for the purchase was lacking. Schmidt tried to get the munificent Raoul La Roche to give the Kunstmuseum another two or three pictures by Braque, Picasso or Gris from his collection, so as to help it acquire the still-life by Braque that was wanted. The collector declined the proposal with his characteristic courtesy, explaining that he "would rather not give the Museum further works from my collection in order for it to sell them and then use the proceeds to acquire pictures that I would not collect myself". He said he had been guided in his donations by the wish to provide the Kunstmuseum with works "that in times to come will be seen as artistic creations of my generation"[295].

In 1962 the collector gave up his Paris domicile, donated his villa to the Le Corbusier Foundation and returned to Basel. He had waited for Franz Meyer, Georg Schmidt's successor, to take up office before handing over a third and last donation. La Roche had once expressed his regret that shortage of space prevented Schmidt from creating a special "Purist Room" to exhibit the pictures by his friends Jeanneret and Ozenfant that he had donated.[296] He must therefore have been very gratified that, as well as eleven drawings and "papiers collés" by Braque, another still-life by Gris, seven paintings by Léger from the 1920s, and four sculptures and reliefs by Jacques Lipchitz, Franz Meyer chose six pictures by Le Corbusier, and six paintings and twenty watercolours by Ozenfant.

Furthermore, in order to give an example of this facet of La Roche's collection, the donation also included a *Mythological Scene* (*Scène mythologique.* 1926) by André Bauchant (1873-1958). This naïve artist, who came to painting relatively late - he was a gardener and arboculturalist by training - exhibited for the first time at the "Salon d'automne" in Paris in 1921, where his work attracted the attention of Le Corbusier and Ozenfant. Writing in the periodical *L'Esprit nouveau* under the pseudonym "de Fayet", Ozenfant was the first to praise Bauchant's gifts.[297] It was also Ozenfant who subsequently obtained pictures by Bauchant for La Roche.[298]

Also in 1962 the Musée national d'art moderne received another gift from Raoul La Roche, the still-life *The White Pot* (*Le pot blanc.* 1925) by Amédée Ozenfant, whose work *Le buffet* (1925) had been donated to the Paris museum by the collector the year before. Finally, there is a further example of La Roche's patronage that deserves mention. When in 1960 the Musée national d'art moderne showed the exhibition organised by Georg Schmidt "Swiss Modern Art from Hodler to Klee", Jean Cassou, the head curator, wanted to acquire for his museum's collection one of the four wire reliefs by the Basel painter and sculptor Walter Bodmer (1903-1973) that were on display. Raoul La Roche heard of this wish and promptly gave the museum the *Relief in Painted Wire* (*Relief en fil de fer peint.* 1954)[299].

At Christmas 1962 Raoul La Roche realised that his first donation of 1952 had coincided with the centenary of his father's birth, while the third, which was to be entered in the inventory as dating from 1963, would coincide with that of his mother's birth. "They were both great art-lovers and would certainly be pleased that I followed them in this respect and that important pieces from my collection are now in the Museum."[300] In the spring of 1963 a combined exhibition of Raoul La Roche's donations held in the Kunstmuseum conveyed an idea, for the first time, of the significance of the works that had been given.[301] The Faculty of Philosophy and History of Basel University had already honoured the generous collector in 1962 by awarding him an honorary doctorate. Raoul La Roche died on 15 June 1965 in Basel.

218 Georges Braque (1882-1963). *The Portuguese (The Emigrant)* (*Le Portugais [L'émigrant]*). 1911-1912
Oil on canvas, 117 x 81.5 cm. Inv. no. 2286. Gift of Raoul La Roche, 1952

219 Pablo Picasso (1881-1973)
The Aficionado
(*L'aficionado [Le Toréro]*). 1912
Oil on canvas, 135 x 82 cm
Inv. no. 2304.
Gift of Raoul La Roche, 1952

220 Pablo Picasso (1881-1973)
Woman with a Guitar (Femme à la guitare). 1911-1914
Oil on canvas, 130.5 x 90 cm
Inv. no. 2307. Gift of Raoul La Roche, 1952

221 Pablo Picasso (1881-1973)
The Pedestal Table (Le guéridon). 1913-1914
Oil on canvas, 130 x 89 cm
Inv. no . 2306 . Gift of Raoul La Roche, 1952

222   Juan Gris (1887-1927)
Woman with a Mandolin (after Corot)
(La femme à la mandoline [d'après Corot]). 1916
Oil on canvas, 92 x 60 cm
Inv. no. G 1956.22. Gift of Raoul La Roche, 1956

223   Juan Gris (1887-1927)
The Violin (Le violon). 1916
Oil on canvas, 116.5 x 73 cm
Inv. no. 2293. Gift of Raoul La Roche, 1952

224   Juan Gris (1887-1927). *Still-Life with Plaque (Nature morte à la plaque)*. 1917
Oil on canvas, 81 x 65.5 cm. Inv. no. 2294. Gift of Raoul La Roche, 1952

225 Fernand Léger
(1881-1955)
Houses among Trees
(Landscape no. 3)
(Les maisons dans les arbres
[Paysage no. 3]). 1914
Oil on canvas, 130 x 97 cm
Inv. no. 2301. Gift of
Raoul La Roche, 1952

226 Fernand Léger
(1881-1955)
Woman in Blue
(La femme en bleu). 1912
Oil on canvas
194 x 130 cm
Inv. no. 2299
Gift of Raoul La Roche, 1952

227 Georges Braque (1882-1963)
The Musician (*La musicienne*). 1917-1918
Oil on canvas, 221.5 x 113 cm
Inv. no. 2289. Gift of Raoul La Roche, 1952

228 Georges Braque (1882-1963)
Café-Bar. 1919
Oil on canvas, 160 x 82 cm
Inv. no. 2292. Gift of Raoul La Roche, 1952

229 Fernand Léger (1881-1955)
Mother and Child (La mère et l'enfant). 1922
Oil on canvas, 171 x 241.5 cm
Inv. no. G 1956.13. Gift of Raoul La Roche, 1956

230 Fernand Léger (1881-1955). *Mechanical Elements (Eléments mécaniques).* 1918-1923
Oil on canvas, 211 x 167.5 cm. Inv. no. G 1956.14. Gift of Raoul La Roche, 1956

231 Amédée Ozenfant (1886-1966)
Flask, Guitar, Glass and Bottles
on a Green Table
(Flacon, guitare, verre
et bouteilles à la table verte). 1920
Oil on canvas, 81 x 100.5 cm
Inv. no. G 1963.24. Gift of
Raoul La Roche, 1963

232 Le Corbusier
(Charles-Edouard Jeanneret)
(1887-1965)
Still-Life with White Jug on a
Blue Ground
(Nature morte à la cruche
blanche sur fond bleu). 1919
Oil on canvas, 65.5 x 81 cm
Inv. no. G 1963.8. Gift of
Raoul La Roche, 1963

The new American painting "made redundant the European standard that was previously the only valid one", was the opinion of the Basel art critic Maria Netter in May 1960, and she warned: "From now on, we shall have to apply a different yardstick. This fact may be painful for the self-assurance of many Europeans, but it cannot be changed even by those voices - and they have been heard in Basel too - that demand 'Europe must be protected from this American painting'". In 1959 the Kunstmuseum in Basel had been the first museum in Europe to come into possession of a group of pictures by contemporary American painters. In the words of Maria Netter this was "a gift that had a shock effect". This effect stemmed not only from the four paintings given to the Kunstmuseum, "but quite fundamentally from the whole of modern American painting". It was welcomed by Maria Netter: "It may well make a lot of people reflect, make them attempt an analysis and define their attitude towards developments in contemporary art."[302]

To mark the 75th anniversary of its foundation, the Schweizerische National-Versicherungs-Gesellschaft (Swiss National Insurance Company) had presented the Öffentliche Kunstsammlung with four works of Abstract Expressionism, namely paintings by Franz Kline, Barnett Newman, Mark Rothko and Clyfford Still. This was an event of more than local significance, for it contained a European dimension so far as the recognition of American artists in Europe was concerned. In the case of Barnett Newman (1905-1970), the painting presented - *Day Before One* (Ill.234, p.265) - was the first of his works to enter a museum collection anywhere. The Museum of Modern Art in New York was, however, soon to follow suit, acquiring its first picture by Newman somewhat later the same year.[303] Not until 1966 did further works by this artist enter the collections of other European museums.[304]

In 1959 there was nowhere else in Europe apart from Basel where a comparable group of works of the new American painting could be seen. At that time the Stedelijk Museum in Amsterdam owned two of Jackson Pollock's pictures - *The Waterbull* (1945) and *Reflections of the Big Dipper* (1947) - which had been given to the museum in 1950 by Peggy Guggenheim, Pollock's first art dealer and patron. In 1959 the Tate Gallery in London acquired its first painting by Mark Rothko (*Light Red over Black*, 1957), and the Friends of the Tate Gallery donated to the gallery one painting each by the American Abstract Expressionists James Brooks and Philip Guston. In the following year, the Friends of the Tate Gallery extended this group with Pollock's *Number 23* (1948).

In the late 1950s Switzerland was probably the best and most directly informed of all European countries about the new American painting. This is principally due to the art historian Arnold Rüdlinger (1919-1967).[305] Rüdlinger headed the Kunsthalle in Berne from 1944 to 1955 and then, until his early death at the age of 48, he was the director of the Kunsthalle in Basel. At the beginning of the 1950s, Rüdlinger organised a series of three exhibitions in Berne that were devoted to the latest developments in art. The exhibitions in 1952 and 1954 were confined exclusively to "Present tendencies of the Paris School", but the third in the series, which was shown in the Berne Kunsthalle in February 1955, no longer included a geographical reference in its title. "Present tendencies 3" was not confined to the Paris School alone but also included pictures by American painters like Sam Francis, Mark Tobey and Pollock, as well as the Canadian Jean-Paul Riopelle. Europe was represented in the exhibition by the Frenchmen Camille Bryen, Georges Mathieu[306] and Henri Michaux, by the Italian Tancredi and by the German Wols. By that time Rüdlinger had become convinced that the fine arts had reached a point, "where in Europe and America a language is spoken that uses the same vocabulary, one that is not acquired or derived but simultaneously created." He referred to this language as "Tachisme".[307]

233   Barnett Newman (1905-1970). *The Command*. 1946. Oil on canvas, 122 x 90.5 cm
Inv. no. G 1988.9. Gift of Mrs. Annalee Newman in honour of Arnold Rüdlinger and Dr. Franz Meyer, 1988

At the end of the 1940s and the beginning of the 1950s, Rüdlinger had got to know a number of American artists living in Paris at the time. First there was Alexander Calder (1898-1976). Their friendship resulted in Calder's exhibition in the Berne Kunsthalle in May 1947. The large mobile *Five Branches with 1000 Leaves* displayed there was loaned to the Kunstmuseum in Basel after the exhibition closed, and was purchased in February 1948 by the Emanuel Hoffmann Foundation. It was the first work by an American artist of the postwar generation to find its way into a Swiss museum.

In 1953 or 1954 Rüdlinger met Sam Francis (born in 1923) and through him other Americans then working in Paris, such as Joan Mitchell and Kimber Smith. Rüdlinger was soon to develop a close friendship with Sam Francis as well. The American was first introduced in the third of the "Present tendencies" exhibitions in the Berne Kunsthalle. Then, in the same year, Rüdlinger acquired Francis' large painting *Deep Orange and Black* (Ill.240, p.271) for the newly founded collectors' association "La peau de l'ours". The following year this work was displayed in the exhibition "Japanese Calligraphy and Western Signs" in the Basel Kunsthalle.[308] In 1967 *Deep Orange and Black* was purchased for the Öffentliche Kunstsammlung.

Sam Francis urged his Swiss friend to visit New York. Rüdlinger went to the USA for the first time in March 1957, with the intention of organising a major exhibition of Abstract Expressionist painting and of showing it in the Basel Kunsthalle, of which he had meanwhile become the director. He visited numerous artists, the first of whom was Clyfford Still, to whom Sam Francis had given him an introduction. Many of these first contacts developed into new friendships, as was the case with Barnett Newman. Rüdlinger planned to organise an exhibition that concentrated on the work of Pollock, Newman, Rothko and Still, but Rothko and Still were opposed to such a narrow selection, because they thought it could give Europeans too one-sided an impression of the new American painting. However, there was another, quite banal, reason why the project could not be realised: the Basel Kunstverein could not afford the associated costs, which would have been considerable. And the short time left for preparing the exhibition also made it impossible to seek financial support from the American side.

Then the International Council of the Museum of Modern Art, New York, came to the rescue. In 1953 it had already assembled an exhibition "Twelve American Painters and Sculptors of the Present" and had sent it on a European tour, which had included the Kunsthaus Zürich in the summer of 1953. In addition to older painters like John Kane, John Marin, Edward Hopper and Stuart Davis, it comprised works by representatives of a younger generation, such as Arshile Gorky and Pollock and the sculptors Calder and David Smith. In 1955/56 another exhibition organised by the International Council toured Europe: "Modern Art from the USA" was based on a selection of works from the collections of the Museum of Modern Art. The section "Abstract Painting of Today" contained pictures by Gorky, Guston, de Kooning, Motherwell, Pollock, Rothko, Still and Tobey. The Kunsthaus Zürich made this survey available to the Swiss public in the summer of 1955.

The travelling exhibition organised by Dorothy Miller in 1958 under the auspices of the International Council of the Museum of Modern Art was the first to be exclusively devoted to "New American Painting". It presented works by seventeen artists. In recognition of Rüdlinger's efforts to mount such a show himself, the exhibition started its tour in the Basel Kunsthalle in the spring of 1958. There it coincided with a retrospective in memory of Jackson Pollock, who had died in a car accident in 1956. By now Rüdlinger considered the new painting to be "an indigenous American event" that had a powerful effect. He saw this double exhibition as a vehicle of information that would allow the European public "to become thoroughly acquainted with the phenomenon of the new American painting and to discuss it."[309] It is hardly necessary to remark that, while the exhibition caused a sensation, the public's reactions were largely negative or absolutely dismissive.

To mark its 75th anniversary in 1959, the Schweizerische National-Versicherungs-Gesellschaft decided to give the City of Basel a present. The director of the "National", Dr. Hans Theler, was also the chairman of the Basel Kunstverein, the organisation which runs the Kunsthalle. His open-mindedness and daring had made it possible for Rüdlinger to show such controversial exhibitions in the Kunsthalle as "The New American Painting". Hans Theler got Rüdlinger to return to New York to acquire some pictures by American painters there, making 100,000 Swiss francs available to him for the purpose.[310] With this sum Rüdlinger bought four large pictures: *Andes* by Franz Kline (Ill.236, p.267), *Day Before One* by Barnett Newman (Ill.234, p.265), *Red, White and Brown* by Mark Rothko (Ill.238, p.269) and a large-format painting by Clyfford Still (Ill.237, p.268). The prices asked for Pollock paintings were, on the other hand, beyond his means. *Day Before One*, which was painted in 1951, is the earliest work of the group; the other three all date from 1957. In order to be able to judge the Newman picture, Rüdlinger had to go specially to Pittsburgh, where *Day Before One* was displayed in the "Bicentennial International Exhibition" in the winter of 1958/59.[311] These four pictures were to be offered to the Öffentliche Kunstsammlung as a gift. If the Kunstkommission declined the offer, the pictures would go to the Kunstverein; they would however, if it were so desired, remain at the disposal of the Kunstmuseum as a loan. The Kunstkommission was informed of this proposal on 20 November 1958.

In the spring of 1959 the four pictures selected by Rüdlinger were displayed in the exhibition "New American Painting" at the Kunstmuseum in St. Gallen, as a loan from the Schweizerische National-Versicherungs-Gesellschaft. James Fitzsimmons, the editor of the periodical *Art International*, devoted a leading article to this "event of international import": "The event marks the first time, so far as the Editor of this magazine is aware, that a European organization, either public or private, has contributed a substantial sum of money for the purchase of paintings by American artists. Insurance companies do not throw their money around, and the event is sure to have repercussions among collectors, dealers and museum officials throughout Western Europe. Its significance may even be grasped in Paris, provoking art critics there - once the best in Europe, in the days of Diderot - to start looking again, to lay down their shovels, put on their thinking caps and leave the stables where most of them pass their time these days."[312]

When the Kunstkommission met on 14 May 1959, it learned from Georg Schmidt that the four American pictures had now arrived in the Kunstmuseum and that he would like to hang them in the gallery as an experiment. On 4 June, the date of a further meeting of the Kunstkommission, the large painting by Clyfford Still was hanging on a wall by the staircase and the other three pictures by Kline, Newman and Rothko were displayed in a room on the second floor, where they were surrounded by pictures by painters of the Paris School like Manessier, De Staël, Vieira da Silva, Hartung and Music, from the museum's own holdings and from the collection of the Emanuel Hoffmann Foundation.[313]

The Kunstkommission did not greet the American pictures with particularly great enthusiasm. However, it is apparent from the minutes of the meetings in which the offer was discussed that its members almost unanimously agreed that they could not afford to refuse the gift, because such a refusal might scare off other potential donors. They also agreed that it would not do to accept the gift and then to leave the pictures in store instead of exhibiting them. The suggestion that they might lend the huge canvases and find a home for them somewhere else in the city in an appropriate modern monumental building did not promise a way out of the dilemma either. Maja Sacher-Stehlin was one of the few members who tried to adopt a more positive attitude. She saw in the four pictures "a significant and quite authentic document of our time" and argued that this offer "cannot be refused even if one has problems with the pictures".[314]

Once it had been decided to accept the gift, the debate was confined to the manner of the pictures' presentation. From today's point of view it is surprising how, in the face of this confrontation between American Abstract Expressionism and the School of Paris, preference was given to the European painting. At the time it seemed unthinkable that the School of Paris could lose out in a new assessment, as was later to happen. Georg Schmidt had his doubts too: for him Newman's *Day Before One* certainly gained "visibly in quality" but he found "a positive attitude to Kline difficult" and he did not want to rule out the possibility "that one or other of these pictures may later be removed".[315] Of course, it never came to that. On the contrary! The jubilee donation of the Schweizerische National-Versicherungs-Gesellschaft opened "a totally new chapter in the museum's history".[316]

The significance of this donation was probably appreciated at the time by only a small circle of enlightened art-lovers. So far as we know, there were no reactions in the daily press, although journalists were invited on 8 December 1959 to the official presentation of the pictures to the Öffentliche Kunstsammlung.

In addition to the four pictures acquired on behalf of the Schweizerische National-Versicherungs-Gesellschaft, Rüdlinger had selected a fifth painting in New York by a younger artist: *The White Spades* (Ill.239, p.270) by Alfred Leslie (born in 1927). The Basel art critic Georgine Oeri, who had been living in New York since 1950 and who from 1959 onwards advised the Geigy Chemical Corporation, Ardsley (New York) on building up its own art collection, persuaded her client to emulate the insurance company and to finance this purchase.[317] Leslie's picture was also exhibited in St. Gallen in the spring of 1959 as a loan from the Geigy Chemical Corporation. Georg Schmidt did not want to add to the difficulties surrounding the acceptance of the insurance company's gift, so he did not submit to the Kunstkommission the offer of a further gift from Geigy. The picture by Leslie was therefore placed on long-term loan with the Basel Kunstverein, until in 1980 it was accepted by the Öffentliche Kunstsammlung.

While the Europeans were still making heavy weather of Abstract Expressionism, the New York public was already being confronted with a more recent development or revolution in American art. At the beginning of 1958 Leo Castelli showed in his gallery the first one-man exhibition by Jasper Johns (born in 1930), whose *Target with Four Faces* (1955) appeared on the front cover of the January issue of *Art News*. Alfred H. Barr not only persuaded a patron to give this picture to the Museum of Modern Art, but also acquired two more of the artist's works, *Green Target* (1955) and *White Numbers* (1957), for the museum at the same time. In the summer of the same year, the 22 year-old Frank Stella (born in 1936) moved to New York after graduating from Princeton University. Soon after that, he began work on the "Black Paintings" series, which was to make him famous. In the winter of 1959, four of these paintings were included in the Museum of Modern Art's exhibition "Sixteen Americans". The museum took the opportunity to buy one of the black pictures - *Marriage of Reason and Squalor* - for its painting collection. Stella was only 23 years old. In the same year the Museum of Modern Art acquired its first picture - *Abraham*, which is also a black painting - by the 54 year-old Barnett Newman. For a younger generation of American painters, events were definitely beginning to speed up!

Jasper Johns' work was first presented in Europe in the summer of 1958 at the 29th International Biennale of Art in Venice, where three of the artist's paintings were displayed in the Palazzo Centrale. In July 1962 the group exhibition "Four Americans", which had been organised by the Moderna Museet, Stockholm, was shown in the Kunsthalle in Bern, and this introduced Switzerland to Johns' works. The first time a painting by Frank Stella was exhibited in Switzerland was in 1963 at the Premier Salon international de galeries-pilotes in Lausanne.[318] A more comprehensive idea of his work was then provided by the six pictures which Alan R. Solomon selected for the special exhibition "Four Younger Artists" at the 32nd Venice Biennale in the summer of 1964.

In presenting the four pictures by American painters to the Kunstmuseum, Hans Theler expressed the hope "that around this rootstock there will very soon be grouped a larger number of works that illustrate the contemporary creativity in our great sister republic beyond the ocean".[319] This hope was not to be realised until the time of Franz Meyer's directorship. Even then, only isolated purchases were made at first: in 1963 Mark Tobey's *Sagittarius Red*, painted in the same year; in 1967 *Deep Orange and Black* and in 1969 *Meaningless Gesture* (1958) by Sam Francis.

In the spring of 1968 Franz Meyer and the Kunstkommission set about revising and redefining the Öffentliche Kunstsammlung's acquisitions policy. It was recognised that with an acquisitions budget of about 400,000 Swiss francs a year, the most promising area for collecting was contemporary art, and that here new specialisations could be created.[320] It seemed to be already a matter of certainty that a picture by Pollock, the most important painter of the first generation, had long since passed beyond the Kunstmuseum's reach. It was all the more important to try to obtain additional works by Newman and Rothko, with whom the Kunstmuseum was on friendly terms. In 1973 Newman's *White Fire II* (Ill. 247, p.278) was purchased at the auction of part of the Robert C. Scull collection, and in 1978 and 1980 respectively the steel sculpture *Here II* (1966) and the painting *White Fire IV* (1968) were acquired from the artist's estate. Rothko's painting *Number 1* (1964) was secured for the collection in 1974. This new speciality was designed to give "the austerity, which is characteristic of the nucleus of the Basel collection, a new relevance for our time".[321]

In 1968/69 a priority list for purchases of works by representatives of the younger generation of artists was also drawn up. The strategy was to prefer Jasper Johns "for the historically significant innovation of 1955" and "indeed before the seemingly more spectacular Rauschenberg"; to give priority to Frank Stella within "Hard Edge Painting" from 1959 onwards (rather than, for example, to Kenneth Noland or Ellsworth Kelly); and in the Pop Art of the early 1960s to concentrate exclusively on Andy Warhol and Claes Oldenburg. In 1970 Jasper Johns' *Figure 2* (Ill.244, p.275), Stella's *Ifafa II* (Ill.248, p.279) and Warhol's *Optical Car Crash* (1962) came into the Kunstmuseum's collection through purchase.

In June 1971, when he was visiting Jasper Johns' studio, Franz Meyer saw the triptych *Voice 2* (Ill. 250, pp.281-282) which the painter had begun in the autumn of 1967 and was then in the process of completing. During those years, Johns had devoted himself principally to making prints. Apart from that, he had painted only *Voice 2*, and had also completely reworked *Map*, which he had created for the USA's pavilion at the World's Fair "Expo'67" in Montreal; this work, which was based on the *Dymaxion Air Ocean World Map* of R. Buckminster Fuller (1895-1983), is five metres high by ten metres wide, and is Johns' biggest painting. "These two works therefore represent a complete phase in the work of one of the most important living painters", Meyer observed in his report to the Kunstkommission. *Voice 2* seeemed to him "an artistic synthesis and purification of previously diverging tendencies in Jasper Johns' work". The work was priced at 100,000 dollars, which was twice what had been spent on *Figure 2* the year before. However, the Kunstkommission confirmed the director in the intention "to acquire other important pictures by Jasper Johns if possible", and judged that the triptych on offer corresponded «particularly well to expectations».[322]

Purchases of further works by the American artists already named, and of others, followed in later years. When Frank Stella was asked in an interview in 1983 which collectors had displayed a continuous interest in his work, he singled out the Kunstmuseum in Basel as "the most convincing patron I've had in the past few years".[323] And in November 1986, when Jasper Johns' picture *Out the Window* fetched the highest price ever paid in an auction for a work by a living artist, the *New York Times* reported the next day that the artist was "not terribly excited about the extraordinary price", but that he was "very happy" that the Kunstmuseum in Basel had been able to buy his early work *Construction with Toy Piano* (Ill.243, p.274) in the auction.[324]

In 1986 the Öffentliche Kunstsammlung received as a bequest a small painting by Robert Motherwell (1915-1991), *Cape de Gata (España)* (Ill.235, p.266), which belongs to the series that later became known under the title *The Elegies of the Spanish Republic*. Marietta von Meyenburg (1900-1986), a Swiss authoress who lived in Basel and Zürich and was a friend of the art critic Georgine Oeri, had bought the picture on 1 December 1953 for 700 dollars in the Kootz Gallery in New York. This was probably the first work of an American Abstract Expressionist to enter a Swiss collection.

Franz Meyer justified the preference for American artists in his purchases with the conviction "that in the period 1950-1970 the most essential artistic achievements stem from them, and so a logical collecting policy should keep to these American 'originals' and not so much their European echo".[325]

234   Barnett Newman (1905-1970)
*Day Before One.*1951
Oil on cotton, 335 x 127.5 cm
Inv. no. G 1959.16. Gift of the Schweizerische
National-Versicherungs-Gesellschaft
(Swiss National Insurance Co.) on their 75th anniversary, 1959

235 Robert Motherwell (1915-1991)
Cape de Gata (España). 1951
Oil on masonite, 76 x 96.5 cm
Inv. no. G 1986.24. Bequest of Marietta von Meyenburg, Zürich, 1986

236 Franz Kline (1910-1962)
Andes. 1959
Oil on canvas, 205.5 x 262 cm
Inv. no. G 1959.15. Gift of the
Schweizerische National-Versicherungs-Gesellschaft
on their 75th anniversary, 1959

237   Clyfford Still (1904-1980)
1957-D No.2. 1957
Oil on cotton, 289 x 408 cm
Inv. no. G 1959.18. Gift of the Schweizerische National-
Versicherungs-Gesellschaft on their 75th anniversary, 1959

238   Mark Rothko (1903-1970). *Red, White and Brown*. 1957. Oil on canvas, 252.5 x 207.5 cm
Inv. no. G 1959.17. Gift of the Schweizerische National-Versicherungs-Gesellschaft on their 75th anniversary, 1959

239   Alfred Leslie (b. 1927). *The White Spades*. 1955
Oil on canvas, 270.5 x 216 cm. Inv. no. G 1980.2. Gift of J.R. Geigy AG, 1959

240   Sam Francis (b. 1923). *Deep Orange and Black*. 1954-1955
Oil on canvas, 371 x 312 cm. Inv. no. G 1967.10. Purchase, 1967

238

241 Cy Twombly (b. 1929)
Untitled (New York City). 1952
Oil on canvas, 74 x 91 cm
Inv. no. G 1982.28. Purchase, 1982

242   Cy Twombly (b. 1929)
Study Presence of a Myth (Delos). 1959
Oil, crayon and pencil on canvas, 178 x 200 cm
Inv. no. G 1979.11. Purchase, 1979

243   Jasper Johns (b. 1930). *Construction with Toy Piano*. 1954
Graphite and collage on canvas laid down on a wooden toy piano
29.3 x 23.2 x 5.6 cm. Inv. no. G 1986.25. Purchase, 1986

244   Jasper Johns (b. 1930). *Figure 2*. 1962
Encaustic and collage on canvas. 127.5 x 102 cm. Inv. no. G 1970.5. Purchase, 1970

245 Frank Stella (b. 1936)
Seward Park. 1958
Oil on canvas, 215.5 x 278 cm
Inv. no. G 1981.3. Purchase, 1981

246   Frank Stella (b. 1936)
West Broadway. 1958
Oil on canvas, 200 x 230.5 cm
Inv. no. G 1982.29. Purchase, 1982

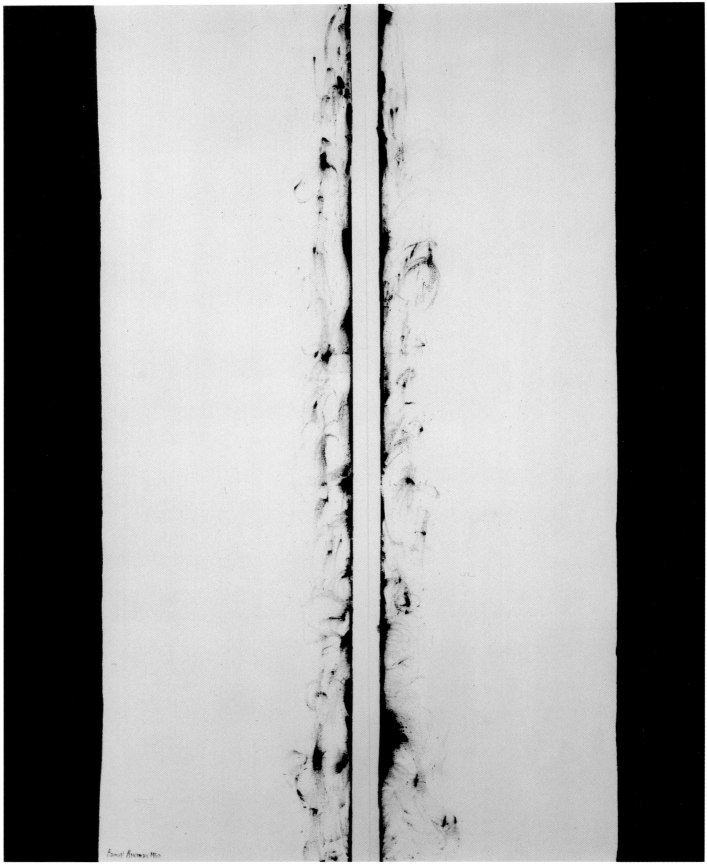

248   Frank Stella (b. 1936)
Ifafa II. 1964
Metal powder in polymer emulsion on canvas
197 x 331.5 cm
Inv. no. G 1970.21. Purchase, 1970

247   Barnett Newman (1905-1970). *White Fire II*. 1960
Oil on canvas, 244 x 193 cm. Inv. no. G 1973.12. Purchase, 1973

249   Jasper Johns (b. 1930)
The Bath. 1988
Encaustic on canvas, 122.5 x 153 cm
Inv. no. G 1988.21. Purchased with a
contribution from the Verein der
Freunde des Kunstmuseums Basel, 1988

From The City of Basel to Its Works of Art (pp. 7-20)

1 *Joachim von Sandrarts Academie der Bau-, Bild- und Mahlerey-Künste von 1675, Leben der berühmten Maler, Bildhauer und Baumeister*, ed. by A.R. Peltzer, Munich, 1925, p.321f.

2 Elias Ashmole's foundation in Oxford, created in 1683, should nonetheless be mentioned.

3 Max Burckhardt, "Europäische Notabilitäten auf der Durchreise in Basel, Ein Einblick in das alte Gästebuch der Basler Universitätsbibliothek", *Basler Zeitschrift für Geschichte und Altertumskunde*, Vol.71, No.1, 1971, pp. 203-250.

4 Ulrich Barth, *Erlesenes aus dem Basler Münsterschatz*, Basel, 1990.

5 Re the following, cf. Georg Germann, Dorothee Huber and collaborators,"Der Bau des alten Museums in Basel (1844-1849)", *Basler Zeitschrift für Geschichte und Altertumskunde*, Vol.78, 1978, pp.5-30 (also published separately in 1979).

6 "Das Fest zur Einweihung des neuen Museums", *Allgemeines Intelligenzblatt der Stadt Basel*, Vol.5, No.281, 27 November 1849, p.1896; see also "Einweihung unseres neuen Museums", *Basler Zeitung*, Vol.19, No.281, 27 November 1849, p.1150.

7 Report of the Committee for the Öffentliche Kunstsammlung, Basel, 1863, p.187f.

8 Reader's letter,"Basel als Kunstplatz", *Schweizerischer Volksfreund*, Vol.20, No.249, 20 October 1880.

9 Minutes of the Kunstkommission's meeting on 28 September 1889.

10 Christian Geelhaar, "'Our Fellow Citizen of Genius' - Arnold Böcklin and Basel", Dorothea Christ/Christian Geelhaar, *Arnold Böcklin, The Paintings in the Kunstmuseum, Basel*, Basel, 1992.

11 *Busoni, Briefe an seine Frau*, ed. by Friedrich Schnapp, Erlenbach-Zürich/Leipzig, 1935, p.33f; re the concert of the Music Society, see '-mm', "Konzertbericht", *Basler Nachrichten*, Vol.56, No.60, 2 March 1900, Supplement.

12 Letter to Justine Rosé of 13 or 14 June 1903 (University of Western Ontario Library, London, Ontario, Canada; Rosé Collection); Henry-Louis de La Grange, *Gustav Mahler*, preface by Pierre Boulez, Vol.2, Paris, 1979, p.352; re the concert on 15 June 1903, see following reviews: 'G.', "Die 39. Tonkünstlerversammlung des Allgemeinen deutschen Musikvereins in Basel, IV", *Basler Nachrichten*, Vol.59, No.164, 18 June 1903, 1st Supplement; E.Th. M., "Vom Tonkünstlerfest, III", *National-Zeitung*, No. 139, 17 June 1903, p.2f.

13 Felix Klee (ed.), *Paul Klee, Briefe an die Familie*, Vol.1, 1893-1906, Cologne, 1979, p.429.

14 Re the following, see the detailed presentation by Nikolaus Meier, *Die Stadt Basel den Werken der Kunst, Konzepte und Entwürfe für das Kunstmuseum Basel 1906-1932*, Basel, 1986.

15 *Basler Nachrichten*, Vol.59, No.222, 15 August 1903, p.2.

16 *Alfred Lichtwark, Briefe an die Kommission für die Verwaltung der Kunsthalle, In Auswahl mit einer Einleitung*, ed. by Gustav Pauli, Vol. 2, Hamburg, 1923, p. 264f; on Lichtwark see also: *Alfred Lichtwark, Erziehung des Auges, Ausgewählte Schriften*, ed. by Eckhard Schaar, Frankfurt am Main, 1991.

17 Cf. the series of articles that appeared before the debate in the Parliament,"Basler Museumsbauten", *Basler Nachrichten*, Vol. 69, No.169, 13 April 1913; II, No.171, 15 April 1913; III, No. 172, 15 April 1913; IV, No.173, 16 April 1913; V, No. 174, 16 April 1913; Conclusion, No.175, 17 April 1913.

18 'U.'(Walter Überwasser), "Die Einweihung des Bachofenhauses und des Augustinerhofes", *Basler Nachrichten*, Vol.78, No. 485, 7 November 1922, p.1.

19 Maurice Denis, *Journal*, Vol.3 (1921-1943), Paris, 1959, p.56.

20 Christian Geelhaar, "Ferdinand Hodler und Basel", *Basler Magazin*, Political and cultural weekend supplement of the *Basler Zeitung*, No.34, 25 August 1979, pp.1-3. By the same author," Ferdinand Hodler und Basel, Dokumente zur Rezeptionsgeschichte", *Zeitschrift für Schweizerische Archäologie und Kunstgeschichte*, Vol.39, 1982, pp.194-198.

21 'k.', "Die Eröffnung des neuen Basler Kunstmuseums", *Basler Nachrichten*, Vol.92, No.238, 31 August 1936, Supplement; '-dt.' (Georg Schmidt), "Die Eröffnungsfeier des Kunstmuseums am St. Albangraben", *National-Zeitung*, Vol.94, No.401, 31 August 1936, p.13.

22 "Kunstmuseum Basel, Zur Eröffnung", special issue of the *National-Zeitung*, Vol.94, No.400, 30 August 1936; this special issue contained articles by Georg Schmidt, "Erster Rundgang - erste Eindrücke" and by Rudolf Riggenbach, "Zur Geschichte der Öffentlichen Kunstsammlung"; see also "Das neue Basler Kunstmuseum", special supplement of the *Basler Nachrichten*, Vol. 92, No.237, of 29/30 August 1936, which contained the following articles: Dr. Walter Überwasser, "Unser Kunstmuseum"; Rudolf Christ, architect, "Die Bau-Idee"; 'k.', "Aus der Geschichte der Basler Kunstsammlung".

23 Schmidt (see Note 22).

24 "Zwölf Jahre Erfahrung im neuen Kunstmuseum Basel", *Bauen und Wohnen*, No.3, 1952. Reprinted in: Georg Schmidt, *Schriften aus 22 Jahren Museumstätigkeit*, Basel, 1964, pp.79-84.

25 Letter to Lyonel and Julia Feininger of 21 August 1954; *Feininger and Tobey, Years of Friendship 1944-1956, The Complete Correspondence*, New York, 1991, p.125f.

26 Cf. Christian Geelhaar, "Bejahung der Gegenwart und Zuversicht auf die Zukunft, Zur Geschichte der Emanuel Hoffmann-Stiftung Basel", and Katharina Steib, "Räume für Kunstwerke", *Emanuel Hoffmann-Stiftung Basel*, Basel, 1991.

27 Cf. the reader's letter quoted on page 108 that appeared in the *Basler Nachrichten* of 7 April 1870.

28 *Exposition Universelle de 1867 à Paris*, Catalogue Général, Œuvres d'art, Groupe I, Peinture à l'huile, Confédération Suisse,Cat. No. 101: "Benjamin Vautier, *Courtier et paysans (Courtier and Peasants) (Wurtemberg)*, Owned by the Basel Museum"; this picture, which was also known under the title *The Indebted Peasant* (1865), was acquired from the artist in 1865 with money from the Birmann Fund.

29 Minutes of the Kunstkommission's meeting on 30 June 1874.

30 Letter of 15 July 1874; *Jacob Burckhardt, Briefe*, Vol.5, ed. by Max Burckhardt, Basel, 1963, p.231f.

31 Cf. "Appendix: the exhibition of the work", William Hauptman, "Charles Gleyre's Penthée and the Creative Imagination", *Zeitschrift für Schweizerische Archäologie und Kunstgeschichte*, Vol. 43, 1986, p.223-225.

32 Léonce Bénédite, "Foreword", *Catalogue de l'Exposition de l'art suisse du XVe au XIXe siècle (de Holbein à Hodler)*, Paris, 1924, p.13.

33 Minutes of the Kunstkommission's meeting on 14 April 1924.

34 Minutes of the Kunstkommission's meeting on 19 May 1924.

35 See also Philippe Kaenel, "Quelques expositions d'art suisse à Paris dans l'entre-deux guerres: images d'une identité artistique et nationale", *Zeitschrift für Schweizerische Archäologie und Kunstgeschichte*, Vol.43, No.4, 1986, pp.403-410.

36 Cf. Nikolaus Meier, *Die Sammlung des Vereins der Freunde des Kunstmuseums Basel*, Exhibition catalogue, Kunstmuseum, Basel, 1983.

37 "Friedrich Rintelen", *Basler Nachrichten*, Vol.82, No.121, 5 May 1926, p.2; Walter Überwasser, "Friedrich Rintelen", *Basler Nachrichten*, Vol.82, No.122, 6 May 1926, 1st Supplement.

38 H.A. Schmid, "Professor Otto Fischer zum Gedenken", *Basler Nachrichten*, Vol.104, No.1160, 16 April 1948, 2nd Supplement; *Otto Fischer, Kunstgelehrter und Museumsmann 1886-1948*, Exhibition catalogue, Graphische Sammlung, Staatsgalerie Stuttgart, 1986; "Otto Fischer, ein Kunsthistoriker des zwanzigsten Jahrhunderts", special issue, *Reutlinger Geschichtsblätter*, New Series No.25, Reutlingen, 1986.

39 Franz Meyer, "Georg Schmidt", *Öffentliche Kunstsammlung Basel, Jahresbericht 1961* , pp.47-49; Robert Hess, "Zur Erinnerung an Professor Georg Schmidt (1896-1965)", *Basler Stadtbuch 1966*, Basel, 1965, pp.194-200.

40 Christian Geelhaar, "Die Öffentliche Kunstsammlung in der Ära Franz Meyer", *Basler Stadtbuch 1981*, 102nd year, Basel, 1982, pp. 89-96.

The Holbeins of Basel (pp. 21-32)

41 F.V. (Félix Vallotton), "Au musée de Bâle, I", *Gazette de Lausanne*, Vol.93, No.273, 17 November 1892.
42 F.V. (Félix Vallotton), "Au musée de Bâle, II", *Gazette de Lausanne*, Vol.93, No.274, 18 November 1892.
43 "Briefe auf einer Reise durch die Niederlande, Rheingegenden, die Schweiz, und einen Teil von Frankreich"; Friedrich Schlegel, *Ansichten und Ideen von der christlichen Kunst*, ed. by Hans Eichner, critical edition of Friedrich Schlegel's works, Vol.4, Paderborn, 1959, p.194.
44 Cf. Andrée Hayum, *The Isenheim Altarpiece, God's Medicine and the Painter's Vision*, Princeton, New Jersey, 1989, pp.128-139; Michael Farin, "Trostfackeln der alten Hoffnung, Grünewald und Huysmans - zwei Naturalisten, zwei Mystiker", *Süddeutsche Zeitung*, No.189, 17/18 August 1991, p.107.
45 Joris-Karl Huysmans, *Les Grünewald du Musée de Colmar, Des Primitifs au Retable d'Issenheim*, Critical edition by Pierre Brunel, André Guyaux and Christian Heck, Paris, 1988, p.126f.
46 Joachim von Sandrarts *Academie der Bau-, Bild- und Mahlerey-Künste von 1675, Leben der berühmten Maler, Bildhauer und Baumeister*, ed. by A.R. Peltzer, Munich, 1925, p.322; see also p.99.
47 Vallotton (see Note 42).
48 Sandrart (see Note 46), p.99.
49 Karl Spazier, *Wanderungen durch die Schweiz*, Gotha, 1790, p.40.
50 Johann Gerhard Reinhard Andreä, "Fortsetzung der Briefe, so aus der Schweiz nach Hannover geschrieben sind", *Hannoverisches Magazin*, No.30, 13 April 1764, Col.471.
51 Johann Rudolf von Sinner, *Historische und literarische Reise durch das abendländische Helvetien*, Part 1, Leipzig, 1782, p.27.
52 Christoph Meiners, *Briefe über die Schweiz*, Part 2, Berlin, 1785.
53 Anna Grigoryevna Dostoyevsky, *Tagebücher, Die Reise in den Westen*, translated from Russian into German by Barbara Conrad, Königstein 1985, p.335.
54 A.G. Dostoyevsky, *Erinnerungen*, Berlin, 1976, p.176.
55 Part I, Chapter V.
56 Gustaf Adolf Wanner, "Lenin war doch in Basel", *Basler Nachrichten*, Vol.130, No.239, 12 October 1974, p.27; reprinted in Gustaf Adolf Wanner, *Berühmte Gäste in Basel*, Basel, 1983, pp. 91-96.
57 Elisabeth Landolt, "Das Amerbach-Kabinett und seine Inventare", *Sammeln in der Renaissance: Das Amerbach-Kabinett, Beiträge zu Basilius Amerbach*, Öffentliche Kunstsammlung, Basel, 1991, p.81.
58 Cf. Landolt (see Note 57), p.92 and p.154, Note 3.
59 Landolt (see Note 57), p.145.
60 Re the following, cf. Paul Ganz and Emil Major, "Die Entstehung des Amerbach'schen Kunstkabinets", *Öffentliche Kunstsammlung in Basel, LIX. Jahres-Bericht*, New Series III, Basel, 1907, pp.1-68; Otto Fischer, "Geschichte der Öffentlichen Kunstsammlung", *Festschrift zur Eröffnung des Kunstmuseums*, Basel, 1936, pp.9 - 21; Elisabeth Landolt, *Kabinettstücke der Amerbach im Historischen Museum Basel*, with contributions by Beatrice Schärli and Hans Chr. Ackermann, Basel, 1984; Elisabeth Landolt, "Zur Geschichte und zum Bestand des Amerbach-Kabinetts", *Sammeln in der Renaissance: Das Amerbach-Kabinett, Die Objekte im Historischen Museum Basel*, Exhibition catalogue, Kunstmuseum, Basel, 1991, pp.9-17; Landolt (see Note 57), pp.77-105.
61 *Sammeln in der Renaissance: Das Amerbach-Kabinett, Die Objekte im Historischen Museum Basel*, Exhibition catalogue, Kunstmuseum, Basel, 1991, Cat.No.1.
62 As in Note 61, Cat.No.11.
63 *Hans Holbein d.J., Zeichnungen aus dem Kupferstichkabinett der Öffentlichen Kunstsammlung Basel*, Catalogue by Christian Müller,

Kunstmuseum, Basel, 1988, Cat.No.65; *Sammeln in der Renaissance: Das Amerbach-Kabinett, Zeichnungen Alter Meister*, selected and commented on by Christian Müller, Exhibition catalogue, Kunstmuseum, Basel, 1991, Cat.No.114; cf. also Elisabeth Landolt, "Zum Nachlass des Erasmus", *Erasmus von Rotterdam, Vorkämpfer für Frieden und Toleranz*, Exhibition catalogue, Historisches Museum, Basel, 1986, p.68f.
64 See Note 61, Cat.No.14.
65 Landolt (see Note 57), p.82.
66 Landolt (see Note 57), p.98.
67 *Sammeln in der Renaissance: Das Amerbach-Kabinett, Die Basler Goldschmiederisse*, selected and commented on by Paul Tanner, Exhibition catalogue, Kunstmuseum, Basel, 1991.
68 *Sammeln in der Renaissance: Das Amerbach-Kabinett, Die Gemälde*, Introduction and catalogue by Paul H. Boerlin, Exhibition catalogue, Kunstmuseum, Basel, 1991, p.9f.
69 *Sammeln in der Renaissance: Das Amerbach-Kabinett, Zeichnungen Alter Meister* (see Note 63), pp.8-10.
70 Landolt (see Note 57), pp.101-105.
71 See Note 61, Cat.No.66.
72 Landolt (see Note 57), pp.123-129.
73 Landolt (see Note 57), pp.131-139.
74 Landolt (see Note 57), pp.141-173.
75 The following is based on Tilman Falk, *Katalog der Zeichnungen des 15. und 16. Jahrhunderts im Kupferstichkabinett Basel*, Part 1, Basel/Stuttgart, 1979, pp.21-23.
76 Letter from Henry Frederic Howard, Lord Maltravers, of 4 August 1637, in Volume Add.MSS.15970, fol.65, in the British Library, London; quoted from Falk (see Note 75), p.21.
77 In the summer of 1988 the exhibition "Hans Holbein the Younger: Drawings from the Collection of H.M. Queen Elizabeth II in Windsor Castle and from the Öffentliche Kunstsammlung Basel" first brought the Holbein drawings of the Royal Library temporarily together with those of the Amerbach Kabinett.
78 Re the Faesch Museum in general, see Emil Major, "Das Fäschische Museum und die Fäschischen Inventare", *Öffentliche Kunstsammlung in Basel, LX. Jahres-Bericht*, New Series IV, Basel, 1908, pp.1-69; Otto Fischer (see Note 60), pp.34-40, 54f. and 67f.
79 Sandrart (see Note 46), p.322.
80 Major (see Note 78), p.1.
81 Peter Vischer-Sarasin acquired around one hundred paintings and miniatures from the collection of the Margraves of Baden-Durlach at the auction in the Markgräfler Hof; cf. Horst Vey, "From Durlach to Wildenstein", *Old Master Pictures from Schloss Wildenstein*, Auction catalogue, Christie's, London, 6 July 1990, pp.11-13.
82 Minutes of the Kunstkommission's meeting on 29 October 1862.
83 Letter to the Committee of the Öffentliche Kunstsammlung Basel of 29 October 1862; *Jacob Burckhardt, Briefe*, ed. by Max Burckhardt, Vol.4, Basel, 1961, p.121f.
84 Minutes of the Kunstkommission's meeting on 5 November 1864.
85 Dieter Koepplin, "Die Schenkung Robert von Hirsch (II): Cranachs 'Urteil des Paris'", *Basler Zeitung*, No.85, 29 March 1978, p.37.
86 Paul H. Boerlin, "Hans Holbein d.Ä.: Bildnis eines Herrn mit Pelzmütze, 1513", *Pantheon*, Vol.XL, No.I, January/February/ March 1982, pp.32-39.

Troops and Generals (pp. 71-77)

87 "Frau Professor L. Bachofen-Burckhardt", *Basler Nachrichten*, Vol.76, No.83, 24 February 1920, Supplement.
88 *Basler Nachrichten*, Vol.76, No.82, 23 February 1920, p.4.
89 Minutes of the Kunstkommission's meeting on 24 February 1920.
90 See Note 88.
91 Minutes of the Kunstkommission's meeting on 23 June 1921.
92 Rudolf F. Burckhardt, *Katalog der Gemäldesammlung von Frau Prof. J.J. Bachofen-Burkhardt*, Basel, 1907.

93 Paul Ganz, "Die Professor Johann Jakob Bachofen-Burckhardt-Stiftung", *Öffentliche Kunstsammlung in Basel, LXVI. Jahres-Bericht*, New Series X, Basel, 1914, pp.41-89.

94 "Basler Museumsbauten", *Basler Nachrichten*, Vol.69, No.169, 13 April 1913, 1st Supplement; cf. also: II, No.171, 15 April 1913; III, No.172, 15 April 1913; IV, No.173, 16 April 1913; V, No.174, 16 April 1913; Conclusion, No.175, 17 April 1913.

95 H.A. Schmid, "Das Bachofen-Burckhardthaus", I, *Basler Nachrichten*, Vol. 78, No.420, 29 September 1922, 2nd Supplement.

96 'U.' (Walter Überwasser), "Die Einweihung des Bachofenhauses und des Augustinerhofes", *Basler Nachrichten*, Vol.78, No.485, 7 November 1922, p.1.

97 H.A. Schmid, "Das Bachofen-Burckhardthaus", II, *Basler Nachrichten*, Vol.78, No.489, 9 November 1922, p.1f.

98 *Catalog der öffentlichen Kunstsammlung zu Basel*, fifth edition, 1860, p.41; cf. the photograph of the Painting Gallery taken in around 1872, *Festschrift zur Eröffnung des Kunstmuseums*, Basel, 1936, p.88.

99 Diary entry of 25 October 1891; "Hans Sandreuter, Briefe und Tagebücher, Schriftlicher Nachlass, Teil 2", *Basler Kunstverein, Berichterstattung über das Jahr 1916*, Basel, 1917, p.28f.

100 *A Corpus of Rembrandt Paintings, I: 1625-1631*, The Hague, Boston, London, 1982, No.C23.

101 See Note 100, No.C16.

102 "Hermann Wirz", *Basler Nachrichten*, Vol.64, No.57, 27 February 1908, 1st Supplement.

103 Cf. Paul Ganz, "Die Sammlung des Herrn Hans Vonder Mühll, Niederländische Gemälde des XVII. Jahrhunderts", *Öffentliche Kunst-Sammlung in Basel, LXIX. Jahresbericht*, New Series XIII, Basel, 1917, pp.37-74.

104 According to Werner Sumowski, *The Baptism of the Chamberlain* was painted not by Salomon Koninck (1609-1656) as previously assumed, but probably by Dirck Bleker (Haarlem 1622 - 1672 The Hague); Werner Sumowski, *Gemälde der Rembrandt Schüler*, Vol.3. Landau/Pfalz 1983, p.1630.

105 See Note 97.

106 For biographical details, cf. 'z.', "Max Geldner", *Basler Nachrichten*, Vol.114, No.298, 18 July 1958, p.2; 't.', "Max Geldner", *National-Zeitung*, Vol.116, No.326, 18 July 1958, p.5.

107 Georg Schmidt, "Max Geldner und seine Sammlung", *Das Vermächtnis Max Geldner*, Catalogue of the Öffentliche Kunstsammlung, Basel, 1958, p.VI; the exhibition of the Max Geldner bequest opened in the Kunstmuseum on 27 November 1958.

108 Christian Geelhaar, "Bilder dieses Sommers", *Schweizer Illustrierte*, No.33, 13 August 1990, p.106.

109 Christian Geelhaar, "Hodler-Landschaft für Basel", *Basler Zeitung*, No.257, 2 November 1983, p.37.

110 Cf. Paul H. Boerlin, "Eine vergessene Abteilung? Die Niederländer in der Öffentlichen Kunstsammlung Basel", *Im Lichte Hollands, Holländische Malerei des 17. Jahrhunderts aus den Sammlungen des Fürsten von Liechtenstein und aus Schweizer Besitz*, Exhibition catalogue, Kunstmuseum, Basel, 1987, pp.51-53.

111 Cf. *Kunstmuseum Basel, Ankäufe und Schenkungen 1988*, with an introduction and commentaries on the pictures by Christian Geelhaar, Basel/Einsiedeln, 1989, p.8f.

The Pious Art of the High-minded Spinster (pp. 93-97)

112 *Allgemeines Intelligenzblatt der Stadt Basel*, Vol.3, No.250, 29 September 1847, p.1120f.

113 Nikolaus Meier, "'Blütezeit des Mittelalters', Zu einem Bilde August Wilhelm J. Ahlborns", *Basler Zeitschrift für Geschichte und Altertumskunde*, Vol.77, 1977, pp.179-195.

114 *Zeichnungen deutscher Künstler des 19. Jahrhunderts aus dem Basler Kupferstichkabinett*, Exhibition catalogue compiled by Eva Maria Krafft, Kunstmuseum, Basel, 1982, Cat.Nos.7-9, pp.29-31.

115 See Note 114, Cat.No.130, pp.228-232.

116 Cf. Paul H. Boerlin's comments, *Im Lichte Hollands, Holländische Malerei des 17. Jahrhunderts aus den Sammlungen des Fürsten von Liechtenstein und aus Schweizer Besitz*, Exhibition catalogue, Kunstmuseum, Basel, 1987, pp.246-249.

117 Ernst von Meyenburg, "Die Kunstsammlung des Johann Konrad Dienast (1741-1824)", *Öffentliche Kunst-Sammlung in Basel, LXII. Jahres-Bericht*, New Series V, Basel, 1909, p.30f.

118 Emilie Linder in a letter to Wilhelm Wackernagel of 22 July 1866; Konrad Escher, "Die Emilie Linder-Stiftung", *Öffentliche Kunst-Sammlung in Basel, LXII. Jahres-Bericht*, New Series VI, Basel, 1910, p.30.

119 Letter from Clemens Brentano to Apollonia Diepenbrock, Munich, mid-October 1833; *Clemens Brentano, Briefe an Emilie Linder*, edited and with a commentary by Wolfgang Frühwald, Bad Homburg/Berlin/Zürich, 1969, pp.13-16; Brentano was presumably referring to Franz von Baader (1765-1841), a religious philosopher.

120 S. Steinle to Brentano, Vienna, 5 November 1838; quoted from Verena Jent, *Emilie Linder, 1797-1867, Studien zur Biographie der Basler Kunstsammlerin und Freundin Clemens Brentanos*, Dissertation, Basel 1967/Berlin 1970, p.89.

121 *Basler Nachrichten*, Vol.18, No.235, 4 October 1862.

122 Cf. the article by Nikolaus Meier, "Die Basler Münsterscheiben, Zur Geschmacksgeschichte des 19. Jahrhunderts", *Basler Zeitschrift für Geschichte und Altertumskunde*, Vol.89, 1989, pp.165-211.

A Modern Swiss Art Collection (pp. 105-114)

123 Paul Ganz, "Samuel Birmann und seine Stiftung", *Öffentliche Kunstsammlung in Basel, LXIII. Jahres-Bericht*, New Series VII, Basel, 1911, p.19f.

124 See Note 123.

125 Cf. the summary in the *Basler Zeitung*, No.275, 22 November 1984, p.29 of a lecture on the subject "Jacob Burckhardt und die Öffentliche Kunstsammlung" that Nikolaus Meier gave to the Historical and Antiquarian Society of Basel on 19 November 1984.

126 Lukas Gloor, *Die Geschichte des Basler Kunstvereins und der Kunsthalle Basel 1839-1988*, Basel, 1989.

127 *Basler Nachrichten*, Vol.30, No.148, 25 June 1874; Gustav Adolf Wanner, "Das Haus 'zum rothen Fahnen' an der Freien Strasse", *Basler Zeitung*, No.164, 16 July 1983, p.24.

128 'L.', Heinrich Lang, *National-Zeitung*, Vol.51, No.12, 14 January 1911, p.3; see also *Basler Nachrichten*, Vol.67, No.15, 15 January 1911, 1st Supplement.

129 *Basler Nachrichten*, Vol.26, No.82, 7 April 1870.

130 Minutes of the Kunstkommission's meeting on 30 June 1853.

131 Valentina Anker, *Alexandre Calame, Vie et œuvre*, Freiburg, 1987, p.428, Cat.No.623.

132 Minutes of the Kunstkommission's meeting on 15 January 1856.

133 Minutes of the Kunstkommission's meeting on 9 July 1868; *Salon de 1868*, 86e exposition officielle, Palais des Champs-Élysées, Paris, 1868, Cat.No.1372: "*Un soir (An Evening)*"; cf. "Aus Paris, Rückblick auf den diesjährigen Salon", *Zeitschrift für bildende Kunst*, Vol.3, 1868, p.279.

134 Letter to Eduard His-Heusler of 22 January 1872; *Jacob Burckhardt, Briefe*, ed. by Max Burckhardt, Vol.5, Basel, 1963, p.152; minutes of the Kunstkommission's meeting on 20 January 1872.

135 Minutes of the Kunstkommission's meeting on 3 December 1859.

136 Minutes of the Kunstkommission's meetings on 23 May and 17 November 1860.

137 Minutes of the Kunstkommission's meeting on 4 February 1865; William Hauptman, "Charles Gleyre's Penthée and the Creative Imagination", *Zeitschrift für Schweizerische Archäologie und Kunstgeschichte*, Vol.43, 1986, pp.215-227.

138 *Verzeichniss der Kunst-Gegenstände auf der schweizerischen Kunstausstellung zu Basel im Jahre 1860*, Cat.No.119: "*Die Ernte (The Harvest)*, 2,000 Swiss francs"; minutes of the Kunstkommission's meeting on 17 November 1860.

139 *Salon de 1859*, Palais des Champs-Elysées, Paris, 1859, Cat. No. 3044: "*La moisson (The Harvest)*".

140 *Basler Kunstverein, Vortrag nebst Berichterstattung über das Jahr 1874*, Basel, 1875, p.22: "Sale of a landscape by Rob. Zünd to the Basel Museum, 2,000 Swiss francs".

141 Minutes of the Kunstkommission's meeting on 18 April 1874.

142 *Verzeichniss der Kunst-Gegenstände auf der Schweizerischen Kunst-Ausstellung in Basel im Jahre 1867*, Cat.No.212: "*Biblische Landschaft (Biblical Landscape)*, 2,000 Swiss francs"; cf. "Zur schweizerischen Kunstausstellung von 1867 in Basel", *Basler Nachrichten*, Vol.23, No.144, 20 June 1867, p.1302f.

143 "Schweizerische Kunstausstellung 1869", *Basler Nachrichten*, Vol.25, No.94, 22 April 1869, p.851f.

144 *Verzeichniss der Kunst-Gegenstände auf der Schweizerischen Kunst-Ausstellung in Basel im Jahre 1869*, Cat.No.27: "*Aussicht vom Hafen von Ouchy (View from the Harbour at Ouchy)*, 1,500 Swiss francs"; minutes of the Kunstkommission's meeting on 18 September 1869; the price was 1,500 Swiss francs.

145 *Basler Kunstverein, Vortrag nebst Berichterstattung über das Jahr 1869*, Basel, 1870, p.13f.; *Verzeichniss der Kunst-Gegenstände auf der Schweizerischen Kunst-Ausstellung in Basel im Jahre 1869*, Cat.No.142: "*La Charmeuse (The Charmer)*, 13,000 Swiss francs".

146 See Note 143.

147 Letter to Eduard His-Heusler of 22 November 1865; *Jacob Burckhardt, Briefe*, Vol.4, ed. by Max Burckhardt, Basel, 1961, p.204.

148 *Rudolf Schick, Tagebuch-Aufzeichnungen aus den Jahren 1866, 1868, 1869 über Arnold Böcklin*, ed. by Hugo von Tschudi, Berlin, 1901, p.334f.

149 *Basler Nachrichten*, Vol.18, No.265, 8 November 1862.

150 Minutes of the Kunstkommission's meeting on 8 March 1862.

151 Christian Geelhaar, "'Our Fellow Citizen of Genius' - Arnold Böcklin and Basel", Dorothea Christ/Christian Geelhaar, *Arnold Böcklin, The Paintings in the Kunstmuseum, Basel*, Basel, 1992, p.18.

152 'B.', "Basler-Museum", *Basler Nachrichten*, Vol.22, No.143, 19 June 1866.

153 *Jahresbericht des Basler Kunstvereins über das Jahr 1866*, Basel, 1876, p.12.

154 Minutes of the Kunstkommission's meeting on 22 February 1868; *Salon de 1868*, 86e exposition officielle, Palais des Champs-Elysées, Paris, 1868, Cat.No.263: "*Pétrarque dans la solitude (Petrarch in his Solitude). Landscape.* (Belongs to Colonel R. Merian-Iselin)"; Cat.No.264: "*La Madeleine et le Christ (Magdalene and Christ).* (Belongs to the Basel Museum.)"

155 Nikolaus Meier (see Note 122), pp.104-107.

156 Minutes of the Kunstkommission's meeting on 10 July 1869.

157 Minutes of the Kunstkommission's meeting on 2 December 1870.

158 Cf. Margarete Pfister-Burkhalter, "Böcklins Basler Museumsfresken", *Arnold Böcklin, Ausstellung zum 150. Geburtstag veranstaltet vom Kunstmuseum Basel und vom Basler Kunstverein*, Basel/Stuttgart, 1977, pp.69-80; cf. also Christian Geelhaar (see Note 151), p.21f.

159 *Exposition Universelle de 1867 à Paris*, Catalogue Général, Confédération Suisse, Œuvres d'Art, Groupe I, Peinture à l'huile, Cat.No. 22: "*L'Abnégation*".

160 *Basler Nachrichten*, Vol.27, No.283, 29 November 1871, p.1.

161 Minutes of the Kunstkommission's meeting on 9 December 1871.

162 Cf. "Die Permanente Kunstausstellung in Basel", I, *Basler Nachrichten*, Vol. 28, No.300, 19 December 1872, Supplement; II, No.302, 21 December 1872, Supplement.

163 Minutes of the Kunstkommission's meeting on 16 December 1872; the two paintings cost 2,000 and 3,000 Swiss francs respectively.

164 *Welt-Ausstellung 1873 in Wien*, Offizieller Kunst-Catalog, Bildende Kunst der Gegenwart, Cat.No.75; minutes of the Kunstkommission's meetings on 4 October and 1 November 1873; the painting cost 10,000 Swiss francs.

165 'K.', "Schweizerische Kunst", *Basler Nachrichten*, Vol.36, No.243, 13 October 1880; minutes of the Kunstkommission's meeting on 23 October 1880; the painting cost 3,600 Swiss francs.

166 *Basler Nachrichten*, Vol.36, No.258, 30 October 1880.

167 Minutes of the Kunstkommission's meeting on 13 January 1877.

168 Minutes of the Kunstkommission's meeting on 25 October 1879; on 11 November 1879 the following notice appeared in the *Basler Nachrichten*, Vol.35, No.267, p.2: "We were delighted to learn that the committee responsible for the local art collection has finally succeeded in acquiring a good-sized picture by the distinguished Berne painter, Anker."

169 *Salon de 1880*, 97e exposition officielle, Palais des Champs-Elysées, Paris, 1880, Cat.No.58: "*Le mège (Charlatan exerçant illégalement la médecine) (The Quack - Charlatan illegally practising medicine)*"; Ph. de Chennevières, "Le Salon de 1880", third and last article, *Gazette des Beaux-Arts*, Year 22, Vol.22, 2nd Period, 1 July 1880, p.60.

170 Letter of 26 December 1879 to Albert de Meuron; *Albert Anker, Katalog der Gemälde und Ölstudien*, Kunstmuseum, Berne, 1962, Cat.No.57.

171 (Reader's letter), "Das Basler Museum und Böcklin's 'Spiel der Wellen'", *Basler Nachrichten*, Vol.41, No.298, 15 December 1885.

172 Xaver Schwegler (1832-1902): *Huntsman with Animal Skins (Jäger mit Tierfellen)*. Acquired in 1877 using money from the Birmann Fund.

173 The picture was purchased in February 1879 at the suggestion of Jacob Burckhardt and Friedrich Weber (minutes of the Kunstkommission's meeting on 1 February 1879); at the same time the artist was given permission to exhibit the picture at the Paris "Salon"; *Salon de 1879*, 96e exposition officielle, Palais des Champs-Elysées, Paris, 1879, Cat.No.159: "*Une scène de 'Fiesco', de Schiller, Acte IV, scène 14 (A Scene from Schiller's 'Fiesco', Act IV, Scene 14)* (Belongs to the Basel Museum)."

174 (Reader's letter), "Die öffentliche Kunstsammlung, ihre Mittel und ihre Ziele", *Basler Nachrichten*, Vol.41, No.311, 29 December 1885.

175 Cf. the book by Christ and Geelhaar quoted in Note 151.

176 Dr.W.M., "Aus der Basler Kunsthalle", *Basler Nachrichten*, Vol.67, No.266, 28 September 1911, 2nd Supplement.

177 *Basler Kunstverein, Jahresbericht 1917*, Basel, 1918, p.12.

178 Letter to Lily Stumpf of 8 May 1902, *Paul Klee, Briefe an die Familie*, Vol.1, 1893-1906, ed. by Felix Klee, Cologne, 1979, p.234f.

179 Re the following, cf. Christian Geelhaar, "Ferdinand Hodler und Basel, Dokumente zur Rezeptionsgeschichte", *Zeitschrift für Schweizerische Archäologie und Kunstgeschichte*, Vol.39, 1982, pp.181-201.

180 "Die Schweizerische Kunstausstellung 1883", *Schweizerischer Volksfreund*, Vol.23, No.261, 4 November 1883, Section 2, p.1.

181 Minutes of the Kunstkommission's meeting on 9 December 1909.

182 Minutes of the Philosophy Faculty 1902-1913, p.332 (Archives of the City of Basel, University Archives, R 3,6).

183 See Note 180.

184 *Basler Nachrichten*, Vol.66, No.170, 25 June 1910, 1st Supplement.

185 Telegram of 24 June 1910 to the Dean, August Hagenbach (University Archives XI, 4,3b).

186 *Gemälde-Galerie L. La Roche-Ringwald, Basel*, Exhibition and sale from 17 May 1910 onwards, Cat.No.13: "*Bettler (Beggar)*", 1891; re La Roche-Ringwald, cf. Geelhaar (see Note 151), p.24f.

187 Letter from Ferdinand Hodler to Max Geldner of 7 December 1910; *Von Hodler bis Gimmi*, Exhibition catalogue, Galerie Kurt Meissner, Zürich, 1977.

188 *Öffentliche Kunst-Sammlung in Basel, LXIV. Jahres-Bericht*, New Series VIII, Basel, 1912, p.15; minutes of the Kunstkommission's meeting on 27 February 1913.

189 *Hodler, Gedächtnis-Ausstellung*, Kunstmuseum, Berne, 20 August-23 October 1921, Cat.No.433: "*Niesengipfel (Summit of the Niesen)*"; the picture's price was not indicated in the "Price List of Works for Sale" of 15 September 1921.

190 *Öffentliche Kunst-Sammlung Basel, Jahres-Bericht 1922*, New Series XIX, Basel, 1922, p.6; the painting cost 13,000 Swiss francs.

191 *International Exhibition of Modern Art*, Association of American Painters and Sculptors, Armory of the Sixty-ninth Regiment, New York, 1913, Cat.No.258: *The Nissen* (sic.); lent by Heinrich Thannhauser. Thannhauser had already exhibited the picture in November and December 1911 in his Moderne Galerie in Munich: *Kollektiv-Ausstellung Ferd. Hodler*, about 100 Works from the Years 1872-1911, Moderne Galerie, Munich, 1911, Cat.No.86: *The Niesen*, 1910.

The Much-praised French Taste (pp. 147-154)

192 Daniel Wildenstein, *Claude Monet, Biographie et Catalogue raisonné, tome III: 1887-1898*, Lausanne/Paris, 1979, pp.23-33; in the autumn of 1990 the Musée d'Orsay, Paris devoted an "exposition-dossier" to the theme: "Il y a cent ans ils ont donné l'*Olympia*".

193 Cf. the minutes of the Kunstkommission's meetings on 23 January and 14 March 1912; excerpts quoted in Lukas Gloor, *Von Böcklin zu Cézanne, Die Rezeption des französischen Impressionismus in der deutschen Schweiz*, Europäische Hochschulschriften, Series XXVIII, Art History, Vol.58, Bern/Frankfurt am Main/New York, 1986, p.177.

194 The picture *L'Hermitage, Pontoise*, which appeared in the catalogue as No. 107, was priced at 7,500 Swiss francs; re the fund-raising campaign, see the report by Paul Burckhardt, "Vom Basler Kunstleben um 1905", *Schweizer Kunst*, No. 7, July 1946, p.62f.

195 Minutes of the Kunstkommission's meeting on 14 March 1912.

196 'C.' (Jules Coulin), "Öffentliche Kunstsammlung", *Basler Nachrichten*, Vol.68, No.129, 12 May 1912, 3rd Supplement.

197 François Daulte, *Alfred Sisley, Catalogue raisonné de l'œuvre peint*, Lausanne, 1959, No.597.

198 Gloor (see Note 193), pp.100-109.

199 'H.K.' (Hermann Kienzle), "Auguste Rodin in der französischen Kunst-Ausstellung zu Basel", *Basler Nachrichten*, Vol.62, No.110, 14 April 1906, 1st Supplement.

200 *Paul Klee, Tagebücher 1898-1918*, new critical edition, edited by Wolfgang Kersten, Stuttgart/Teufen, 1988, p.236, Entry No.758.

201 See Klee's review of the exhibition in the monthly *Die Alpen*, No.6, February 1912. Reprinted in *Paul Klee, Rezensionen und Aufsätze*, ed. by Christian Geelhaar, Cologne, 1976, p.98f.

202 18 sculptures by Rodin were exhibited but they were not individually listed in the catalogue. For their identification see Alain Beausire, *Quand Rodin exposait*, Musée Rodin, Paris, 1989, p.275.

203 See Note 199.

204 The pictures by Monet that were for sale cost between 12,000 and 15,000 Swiss francs; the two female portraits by Renoir cost as much as 15,000 and 20,000 Swiss francs.

205 See Note 199.

206 Wilhelm Barth, "Die welschen Maler in der Kunsthalle", *Basler Nachrichten*, Vol.71, No.600, 26 November 1915, Supplement.

207 Minutes of the Kunstkommission's meeting on 19 December 1916.

208 Christian Geelhaar, "Es war immer meine Auffassung, möglichst hohe Qualität zu kaufen", Hans-Joachim Müller, *NAFEA, The Rudolf Staechelin Collection, Basel*, with contributions by Christian Geelhaar, Franz Meyer, Simon de Pury, Ruedi Staechelin, Basel, 1990, p.151f.

209 *Öffentliche Kunstsammlung Basel, Jahresberichte 1946-1950*, p.7; re Rudolf Staechelin, cf. the publication quoted in Note 208.

210 Letters from Wilhelm Barth to Léonce Bénédite of 27 April and 27 September 1918, 6 and 13 June 1919; archives of the Musée Rodin, Paris.

211 *Basler Nachrichten*, Vol.75, No.279, 20 June 1919, 2nd Supplement; see also *National-Zeitung*, Vol. 78, No. 283, 20 June 1919, Supplement.

212 "Report of the Committee for the Sculpture Hall for 1919", Basler *Kunstverein, Berichterstattung über das Jahr 1919*, Basel, 1920, p.17.

213 Minutes of the Kunstkommission's meeting on 13 January 1920; report of the Committee for the Sculpture Hall for 1920, *Basler Kunstverein, Berichterstattung über das Jahr 1920*, Basel, 1921, p.25.

214 Venturi 344; minutes of the Kunstkommission's meeting on 15 February 1921.

215 *Basler Nachrichten*, Vol.81, No.209, 1/2 August 1925, 1st Supplement.

216 Venturi 210.

217 De la Faille 488.

218 Minutes of the Kunstkommission's meetings on 6 January and 15 February 1926.

219 Minutes of the Kunstkommission's meeting on 22 March 1955.

220 Cf. Christian Geelhaar, "The Painters Who Had the Right Eyes, On the reception of Cézanne's Bathers", Mary Louise Krumrine, *Paul Cézanne, The Bathers*, Exhibition catalogue, Kunstmuseum, Basel, 1989, pp.275-303.

221 Minutes of the Kunstkommission's meeting on 21 June 1926; the picture cost 8,000 Swiss francs; in April 1916 it had been included in the "Exhibition of Recent Art from Basel Private Collections" in the Kunsthalle, as a loan from Dr. Paul Linder.

222 'O.F.' (Otto Fischer), "Neuerwerbungen der Öffentlichen Kunstsammlung in Basel", *Basler Nachrichten*, Vol.86, No.44, 14 February 1930, 1st Supplement.

223 Minutes of the Kunstkommission's meeting on 6 July 1931.

224 De la Faille 433; privately owned in the USA; minutes of the Kunstkommission's meetings on 26 September, 24 October and 14 November 1932.

225 De la Faille 795; The St. Louis Art Museum; minutes of the Kunstkommission's meetings on 8 and 23 June and 23 October 1933.

226 De la Faille 348; acquired by the Museum of Buenos Aires in 1934; minutes of the Kunstkommission's meeting on 23 October 1933.

227 De la Faille 375; Metropolitan Museum of Art, New York; minutes of the Kunstkommission's meeting on 23 October 1933.

228 De la Faille 650; minutes of the Kunstkommission's meetings on 2 and 23 October 1933.

229 De la Faille 762; The St. Louis Art Museum; minutes of the Kunstkommission's meetings on 2 and 23 October 1933.

230 De la Faille 594; minutes of the Kunstkommission's meetings on 6 November, 18 and 20 December 1933.

231 De la Faille 444; minutes of the Kunstkommission's meetings on 6 November, 18 and 20 December 1933, as well as on 16 and 31 January 1934.

232 Minutes of the Kunstkommission's meeting on 5 July 1934.

233 Minutes of the Kunstkommission's meeting on 11 June 1934.

234 Venturi 725; minutes of the Kunstkommission's meeting on 2 July 1935.

235 Dieter Koepplin, "Der Erwerb der Cézanne-Zeichnungen in Basel 1934/35", *Paul Cézanne: Die Basler Zeichnungen*, Kupferstichkabinett, Basel, 1988, pp.12-18.

236 Paul Fechter, "Die Sammlung Schmitz", *Kunst und Künstler*, Vol.VIII, No.1, 1910, pp.15-25; Karl Scheffler, "Die Sammlung Oskar Schmitz in Dresden", *Kunst und Künstler*, Vol.XIX, No.5, 1921, pp.178-190.

237 Christian Geelhaar, "Die Anfänge des Impressionismus, Renoirs 'Dame mit dem Möwenhütchen'", *Basler Zeitung*, No.242, 14 October 1988, p.51; reprinted, *Kunstmuseum Basel, Ankäufe und Schenkungen 1988*, with an introduction and commentaries on the pictures by Christian Geelhaar, Basel/Einsiedeln, 1989, p.16f.

238 Minutes of the Kunstkommission's meeting on 27 November 1939.

239 '-dt.' (Georg Schmidt), "Paul Cézanne in der Kunsthalle", III, *National-Zeitung*, Vol. 80, No.121, 13 March 1921, p.2.

240 Minutes of the Kunstkommission's meeting on 22 December 1959; the picture cost 780,000 Swiss francs.

241 Franz Meyer, "Die Schenkung Martha und Robert von Hirsch an das Kunstmuseum", *Basler Stadtbuch 1977*, 98th year, Basel, 1978, pp.221-236; Paul H. Boerlin, "Die Schenkung von Hirsch: Holbeins Verkündigungsengel", *Basler Zeitung*, No.74, 16 March 1978, p.46; Dieter Koepplin, "Die Schenkung Robert von Hirsch (II): Cranachs 'Urteil des Paris'", *Basler Zeitung*, No. 85, 29 March 1978, p.37; Christian Geelhaar, "Die Schenkung Robert von Hirsch (III): Ingres' verwundete Venus", *Basler Zeitung*, No.87, 31 March 1978, p.45; Nikolaus Meier, "Die Schenkung Robert von Hirsch (IV): Daumiers Don Quixote", *Basler Zeitung*, No.93, 6 April 1978, p.43; Franz Meyer, "Die Schenkung Robert von Hirsch (V): Edgar Degas' Pferderennen", *Basler Zeitung*, No.95, 8 April 1978, p.57; Franz Meyer, "Die Schenkung Robert von Hirsch (VI): Cézannes Taubenschlag", *Basler Zeitung*, No.98, 11 April 1978, p.35.

242 Christian Geelhaar, "Paul Cézannes Porträt von Fortuné Marion", *Basler Zeitung*, No.177, 4 July 1978, p.29.

Dance Halls for Music of the Future (pp. 185-192)

243 *National-Zeitung*, Vol.75, No.73, 29 January 1916, p.9.

244 "Die welschen Maler in der Kunsthalle", II, *Basler Nachrichten*, Vol.71, No.610, 1 December 1915, p.1.

245 Cf. Christian Geelhaar, "Basel an einer Welten- und Kunstwende", Christian Geelhaar und Monica Stucky, *Expressionistische Malerei in Basel um den ersten Weltkrieg*, Basel, 1983, p.18f.

246 *Öffentliche Kunstsammlung Basel, Jahresbericht 1927*, New Series XXIV, Basel, 1928, p.7; cf. also Christian Geelhaar, Introduction, *Edvard Munch, Sein Werk in Schweizer Sammlungen*, Exhibition catalogue, Kunstmuseum, Basel, 1985, p.7f.

247 'O.F.' (Otto Fischer), "Neuerwerbungen der Öffentlichen Kunstsammlung in Basel", *Basler Nachrichten*, Vol.86, No. 44, 14 February 1930, 1st Supplement.

248 Christian Geelhaar, "Paul Klee und Basel", *Basler Magazin*, Political and cultural weekend supplement of the *Basler Zeitung*, No.50, 15 December 1979, p.7.

249 Helga Tratz, *"Entartete Kunst": ein Kapitel zur Geschichte der Kunsthalle von 1933-45*, publication of the Staatliche Kunsthalle, Karlsruhe, 1987.

250 The Walter Schwarzenberg collection was auctioned by the Galerie Georges Giroux in Brussels on 1 and 2 February 1932.

251 Nikolaus Meier, *Die Stadt Basel den Werken der Kunst, Konzepte und Entwürfe für das Kunstmuseum Basel 1906-1932*, Basel, 1986.

252 Re the acquisition of Hodler's *View into Infinity*, cf. Christian Geelhaar, "Ferdinand Hodler und Basel", *Basler Magazin*, Political and cultural weekend supplement of the *Basler Zeitung*, No.34, 25 August 1979, p.1f.; cf. by the same author, "Ferdinand Hodler und Basel, Dokumente zur Rezeptionsgeschichte", *Zeitschrift für Schweizerische Archäologie und Kunstgeschichte*, Vol.39, 1982, pp.181-201.

253 Letter to Councillor Fritz Hauser of 19 May 1939; Georg Kreis *"Entartete" Kunst für Basel*, Basel, 1990, p.41, Note 95.

254 Letter to Councillor Fritz Hauser of 19 May 1939; Kreis (see Note 253), p.81.

255 '-dt.' (Georg Schmidt), "Max Beckmann, Zur Ausstellung in der Kunsthalle", II, *National-Zeitung*, Vol.88, No.393, 28 August 1930, Supplement.

256 '-dt.' (Georg Schmidt), "Lovis Corinth, Zur Ausstellung in der Kunsthalle", III, *National-Zeitung*, Vol.94, No.164, 7 April 1936, p.5.

257 Minutes of the Kunstkommission's meeting on 27 November 1939.

258 Cf. Beat Stutzer, "Zu Hermann Scherers 'Atelierfest', Oder: Ein Dokument für die Basler Künstlergruppe 'Rot-Blau'", *Kunst-Nachrichten*, Vol. 15, No.5, September 1979, p.132f.

259 In a letter to Gustav Schiefler written in 1927 of which only a fragment remains; *Ernst Ludwig Kirchner-Gustav Schiefler, Briefwechsel 1910-1935/1938*, Stuttgart/Zürich, 1990, p.493.

260 Letter to Gustav Schiefler of 9 September 1927; *Kirchner-Schiefler* (see Note 259), p.489; cf. also Kirchner's comments in his *Davoser Tagebuch* on 21 December 1926: "In Basel, too, they haven't bought one picture or one print for the collections, *but they have bought a great deal by young artists*", Lothar Griesebach, *E.L. Kirchners Davoser Tagebuch*, Cologne, 1968, p.138.

261 *Amselfluh* had been displayed in the Kunstmuseum since 1941 as a loan from Mrs. Erna Kirchner.

262 Beat Stutzer, "Ernst Ludwig Kirchner und Basel", *E.L. Kirchner im Kunstmuseum Basel*, Exhibition catalogue, Kunstmuseum, Basel, 1979/1980, pp.7-36.

263 Minutes of the Kunstkommission's meeting on 27 November 1939.

264 Georg Schmidt, "Die Entstehung der Öffentlichen Kunstsammlung", Georg Schmidt, *Schriften aus 22 Jahren Museumstätigkeit*, Basel, 1964, p.140.

265 Christian Geelhaar, "Bejahung der Gegenwart und Zuversicht auf die Zukunft, Zur Geschichte der Emanuel Hoffmann-Stiftung Basel", *Emanuel Hoffmann-Stiftung Basel*, Basel, 1991, pp.9-34.

266 Franz Meyer, "Die Schenkung Hans und Marguerite Arp von 1966", *Öffentliche Kunstsammlung Basel, Jahresberichte 1964-1966*, p.199-211; cf. also Geelhaar (see Note 265), p.21f.

267 Hans-Joachim Müller, *NAFEA, The Rudolf Staechelin Collection, Basel*, with articles by Christian Geelhaar, Franz Meyer, Simon de Pury and Ruedi Staechelin, Basel, 1990; Bernhard Scherz and Kurt Wyss, *Die Basler Picasso-Story*, Basel/Boston/Stuttgart, 1981.

Treasure-house of Cubism (pp. 237-344)

268 *Impressionist and Modern Paintings and Sculpture*, Sotheby's, London, 2 December 1986, Lot 58; Beyeler Collection, Basel.

269 *Impressionist and Modern Paintings and Sculpture*, Sotheby's, London, 1 December 1987, Lot 46; private collection.

270 The catalogue entry was: "141 - Still-life. (Signed on the back.) 1.90m. high x 0.81 m. wide." These dimensions exactly correspond to *Woman Reading*, Braque's largest Cubist painting.

271 'G.A.W.' (Gustav Adolf Wanner), "Dr. h.c. Raoul La Roche", *Basler Nachrichten*, Vol.121, No.250, 17 June 1965, p.5; speeches given at Raoul La Roche's funeral on 18 June 1965, privately printed.

272 Daniel-Henry Kahnweiler, *Mes galeries et mes peintres*, Entretiens avec Francis Crémieux, Paris, 1982, p.108.

273 Kahnweiler (see Note 272), p.107.

274 Daix 414.

275 Daix 569.

276 1914. Bauqier No.83. The still-life listed in the auction catalogue as No.108 cost 90 French francs.

277 Pierre Assouline, *L'homme de l'art, D.-H. Kahnweiler (1884-1979)*, Paris, 1988, p.227.

278 Tim Benton, "La collection et la villa La Roche", *L'Esprit nouveau*; *Le Corbusier et l'industrie 1920-1925*, Exhibition catalogue, Museum für Gestaltung, Zürich, 1987, p.84.

279 *Daniel-Henry Kahnweiler, marchand, éditeur, écrivain*, Exhibition catalogue, Centre Georges Pompidou, Paris, 1984/85, p.140; *André Breton, La beauté convulsive*, Exhibition catalogue, Centre Georges Pompidou, Paris, 1991, p.177.

280 Zervos IV:430; with the reproduction of a different picture.

281 Cooper, Nos. 343, 351 and 357.

282 Letter from Raoul La Roche to Le Corbusier of 24 May 1926; Benton (see Note 278), p.88; cf. also Timothy J. Benton, *Le Corbusiers Pariser Villen*, Stuttgart, 1984, p.70.

283 Re the story of the building work, cf. Benton (see Note 282), pp.44-75.; cf. also the Exhibition catalogue *Le Corbusier und Raoul La Roche, Architekt und Maler, Bauherr und Sammler*, Architekturmuseum, Basel, 1987.

284 Letter from Raoul La Roche to Le Corbusier of 13 March 1925; cf. Benton (see Note 278), p.93.

285 Letter from Raoul La Roche to Le Corbusier of 24 May 1926; cf. Benton (see Note 282), p.70.

286 Letter from Le Corbusier to Ozenfant of 16 April 1925; cf. Benton (see Note 278), p.87; cf. also Benton (see Note 282), p.65.

287 See Note 286.

288 *Zürcher Kunstgesellschaft, Jahresbericht 1932*, p.5.

289 Known at the time as *La veille*; Cooper No. 331; cf. *Zürcher Kunstgesellschaft, Jahresbericht 1933*, p.6.

290 Cf. *Öffentliche Kunstsammlung Basel, Jahresberichte 1946-1950*, p.127.

291 Minutes of the meeting of the Kunstkommission on 28 March 1950.

292 *Öffentliche Kunstsammlung Basel, Jahresbericht 1951/1953*, p.41.

293 Letter from Raoul La Roche to Georg Schmidt of 9 May 1956.

294 Letter from Raoul La Roche to Georg Schmidt of 28 May 1955.

295 Letter from Raoul La Roche to Georg Schmidt of 9 January 1961.

296 Letter from Raoul La Roche to Georg Schmidt of 28 September 1957.

297 De Fayet, "Le talent, à propos de Bauchant-Jeune", *L'Esprit nouveau*, No.17, 1922, no page number.

298 Ozenfant, *Mémoires 1886-1962*, Paris, 1968, p.135.

299 *L'art suisse de Hodler à Klee*, Musée national d'art moderne, Paris, 1960, Cat.No.108.

300 Communication from Raoul La Roche to Franz Meyer of 25 December 1962.

301 Cf. *Die Schenkungen Raoul La Roche*, Exhibition catalogue, Öffentliche Kunstsammlung, Basel, 1963, with a foreword by Franz Meyer; Franz Meyer, "Die Schenkungen Raoul La Roche an das Kunstmuseum", *Jahresbericht 1963 der Öffentlichen Kunstsammlung Basel*, pp.55-70.

A Gift that had a Shock Effect (pp. 257-264)

302 Maria Netter, "Die Jubiläumsschenkung der Schweizerischen National-Versicherungs-Gesellschaft an das Basler Kunstmuseum", *Werk*, Schweizer Monatsschrift für Architektur, Kunst, Künstlerisches Gewerbe, Vol.47, No.5, May 1960, pp.182-184.

303 *Abraham* (1949) was acquired for the Museum of Modern Art with money from the Philip Johnson Fund.

304 In 1966 the Moderna Museet in Stockholm acquired *Tertia* (1964), in 1967 the Stedelijk Museum in Amsterdam acquired *The Gate* (1954) and in 1968 the Tate Gallery acquired *Adam* (1951-52).

305 Franz Meyer, "Arnold Rüdlinger", *Neue Zürcher Zeitung*, No.4977, 21 November 1967, Section 7; by the same author, "Arnold Rüdlinger und die amerikanische Kunst", *Amerikanische Kunst von 1945 bis heute, Kunst der USA in europäischen Sammlungen*, ed. by Dieter Honisch/Jens Christian Jensen, Cologne, 1976, pp.114-116.

306 Maja Sacher-Stehlin acquired a picture by Mathieu, *Composition on a blue ground* (1953), at the exhibition. The picture, which was acquired for the Emanuel Hoffmann Foundation, was exchanged in 1960 for another work by the same artist *Cardinal Mathieu asks St. Bernard to act as secretary to the Council of Troyes* (1958).

307 Foreword in the catalogue, *Tendances actuelles, Troisième exposition*, Kunsthalle, Berne, 1955.

308 Although *Deep Orange and Black* was not listed in the catalogue for the exhibition "Japanese Calligraphy and Western Signs", a photograph of the installation of the exhibition, which was reproduced in the catalogue for the Sam Francis exhibition held in the Basel Kunsthalle in the spring of 1968, proves that it was included.

309 "Aus europäischer Sicht", *Die neue amerikanische Malerei*, Exhibition catalogue, Kunsthalle, Basel, 1958.

310 Cf. Hans Theler, "Schwierigkeiten mit Amerikanerbildern, Zur Rothko-Ausstellung in der Basler Kunsthalle", *Basler Zeitung*, No.60, 11 March 1989, p.79.

311 *The 1958 Pittsburgh Bicentennial International Exhibition of Contemporary Painting and Sculpture*, Carnegie Institute, Pittsburgh, 5 December 1958 - 8 February 1959, Cat.No.323.

312 "Editorial on an event of international import in St.Gall, Switzerland", *Art International*, Vol.III, Nos.1-2, 1959, p.17.

313 Two photographs by Maria Netter, which illustrate the article quoted in Note 302, show how Franz Kline's picture was hung in the gallery between pictures by Hartung and Music, and how Clyfford Still's picture and Calder's mobile were hung by the staircase of the Kunstmuseum.

314 Minutes of the Kunstkommission's meeting on 4 June 1959.

315 See Note 313.

316 Franz Meyer, "Das 19. und 20. Jahrhundert im Kunstmuseum Basel", *Katalog 19./20. Jahrhundert*, Kunstmuseum, Basel, 1970, p.343.

317 Georgine Oeri (1914-1968) wrote art reviews for various Swiss and American newspapers and periodicals, and worked in the Solomon R. Guggenheim Museum in New York from 1953 to 1957; she subsequently taught art history and composition at the Parsons School of Design. In her book, *Man and His Images: A Way of Seeing*, New York, 1968, she devoted a whole chapter ("The Inner Landscape") to Abstract Expressionism. Cf. Maria Netter, "Georgine Oeri zum Gedenken", *Basler Nachrichten*, Vol.124, No.295, 17 July 1968, p.5.

318 Musée Cantonal des Beaux-Arts, Lausanne, 20 June to 6 October 1963; the picture by Stella was shown by the Leo Castelli Gallery, New York.

319 *Neue amerikanische Malerei*, Exhibition catalogue, Kunstmuseum, St. Gallen, 1959.

320 Minutes of the Kunstkommission's meeting on 5 September 1969.

321 Franz Meyer, "Die Sammlungspolitik des Kunstmuseums im Bereich von Malerei and Skulptur, 1968-1977", *Kunstmuseum Basel, Jahresbericht 1977*, p.44.

322 Minutes of the Kunstkommission's meeting on 25 June 1971.

323 *Art & Auction*, Vol.V, No.6, February 1983, p.61.

324 Rita Reif, "Jasper Johns Painting Brings Record Price", *The New York Times*, 11 November 1986, p.C16.

325 See Note 321.

Paul Ganz, *Meisterwerke der Öffentlichen Kunstsammlung in Basel, Meisterwerke der bedeutendsten Galerien Europas*, Vol. X, Munich, 1924.

Festschrift zur Eröffnung des Kunstmuseums, Basel, 1936. In this publication: Otto Fischer, "Geschichte der Öffentlichen Kunstsammlung".

Rudolf Christ and Otto Fischer, *Kunstmuseum Basel*, Basel, 1937.

Das Vermächtnis Max Geldner, Öffentliche Kunst-Sammlung Basel, Basel, 1958.

Die Schenkungen Raoul La Roche, Öffentliche Kunstsammlung Basel, Basel, 1963.

Georg Schmidt, *Museum of Fine Arts, Basle, 150 paintings 12th-20th century*, Basel, 1964.

Öffentliche Kunstsammlung, Kunstmuseum Basel, Catalogue 1st part, *Die Kunst bis 1800*, Basel, 1966. In this publication: Georg Schmidt, "Zur Geschichte der Öffentlichen Kunstsammlung im Kunstmuseum Basel".

Öffentliche Kunstsammlung, Kunstmuseum Basel, Catalogue, *19./20. Jahrhundert*, Basel 1970. In this publication: Franz Meyer, "Das 19. und 20. Jahrhundert im Kunstmuseum Basel".

Annemarie Monteil, *Basler Museen, Les Musées de Bâle, The Museums of Basel*, Basel, 1977.

Kunstmuseum Basel, Vol. "museum", Braunschweig, 1980.

Erich Steingräber (Ed.), *Große Gemäldegalerien*, Munich, 1980.

Nikolaus Meier, *Die Sammlung des Vereins der Freunde des Kunstmuseums Basel*, Exhibition catalogue Kunstmuseum Basel, Basel, 1983.

Nikolaus Meier, *Die Stadt Basel den Werken der Kunst, Konzepte und Entwürfe fur das Kunstmuseum Basel 1906-1932*, Basel, 1986.

Kunstmuseum Basel, Ankäufe und Schenkungen 1988, With an introduction and commentaries on the pictures by Christian Geelhaar, Basel and Einsiedeln, 1989.

Georg Kreis, *"Entartete" Kunst fur Basel*, Basel, 1990.

Hans-Joachim Müller, *NAFEA, The Rudolf Staechelin Collection Basel*, With contributions by Christian Geelhaar, Franz Meyer, Simon de Pury, Ruedi Staechelin, Basel, 1991.

Emanuel Hoffmann-Stiftung Basel, Basel, 1991. In this publication: Christian Geelhaar, "Bejahung der Gegenwart und Zuversicht auf die Zukunft, Zur Geschichte der Emanuel Hoffmann-Stiftung".

Dorothea Christ/Christian Geelhaar, *Arnold Böcklin*, Basel, 1992.

Sammeln in der Renaissance: Das Amerbach-Kabinett, Beiträge zu Basilius Amerbach, Öffentliche Kunstsammlung, Basel, 1991. In this publication: Elisabeth Landolt, "Das Amerbach-Kabinett und seine Inventare".

Sammeln in der Renaissance: Das Amerbach-Kabinett, Die Gemälde, Introduction and catalogue by Paul H. Boerlin, Öffentliche Kunstsammlung, Basel, 1991.